Advance Praise for *Engaging Human Services with Evidence-Informed Practice*

"At last we have a book on evidence-informed practice (EIP) that public services and particularly social work have waited for far too long. It provides what has been a missing ingredient in the creative mix essential to service improvement—that is, enhancing or changing an organization's response to gathering compelling evidence about its impacts on individuals, groups, and communities. Dr. Plath's excellent and accessible book is no reductionist, 'what works' plug-and-play manual for the hard of thinking. Rather, it is a rigorous, complex, and demanding approach to constructing an organizational and strategic response to preparing and implementing EIP. It is aimed at managers but is highly relevant to a wide range of professionals who need to think, plan, and devote time, resources, and effort to reshape key aspects of the organization that will promote better transparency of decision making through evidence of interventions that need to be congruent with public service values, relationships, and cultures. At the heart of the book is a clear model of implementation that focuses on practical strategies of leadership and change that will mobilize key organizational processes, resources, structures, and decision making that can support frontline workers and teams in using research evidence. Critical realism and social justice inform the analysis throughout and practice examples, and real-world settings feature prominently in this very essential text for progressive leaders of public services—be they managers or practitioners."

Andrew Pithouse
Cardiff University, Wales

"This book offers a thought-provoking and practical guide to evidence-informed practice. Debbie Plath outlines how human services leaders, managers, and practitioners can effectively use evidence to inform their practice to produce best outcomes with and for the people who use human services. A well-written book that demonstrates the integration of theory, knowledge, and research at its finest. It will become a classic."

Karen Healy, AM
University of Queensland, Australia
President, Australian Association of Social Workers

"This book is a welcome addition to the human services literature on evidence-informed organizational practice. The pragmatic approach taken by Debbie Plath has produced an immensely practical resource for managers, leaders, and practitioners in human services organizations. Building on her considerable research and experience, Plath highlights the importance of a team approach in developing an organizational culture conducive to evidence-informed practice. An organizational environment committed to the best available evidence, reflective thinking, and sound relationships with service users is, Debbie Plath argues, the ideal mix to respond to, and withstand, the pressures of contemporary human services provision."

Mel Gray
University of Newcastle, Australia

"Debbie Plath provides a searching but comprehensive account of the uses of evidence-informed approaches in the human services. It is the foremost practice guide for human services professionals currently available. Her deep understanding helps carefully unpick for the reader the advantages of an organizational model for practice."

Stephen Webb
Glasgow Caledonian University, Scotland

ENGAGING HUMAN SERVICES

WITH
Evidence-Informed Practice

DEBBIE PLATH

NASW PRESS

National Association of Social Workers
Washington, DC

Kathryn Conley Wehrmann, PhD, MSW, LCSW, *President*
Angelo McClain, PhD, LICSW, *Chief Executive Officer*

Cheryl Y. Bradley, *Publisher*
Stella Donovan, *Acquisitions Editor*
Julie Gutin, *Managing Editor*
Sarah Lowman, *Project Manager*
Katherine H. Loomis, *Copyeditor*
Juanita R. Doswell, *Proofreader*
Bernice Eisen, *Indexer*

Cover by Britt Engen, Metadog Design Group
Interior design, composition, and eBook conversions by Xcel Graphic Services
Printed and bound by Sheridan

First impression: September 2017

Library of Congress Cataloging-in-Publication Data

Names: Plath, Debbie, author.
Title: Engaging human services with evidence-informed practice / Debbie Plath.
Description: Washington, DC : NASW Press, [2017] | Includes bibliographical
    references and index.
Identifiers: LCCN 2017029078| ISBN 978-0-87101-520-4 (pbk.) |
    ISBN 978-0-87101-521-1 (ebook)
Subjects: LCSH: Human services. | Social service—Practice.
Classification: LCC HV40 .P585 2017 | DDC 361.0068/4—dc23 LC record available at https://
lccn.loc.gov/2017029078

Printed in the United States of America

To my Mum, Anne Plath, for your 90th birthday on July 9, 2017,
in appreciation for the lifetime of unconditional love and pride
that has kept me grounded and secure

Contents

About the Author

Debbie Plath, PhD, is an Australian social work practitioner, educator, and researcher. Following a social work academic career at the University of Newcastle, she established a consulting business. Her driving aspiration in this role is to facilitate research-minded and evidence-informed approaches to practice in human services organizations. Dr. Plath is coauthor (with Mel Gray and Stephen A. Webb) of the book *Evidence-Based Social Work: A Critical Stance.*

Acknowledgments

This book would not have been written without the initial approach and encouragement of Stella Donovan at NASW Press. I am grateful for her positive support and manuscript edits. The enthusiasm for this project shown by my family, Greg, Thomas, and Aidan, has been instrumental in seeing it through. I am fortunate to be surrounded by their love and support. My thanks also go to Penny Crofts and to Alison Ferguson for their careful reading and wise comments on a draft manuscript.

1

Using Evidence in the Human Services

Human services practitioners, managers, leaders, and service users are increasingly asked to demonstrate how evidence informs practice in their organization. Organizational credibility, funding, and service utilization can be influenced by their response. Although there are many empirically supported intervention programs that are marketed as evidence based, evidence-informed practice (EIP) involves much more than purchasing or selecting such programs and delivering them. EIP entails gathering credible and relevant information about the impact of interventions, applying this information to the specifics of the practice context, and using new knowledge to guide the delivery of human services practice so that positive outcomes are maximized for service users. From an organizational perspective, EIP requires processes, structures, and resources that support the critical use of research evidence to inform decisions about practice, program development, and strategic planning.

This book is designed for use in human services organizations that strive to strengthen their approaches to finding and appraising research evidence and using this evidence to inform practice. It is a resource for human services practitioners and managers seeking to understand and respond to pressures to demonstrate evidence-based practice (EBP). In particular, this book is for those in leadership roles who are looking for guidance and strategies to enhance an evidence-informed approach in their organization. These leadership roles can be filled by chief executives, directors, middle management staff, and team leaders, but also by team members who take on a level of responsibility in promoting the use of research evidence by the practice team. The material presented in this book is also relevant to organizations tasked with gathering and disseminating evidence to human services organizations.

1

Discourse on evidence is a prominent feature in the current human services landscape. Human services providers are required to engage with evidence at some level. EIP is not, however, just about organizational survival in the current political context. Successful EIP involves a critically reflective approach to the use of research evidence in a way that guides practice toward better outcomes for service users. It is part of a professional approach to practice that also attends to relationship building and respectful collaboration with service users and colleagues. The approach taken to EIP in this book will appeal to those seeking to engage in critical reflection on research–practice links while also maintaining a focus on relationship building with service users as a vital part of respectful, responsive practice in the human services.

The route that led me to write this book includes over three decades of practice as a social worker, educator, researcher, and consultant to human services organizations. During this time, EBP discourse has gradually established a firm presence in social work and the human services. My social work background has influenced the approach taken in this book. The ideas and resources presented here are, however, broadly applicable beyond social work practice to the wider human services field.

Although diverse in its approaches and practice settings, the discipline of social work has been strongly influenced by the medical model of service delivery. It is therefore unsurprising that the evidence-based medicine movement has influenced social work thinking and literature on EBP. In particular, the five-step approach to evidence-based clinical decision making is referred to widely as the template for EBP in social work (Gambrill, 2010; Gibbs & Gambrill, 2002; Thyer & Myers, 2010).

FIVE STEPS IN EVIDENCE-BASED CLINICAL DECISION MAKING

Physician David Sackett was the early proponent of evidence-based medicine, which is defined as "the conscientious, explicit and judicious use of current best evidence in making decisions" (Sackett, Richardson, Rosenberg, & Haynes, 1997, p. 71). The purpose of evidence-based medicine is to promote the use of research evidence to inform the diagnosis and treatment of individual patients, placing the onus on individual clinicians as decision makers. The clinical decision-making model of evidence-based medicine and, subsequently, evidence-based social work assumes that there is a relationship between the clinician and the individual service user or patient and that the clinician delivers the intervention. Evidence-based clinical decision making requires that the clinician engage in the following five-step process:

1. Define a practice question that stems from the client's circumstances.
2. Find the best evidence to answer the question.
3. Critically appraise the evidence.
4. Integrate new knowledge into decisions about interventions for the client.
5. Monitor and evaluate client outcomes.

Each of the five steps demands a lot from individual practitioners. Because individual clinicians generally do not have the time and resources to adequately complete each of these steps alone in their day-to-day clinical decision making, resources such as evidence banks of reviewed and summarized research are needed to support the process. The five-step model is intended for clinical decision making by practitioners who are in a position to implement the interventions that have the best evidence for positive outcomes in the service user's circumstances.

The term "intervention" is used in a very broad sense in this book to encompass any purposive actions undertaken by a human services provider with the intention of effecting change for an individual, group, or society. Soydan (2015) described the purpose of a social work intervention as being "to induce change to intentionally isolate or eradicate risk factors, activate and mobilize protective factors, reduce or eradicate harm, or introduce betterment beyond harm eradication" (p. 324). Interventions can include single events (for example, providing information to an individual on benefits he or she is eligible for) or multiple actions (for example, a series of family therapy sessions provided over several months, or a targeted program of services to a population group) that can occur at the individual, group, organizational, community, regional, or national level.

In human services contexts, the type of interventions that can be offered to service users is often dependent on factors beyond the practitioner–client dyad. Although many human services practitioners do make clinical decisions about individual service users and are able to control the choice and implementation of interventions in their individual therapeutic work, evidence-informed decision making in the human services is also relevant at the policy, resource allocation, organizational, and program implementation levels. Decisions at these levels, along with other contextual factors, shape the nature of interventions and decision making undertaken by practitioners as they work with service users.

SWITCHING LENSES FROM CLINICAL DECISION MAKING TO ORGANIZATIONAL PRACTICE: A PRACTICE EXAMPLE

For some time, I have been mindful of the need to take a wider perspective than clinical decision making for EBP in social work and the human services. In particular, an organizational approach is needed so that the links between research evidence and practice are strengthened not only in clinical decision making by individual practitioners, but also in decisions about practice principles, priorities, programs, and processes at the team and organizational levels.

A practice example can be helpful in illustrating an organizational or program-level approach to EIP. In this example, a human services organization that has provided a youth drop-in service for many years is now being pushed by its funding body and management to offer an evidence-based approach that demonstrates effective outcomes. Over the years, clinical decisions have been made by practitioners to engage young people with the service and to support them to achieve social, educational, and employment outcomes. Within the demands of day-to-day work, practitioners have done their best to keep up to date with current views on best practice, and several of programs and courses have been offered to young people. Practice has been guided by individual relationships between practitioners and young people and professional decision making about how best to work with individuals. Managers are now interested in gathering outcome data and research findings to substantiate a case for program effectiveness. It is program-level evidence that the organization now requires to secure the future funding of the program.

Relationship building and individually focused decision making are important for the youth drop-in service, but an evidence-informed approach for this service involves more than decisions on interventions with individual young people because it is more than an individual counseling service. Evidence can inform decisions about how the program is run and the opportunities offered to young people within the center to connect with other young people, build capacities, and learn new skills. Service delivery relies on longer term program planning, teamwork approaches, and collaboration with several players both internal and external to the organization. These players include funders, managers, multidisciplinary teams, practitioners, service users, families, referral organizations, and advocacy groups. These stakeholders have contributed over a long period of time to the establishment, delivery, and maintenance of the youth drop-in service. Evidence can be drawn on in making decisions about what resources the youth drop-in service needs, how it is to be operated, and what programs and practice principles should be adopted.

An organizational approach requires taking a step back to look at services and programs as a whole, asking questions about assumptions (strengths, needs, and goals of young people) and alternatives (types of programs and practice principles that could address social, emotional, educational, employment, and health goals) and seeking evidence (internally generated data and external research findings) that can assist in making choices among alternative ways of practicing. An organizational approach entails engaging with the relevant stakeholders to review the gathered evidence critically and determine how it can be incorporated with the particular demographic, cultural, social, economic, political, and historical characteristics of the practice context. Organizational resources and strategies are required to implement, evaluate, and sustain new practices. It is clear that interventions offered by the youth drop-in center—and in fact, all human services interventions—are complex in nature. Human services interventions involve multiple players beyond the clinician–client dyad in clinical decision making. Making and implementing decisions about interventions can be long-term processes.

A few years ago, I undertook a case study research project to examine the implementation process in a human services organization that had formally adopted an evidence-based approach to practice. Through interviews, surveys, and observation, I sought to document the ways EBP was understood in the organization and the processes used to achieve EBP goals (Plath, 2013a, 2013b, 2014). I found that practices in the organization sometimes mirrored the five steps in evidence-based clinical decision making, but the tasks of defining practice questions or issues, gathering and appraising evidence, making decisions about interventions, and evaluating and monitoring outcomes were undertaken in a variety of ways by practitioners and staff both within and outside the organization, as well as by individual clinicians. There is a need to consider EIP in the human services as a process that draws on resources from different parts of the organization and beyond the organization. This process includes supporting evidence-informed decision making by individual clinicians but also attends to the processes and relationships in teams, programs, departments, organizations, and external partnerships. This approach prioritizes research and critical thinking in practice decision making.

Returning to the practice example of the youth drop-in service, both an immediate organizational response and a longer term strategy are required when new program funding conditions require the demonstration of evidence for effectiveness. Having received information on the new funding requirement, the manager, through the team leader, informs the practitioners about the potential funding threat and consults with them to develop an action plan. The action plan includes compiling service user outcome data from service reports and from a review of service user records. In addition, the youth services advocacy organization is consulted to obtain advice on available evidence reviews on the role of youth drop-in services. To supplement this information gathering, a more targeted review of research literature that relates to Indigenous youths (a service user group that the program has successfully engaged) is undertaken.

This reactive style of evidence gathering secures funding for another year, but the experience prompts managers and practitioners in the organization to consider how gathering and reviewing research evidence could become embedded in the day-to-day practice of the organization for the future. Their goals are for service planning to be proactive rather than reactive, for alternative types of services and programs to be given informed consideration, and for the offered interventions to produce good outcomes and be responsive to the issues facing local young people. To prepare the organization for a more evidence-informed approach to practice, processes are set in place to

- define the key practice questions for the organization
- use internal and external resources to generate evidence that will inform answers to the practice questions
- ensure that the research evidence is appraised critically for its strength and suitability to the practice context in the organization
- engage staff with new knowledge and decision making about effective programs and interventions to be offered by the organization
- establish a systematic approach to monitoring service user outcomes and evaluating programs.

The alignment between the steps in the clinical decision-making model of EBP and the organizational model of EIP, as shown in Table 1.1, is obvious. In this book, readers will engage with an appraisal of organizational strategies and processes that can assist movement through these five steps. The book offers guidance for managers and other leaders in organizations in designing strategies and mobilizing resources so that an EIP approach can be integrated into the life of the organization.

HUMAN SERVICES CONTEXT

The human services comprise a wide range of service types established to address human needs and remediate problems. They include services to families and individuals across the life span who are facing hardships and challenges that result from wider social, economic,

Table 1.1 Alignment between the Five Steps in Evidence-Based Practice Decision Making and the Organizational Approach to Evidence-Informed Practice

Evidence-Based Practice Decision-Making Step	Organizational Approach to Evidence-Informed Practice Step
1. Define a practice question that stems from the client's circumstances.	Define key practice questions for the organization.
2. Find the best evidence to answer the question.	Use internal and external resources to generate evidence that will inform answers to the practice questions.
3. Critically appraise the evidence.	Ensure that research evidence is appraised critically for strength and suitability to the practice context in the organization.
4. Integrate new knowledge into decisions about interventions for the client.	Engage staff with new knowledge and decision making about effective programs and interventions to be offered by the organization.
5. Monitor and evaluate client outcomes.	Establish a systematic approach to monitoring service user outcomes and evaluating programs.

political, and environmental factors as well as physiological, psychological, emotional, and relationship factors. The types of organizations in which human services practitioners work range from small community-based groups to large government departments. The diversity of human services is further shaped by the fact that the human services workforce comprises a range of professions. An interdisciplinary approach to practice is common, given that different perspectives and knowledge bases contribute to a more holistic understanding of how to assist people in need. The evidence base for human services practice is therefore sourced from a variety of disciplines. As a result, there are challenges associated with locating all of the relevant evidence and determining how to apply this evidence to diverse practice situations.

Social work is one of the professions in the realm of human services practice that has grappled with how to engage with and implement EBP. Because this is my own professional background, the social work literature on the nature of EBP and the barriers and facilitators to its implementation has informed my thinking and writing. The contents and approach of the book are, however, relevant to the wider human services field. Ultimately, this book is intended for a multidisciplinary audience in human services practice and management.

Although this book is offered as a guide to the implementation of EIP for human services practice leaders and managers, it does not take a one-size-fits-all approach. Diversity in the human services demands a range of perspectives and strategies for the implementation of EIP. Although a common guiding framework and approach are provided, it is intended that readers will draw out the strategies that are suited to their own practice contexts. Reflective questions are included at the end of each chapter to assist with this process.

WHY USE RESEARCH EVIDENCE TO INFORM PRACTICE?

EBP has been criticized as a fad or managerial tactic to rationalize service provision. The language of EBP is sometimes used in a reductionist way to label and support certain defined practices and dismiss or disregard others. It can be used by management as a way of controlling and justifying practice without an appreciation of the complex nature of good practice and relationship building with service users.

Confining EIP to a list of programs labeled as evidence based is not advocated here. Such an approach fails to recognize a number of important issues. First, diverse human needs and circumstances require diverse interventions. So-called effective interventions are often not beneficial to everyone. Second, the opportunities and potential presented through trialing innovative new practices would be missed if only tried and tested interventions were used. Third, a lack of research evidence for alternative interventions is an indicator not of poor intervention outcomes but rather of a need for ongoing research and evidence gathering. Finally, it is often not possible to fully emulate tested practices within the constraints of real-world practice. Although the identification and promotion of programs with strong evidence for effective outcomes are certainly important, this activity is not the only aspect of EIP.

Although a simplistic conceptualization of EBP deserves to be challenged, there remain compelling arguments to pursue evidence-informed approaches. First, there is an ethical responsibility to provide the most effective services to service users. Research evidence informs an understanding of the types of interventions that have been found to be effective. Second, an evidence-informed approach enhances the credibility and accountability of services to service users, funding bodies, and the public, who directly and indirectly support organizations through donations and taxes. Third, when an evidence-informed approach includes monitoring outcomes and contributing to the knowledge base, the body of information on the impact of human services interventions is increased.

Finally, the approach to EIP promoted in this book enhances professionalism in human services organizations through the development of a research culture and critically reflective practice. This approach aligns with Macdonald's (2001) definition of *evidence-based practice* as "an approach to decision-making which is transparent, accountable and based on the careful consideration of the most compelling evidence we have about the effects of particular interventions on the welfare of individuals, groups and communities" (p. xviii).

The relationship between research and practice is not a simple one. Research evidence does not lead automatically to answers about best practice and outcomes for service users. A program for young people with anorexia nervosa, for example, may have very strong research evidence for success in assisting young people to return to a healthy weight, but this evidence does not mean that the program will work for all young people. It is important to interpret research findings in light of the characteristics of the research participants, the dropout rate, and the context in which the research was conducted. If the service user group, culture, or professional team is different from those in the research studies, there may be good reasons to implement an alternative program. There are also economic, political, and social factors that can influence the types of programs that are regarded as suitable and worthy of the resources required for their implementation.

The processes involved in gathering, interpreting, and applying evidence; promoting the implementation of interventions; and monitoring the outcomes of new practices are multifaceted. Time is required to gather evidence, make program decisions, develop intervention programs, and implement the interventions in organizational settings. The implementation of EBP entails a long-term organizational commitment that is likely to face challenges and pitfalls. A model for organizational implementation is offered in this book to assist with that process, but commitment to what may be a lengthy change process is also needed. For many human services organizations, a shift in organizational culture is required to embed a research-minded approach. Bringing about this shift entails working both with organizational structures and processes and with interpersonal relationships to get others on board with the implementation of EIP.

KEY COMPONENTS OF THE APPROACH: EVIDENCE, CRITICAL REFLECTION, AND RELATIONSHIP BUILDING

Up to this point, the terms "evidence-based" and "evidence-informed" have both been used. The term "evidence-informed practice," rather than the more commonly used "evidence-based practice," was chosen for the title of the book and to describe the proposed organizational process. There is a subtle differentiation in meaning that can be drawn between these two terms. "Evidence-based" implies that research evidence is the starting point that leads to particular practices being defined and implemented. That is, the practice is based in or stems from the evidence. In contrast, "evidence-informed" leaves room for practice to be grounded in values, theory, relationships, culture, and other relevant factors alongside evidence. The choice of the term "evidence-informed" reflects a stance on the role of evidence. That is, evidence does not stand alone in determining practice effectiveness: It should be integrated with critical reflection on practice circumstances and outcomes for service users and relationship building with service users and other stakeholders in practice implementation.

Although the focus of this book is on building and using evidence, critical thinking and critical reflection are needed to determine what to make of this so-called evidence. Because there are many personal and contextual factors that mediate the translation of evidence into practice, there is never an automatic link between research and best practice. Critical thinking and reflection are required to analyze and make sense of research and come to an understanding of how it may or may not apply in particular contexts, in the circumstances of particular service users, and in specific human services organizations. Links between research and practice are made in complex and contested terrains that critical reflection can help to navigate. Critical reflection is a process that examines the personal, relational, historical, social, and political factors that influence understanding and experiences. The process involves identifying and challenging values and assumptions that have an impact on understanding; questioning dominant or accepted interpretations of information, situations, and behaviors; and considering alternative interpretations.

A team may, for example, embark on a process of developing an evidence-informed approach to an early intervention program for children with autism. Faced with a body of research supporting multidisciplinary center-based interventions and a body of research supporting caseworker home-based interventions, the team will need to examine the alternatives to decide how their limited resources can be most effectively used. This examination involves a process of carefully appraising the research, including its values, assumptions, and interpretations, to understand how findings for the study participants relate to requirements in their own practice context.

Relationship building with service users also plays a key role in deciding what the best practices are in particular contexts. Understanding and respecting the values and wishes of service users is an ethical principle that manifests in relationship building and collaborative approaches to practice. This principle influences decision making about which interventions are appropriate. The quality of the relationship between practitioner and service user shapes how the service is experienced and how effective it is from the service user's perspective. Continuing with the previous example, canvassing the views and wishes of parents of young children with autism will be useful in identifying the type of early intervention service that is likely to be positively received and engaged with by service users. Whether a caseworker or multidisciplinary approach is adopted, effective engagement with families will be important if families are to receive adequate resources and support to continue with interventions in the home environment.

Attention to relationship building is not only important between practitioners and service users; the quality of relationships between coworkers and with managers will also affect how smoothly and successfully new evidence-informed programs are incorporated into organizations. The nature of relationships with funding bodies and external research organizations can also influence access to resources and relevant evidence. In the early intervention example, if the team recommends a shift from a center-based service to a home-based service on the basis of an evidence review, successful implementation will depend on management support and possibly additional funding for resources and vehicles. Apart from the evidence presented to management, interpersonal skills in negotiation and lobbying in the context of respectful relationships will support program implementation. Strong team relationships with attention to relationship building and collaborative planning underlie a successful approach that optimizes input from the different professional disciplines.

Throughout this book, reference is made to three key components underpinning EIP: evidence, critical reflection, and relationships (see Figure 1.1). It is proposed that in order to achieve quality, responsive, and effective practice, evidence should not be the dominant discourse but rather should be integrated and balanced with relationship building and critical reflection. A critical, informed, and relational process is advocated as the way forward for the implementation of EIP in human services organizations.

PREPARING FOR AN ORGANIZATIONAL APPROACH

The steps entailed in an organizational approach to EIP are listed in Table 1.1. Implementing these steps at an organizational level requires a commitment of resources and a rethinking of organizational priorities and processes. So why would decision makers

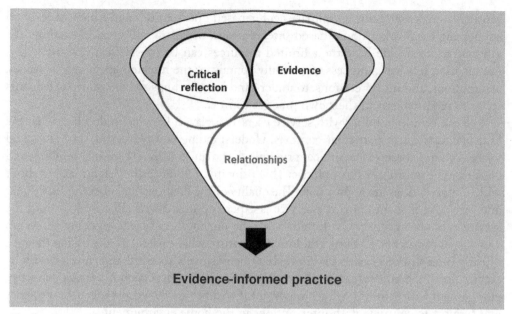

Figure 1.1 Three Key Components Underpinning Evidence-Informed Practice

in an organization be inclined to devote time, money, and effort to reshaping aspects of the organization in this way?

A compelling argument for taking an organizational approach to EIP is that the viability of organizations may depend on doing so. Organizations that take a strategic approach to EIP can demonstrate that their practice is research informed and that its services produce good outcomes for service users. Organizations adopting an evidence-informed approach are positioned better in the current climate of human services provision because they are able to respond to pressure from governments, funding bodies, media, and the general public to have reasoned and substantiated evidence for interventions and programs. It is no longer sufficient for organizations to rely on consumer satisfaction surveys. Organizations need to draw on independent and rigorous research evidence from both within and beyond the organization. The implementation of EIP supports both the quality of services to service users and the viability of organizations in a political context.

Human services practitioners naturally draw on their own professional knowledge from training, professional development, and evidence-gathering activities when they choose interventions, but there are often organizational barriers to doing independent practice consistently. Such barriers can relate to limited time, resources, and influence within the organization to gather evidence and to shape practices. Leadership- and organizational-level strategies are needed if an evidence-informed approach is to become embedded in individual practice and decision making about programs and priorities at the organizational level. From a review of research on the implementation of EBP in the human services, Austin and Claassen (2008) identified five components of an organizational approach to implementation that support EIP in the human services:

1. leadership by middle and top management that demonstrates open and honest communication, adopts a supportive approach to change, and mobilizes resources for change
2. involvement of stakeholders in the implementation of EIP by bringing together service users and staff from different parts of the organization
3. teamwork in collaboratively reflecting on practice and questioning assumptions
4. commitment of organizational resources to professional growth, skill development, staff engagement, and organizational change
5. readiness to become a learning organization that values ongoing questioning, information gathering, reflection, and reevaluation of practice.

Leadership is needed to implement EIP in any organization. The attitudes and activities of organizational leaders, including executives, middle management, and team leaders, can influence the attitudes of other staff in the organization toward the use of evidence. Leaders can provide guidance and support that strengthen practitioners' capacity to access evidence and integrate it into practice. Although managers widely recognize both the benefit in adopting an EIP approach and their own role in supporting implementation, they can struggle to formulate strategies to support and sustain the implementation process (Gray, Joy, Plath, & Webb, 2014; Mosson, Hasson, Wallin, & von Thiele Schwarz, 2017; Plath, 2013b).

Leaders can support the implementation of EIP by

- providing resources to help practitioners access, understand, and apply evidence;
- conveying a vision and goals around the use of research evidence;
- modeling behavior;
- generating enthusiasm and providing encouragement for the use of evidence;
- sharing information;
- promoting a research culture;
- implementing and using data collection systems;
- providing professional development opportunities; and
- addressing emerging barriers (Mosson et al., 2017).

This book provides a practical framework for organizations preparing to implement or strengthen their approach to EIP. Guidance is offered to assist organizational leaders in analyzing their organization and designing strategies to implement, support, and sustain EIP. The incorporation of evidence-informed approaches to decision making and practice is a cumulative process that develops over time. Likewise, readiness develops over time as organizations develop the capacity to expand and enhance their evidence-informed approach.

WHO IS THIS BOOK FOR, AND HOW WILL IT HELP?

This book is written primarily for managers and team leaders in social work and human services who wish to enhance an evidence-based approach to practice in their organization. But it is not only managers who play a leadership role in the implementation of EIP; the contents of the book will also be useful for frontline human services practitioners and students wanting to understand the implementation of EIP and learn how to contribute to EIP in the organizations in which they work. The material will also enhance learning about how organizations function and how research and practice relate to one another in social work and the human services.

The book does not contain appraisals of evidence for particular practices or interventions. Rather, it is concerned with examining organizational processes that support the use of evidence in practice and promoting the implementation of these organizational processes. This organizational approach gives consideration to resources, structures, processes, culture, and decision making in organizations and the ways these can be mobilized to support practitioners, teams, and programs in using research and evidence to guide practice. Evidence reviews and bodies of research evidence that relate to particular approaches to practice play a vital role in EIP. This book is a complementary resource to such bodies of evidence. It is intended that the ideas and strategies presented in this book will function as a realistic and practical guide to assist practitioners, managers, and human services organizations in changing workplace practices so that research evidence is more effectively used.

The organizational implementation of EIP entails a process of organizational change. As such, much can be learned from the literature on organizations and management. The new perspective offered by this book is the appreciation of, and attention to, the particular features, values, and political context of human services organizations. The demands and challenges of EIP for organizations are confronted, and strategies to address these challenges are proposed.

The book can help managers and practitioners analyze and navigate the complexities of EIP and understand the barriers to and facilitators of EIP. By offering a framework for implementation and practical strategies, the book responds to the current pressures on human services practitioners, managers, and organizations to provide EIP. It assists readers in deciding where they and their organization are situated in relation to different approaches to EIP.

Research on organizational change and the implementation of EIP has not resulted in a consensus about the strategies that can lead to successful change. Therefore, the book should not be used as a technical how-to guide. Rather, it is a resource for practitioners and managers who wish to implement EIP within the context of a critically reflective approach to management and practice that recognizes the centrality of relationship-building skills for effective social work and human services practice.

CRITICAL REALIST AND SOCIAL JUSTICE APPROACH

Critical realism is a theory that has been applied in social work by a number of authors (Craig & Bigby, 2015; Houston, 2001; Pawson, 2006) and aligns well with the approach to EIP adopted in this book. Critical realism recognizes a social reality that is independent of the thoughts and impressions of individuals but avoids the causal determinism of positivism, criticized for reducing complex human experiences to quantifiable variables (Shaw, 1999; Witkin, 1996). For example, from a critical realist perspective, an organization can be regarded as having a life of its own that is sustained by dominant values, patterns of behavior, and organizational systems. All activities and decisions in organizations cannot, however, be reduced to, or explained by, these organizational structures and systems. There are other personal and social factors that shape behaviors and experiences. In critical realism, both objective knowledge and social meaning are valued as important for understanding the social world. Critical realism argues that several open systems interact to produce events and outcomes for individuals and social groups. Human services practice cannot be reduced to direct causal relationships between intervention and service user outcomes (the simplistic "What works?" mentality). Critical realism requires situations to be closely analyzed to identify the social meanings, systems, mechanisms, and processes that are operating and to understand the likely impact of these on experiences, behaviors, and outcomes for individuals and groups in particular circumstances.

If a critical realist stance is taken to analyzing decision making in organizations, it may be identified that an organization has formal decision-making mechanisms that include consultation, committee meetings, resolutions, and documentation. Alongside these formal processes, however, there are personal, professional, cultural, and social networks that also operate as systems within organizations (for example, friendship groups, discipline groups, organizational units, hierarchy levels, historical associations). These informal systems interact with the formal organizational systems. Chance discussions, past decisions, individual values, behavior patterns, and charismatic individuals within groups can influence decisions and behavior patterns within the organization. Hence, practices and behaviors in organizations do not always match with the formal processes and policies adopted within those organizations.

Similarly, if critical realism is applied at the service user level, each individual's experience of a service provided by a human services organization is different because of the circumstances, relationships, personal history, values, and resources that shape the individual's own life and worldview. The fact that each service user presents with unique circumstances and characteristics has implications for how EIP is approached. Through a process of information gathering and critical analysis, researchers, managers, and practitioners can seek to understand and explain tendencies in service provision and service user responses. Because of the mechanisms operating in different systems, however, it is generally easier to establish trends rather than definitive outcomes.

The critical realist approach to EIP taken in this book shapes how evidence is viewed. Rather than viewing particular interventions as effective on the basis of a defined body of evidence (that is, interventions that "work"), evidence is conceived as provisional and context bound. Particular contexts must be examined to understand how interventions are operating and how to improve interventions. Evidence is derived from robust research (both qualitative and quantitative), practice evaluation, systematic information gathering, professional practice wisdom, and critical reflection. In the human services, it is necessary to come to terms with never fully understanding the individual, organizational, or social world on which evidence may shed some light. Evidence is continually reviewed, updated, and refined to suit the practice context. By seeking out evidence that is relevant and useful, this pragmatic approach explains practice and guides decision making in the real world of policy and practice uncertainty. This approach also recognizes that evidence is negotiated in a political context of power, influence, and power imbalances.

Critical realism provides a framework not only to identify systems and mechanisms, but also to pursue a social justice agenda by challenging processes when they lead to oppression and marginalization of particular groups—for example, by identifying and challenging cultural, economic, and gender-based mechanisms that have a negative impact on access to services, supports, and opportunities. The pursuit of social justice is a fundamental goal of the profession of social work and a driving principle for many human services organizations. A social justice perspective has also been brought to EIP and the critical realist approach taken in this book.

In considering EIP from a social justice perspective, it is important to recognize when certain interventions are ineffective for particular social groups and to consider how interventions can better respond to diverse circumstances. This recognition is particularly pertinent if these social groups are already marginalized in society on economic, cultural, or social grounds. A social justice perspective also prompts consideration of the characteristics and experiences of service users who are withdrawing from services. Without such a critical eye, services can further marginalize users by providing interventions that may be suited to some groups in the community but experienced as alienating by others. For example, a new parents support group could be well received by many parents but experienced as alienating for very young parents, single parents, fathers, or parents who are not from the dominant cultural group, even though the program has strong evidence for effectiveness in supporting baby and parent well-being goals. A critical approach includes the analysis of privilege and disadvantage and prompts the search for fuller evidence on the suitability of interventions, or aspects of interventions, for different groups in the community. In examining the evidence for interventions, a critical approach entails scrutinizing the characteristics of research participants as part of the process of evaluating how applicable the evidence is to other population groups.

The following definition of evidence is used in this book: *Evidence* is provisional, well-informed, negotiated knowledge about what is expected to work well in a particular context. Evidence comprises knowledge from robust research (both qualitative and quantitative), practice evaluation, systematic information gathering, professional practice wisdom, and critical reflection. Evidence is gathered with the understanding that individual, organizational, and social worlds can never be fully understood. Evidence is continually reviewed, updated, and refined to suit the practice context. The approach to evidence is pragmatic. The goal is real-world applicability, which is negotiated in a political context.

OVERVIEW OF THE BOOK

The chapters in this book examine issues surrounding the implementation of EIP. Readers are prompted to reflect on their own practice experiences and organizational settings to develop an understanding of evidence-informed practice and how it is, could be, or should be approached in organizations.

Chapters 2 and 3 provide a conceptual and theoretical basis for the organizational implementation of EIP and analyze implementation requirements. Chapter 2 explores the EIP landscape. Key terms, concepts, principles, and alternative views of EIP are examined alongside existing tensions and debates. Readers are encouraged to consider their own stance in the context of a range of differing definitions and positions on EBP and EIP. Chapter 3 examines how organizations work and why an organizational approach is needed for the implementation of EIP in the human services. The features of an organizational approach are explained more fully, and a pragmatic, realist approach to negotiating organizational processes is presented. An implementation model, based on the five steps outlined in Table 1.1, is presented at the end of chapter 3 as a framework for purposeful action in organizations.

Chapters 4 to 8 cover the five phases of the implementation model in turn. In addition to examining each of the five phases, these chapters offer guidance and practical suggestions for planning and implementing strategies. Practice examples, reflective questions, and strategies for implementation are incorporated throughout to encourage readers to analyze their own organizations, apply ideas to real-world settings, and prepare action strategies that suit their individual situations. Practitioners and managers are guided through this framework and prompted to develop purposeful action plans that will facilitate the implementation of EIP, including integrating EIP principles into existing structures and processes in the organization and building on existing strengths. Within the implementation framework that is offered, it is anticipated that readers will find ideas and strategies that can be shaped to suit the requirements of specific contexts, service user groups, and workforces.

The final chapter provides a summary and integration of the key features and components of the implementation model. It also revisits the issue of organizational readiness for the implementation of EIP and the ways such readiness could be assessed. The book may be used to better understand the implementation of EIP in the human services, to inform organizational preparation for EIP, and as a reference and troubleshooting guide through the implementation process.

2

The Evidence-Informed
Practice Landscape

What is evidence-informed practice (EIP)? What counts as evidence? Answers to these questions are fundamental to the implementation of EIP. There is an abundance of literature devoted to debating different perspectives on evidence-based practice (EBP) in social work and the human services and teasing out its key concepts. This chapter offers an overview of definitions and perspectives and describes the stance on EIP that underpins the organizational implementation process presented in this book. Readers are encouraged to consider differing views on EIP and how these lead to different approaches in practice. This chapter also provides further insights into what is meant by "evidence" in the human services.

As the starting point, an adaptation of the definition of evidence-based medicine provided by Sackett, Richardson, Rosenberg, and Haynes (1997) conveys the essential nature of the approach: "Evidence-based practice is the conscientious, explicit and judicious use of current best evidence in making decisions about interventions for patients" (p. 71). From a social work perspective, Macdonald (2001) proposed a similar definition of EBP that focuses on informed, critical decision making: "Evidence-based practice is an approach to decision-making which is transparent, accountable and based on the careful consideration of the most compelling evidence about the effects of particular interventions on the welfare of individuals, groups and communities" (p. xviii).

Like social work, the psychology discipline is prominent in the provision of human services and has also derived a definition of EBP from medicine. The American Psychological Association (2005) has stated,

> Evidence-based practice in psychology (EBPP) is the integration of the best available research with clinical expertise in the context of patient characteristics,

culture, and preferences. . . . The purpose of EBPP is to promote effective psychological practice and enhance public health by applying empirically supported principles of psychological assessment, case formulation, therapeutic relationship, and intervention. (para. 1)

These are broad, important definitions that establish the fundamental nature and purpose of EBP—that is, the process is rigorous and informed, and the purpose is to achieve the best outcomes for service users. These are worthy guiding principles for social work and human services practice.

It is when the finer details of EIP are examined that questions and differing viewpoints emerge. These questions relate to what is accepted as evidence, what the decision-making process entails, who makes the decisions, what role economic and political factors play, what counts as a good outcome, and who defines effectiveness.

As explained in chapter 1, "evidence-informed practice," rather than "evidence-based practice," is the preferred term in this book. However, these terms are sometimes used interchangeably. The language of EBP is dominant in the human services context and organizational settings. This term is therefore used at times in this book to reflect EBP as a movement that is part of the organizational environments in which human services organizations operate. The term "evidence-informed practice" is used in the recognition that although research should inform practice, human services practice is not based in research evidence alone. Other factors that inform practice include wider structural influences (cultural, economic, and political) as well as individual relational circumstances. Use of the term "evidence-informed practice" is an acknowledgment of both the benefits and the limits of evidence in specific practice contexts.

When EIP or EBP is discussed in practice contexts, confusion and conflict can arise if people are approaching the topic with different understandings and perspectives, limiting the potential to move forward with practice and policy decision making. Taking time to consider the components and processes of EIP can help readers illuminate their own position and better understand the different standpoints and reactions of others. This chapter helps readers reflect on and clarify definitions of EIP and become familiar with the EIP landscape in the human services. Definitions and classifications of EIP are presented to show that EIP is not a standardized process, but rather is open to interpretation in different contexts. The following practice scenario illustrates how different views and tensions relating to EIP can emerge in an organization.

Case Study: Family Focus (Organizational Scenario 1)

Family Focus is a fictitious organization providing case management, group programs, and home visiting services for families with young children. It offers universal, community-based programs and targeted interventions for families under stress or at risk of increased difficulties. The government program that funds a large proportion of the organization's operating costs has instituted funding criteria that require organizations to demonstrate their evidence base for programs, so the manager decides to engage a consultant to work with the organization to strengthen its approach to EIP. This decision is announced at a staff meeting in which staff are also advised of a workshop that the consultant will facilitate in the coming weeks.

After the announcement, people move off into their separate offices and work groups, preoccupied with what this new effort may mean for them and the work they carry out. The parent educators discuss their concerns that in the future they will be able to offer only standardized, evidence-based parenting education programs that may be too rigid and culturally inappropriate for many families. They fear that they will be no longer allowed to be creative or adaptable in their approach.

In another office, one of the case managers is feeling anxious because he struggled with research methods during his university studies. He worries that reading scientific articles and critically appraising randomized controlled trials (RCTs) and statistics will become a feature of his daily work and a precursor to trying any new approaches with families. He decides that it may be time for a job change and goes online to scour employment sites.

The other case managers discuss the possibilities that the future may hold for undertaking research into the experiences of the families that use their case management services. They see a potential to highlight unmet needs and to demonstrate the usefulness of the work they are doing with families.

One of the home visiting social workers remembers the weekly e-mails she receives from a clearinghouse concerned with research into family interventions. She usually deletes these e-mails without reading them, but a colleague at an interagency group meeting recently told her that the newsletter contains useful summaries of research evidence for different aspects of practice. She looks in her deleted e-mail folders to see whether she can find something relevant.

Meanwhile, in her office, the Family Focus manager is imagining a future in which a neat, matching set of best practice guidelines will sit in her bookcase, clearly outlining the principles and procedures for the different service streams offered by the center. She then thinks about the cost associated with writing and producing these practice guidelines and pulls out the annual budget spreadsheet to see where some funds for this EIP project might lie.

By the time the workshop with the consultant takes place a few weeks later, participants have formulated some opinions on what EIP could mean for them and the organization in the future. Some are feeling defensive, some are curious, and some are worried about the possible implications for themselves, the service users, and the operation of the organization. The consultant begins by asking them to share their views and expectations. Meeting participants are surprised and confused by the diversity of opinions. Four views of what constitutes EIP emerge:

1. empirically supported standardized interventions
2. research-informed clinical decision making
3. best practice guidelines
4. local practice-based research activities

When the consultant says that all of these aspects could be incorporated into an organizational approach to EIP, they begin to appreciate the scope and complexity of the process they are embarking on. They look in turn at what each of these perspectives on EIP could entail.

FOUR VIEWS ON EIP

Empirically Supported Standardized Interventions

Empirically supported interventions, programs, or treatments (also called "evidence-based programs") are therapeutic, educational, or treatment programs that have an associated body of empirical research demonstrating effective outcomes. The extent and strength of the supporting research vary among interventions and programs, but several studies conducted in different settings with intervention and control groups are generally required to gain credibility as an empirically supported intervention. There are professional bodies and advocacy organizations that maintain lists of empirically supported interventions; these groups review the body of outcome evidence before adding an intervention to their lists. Such interventions are relevant to a range of fields of human services practice and concerns—for example, mental health, substance use, parenting, relationship counseling, and antisocial behavior.

Empirically supported interventions are manualized. That is, a manual is available that details the principles, practices, and procedures that are to be followed in implementing the intervention. Training to deliver the intervention and supervision of practice standards by trained specialists are also typical components of empirically supported interventions. Because the manual, training, and program oversight are often bundled together, empirically supported interventions are sometimes referred to as "packaged programs." The manuals, training, and supervision are designed to ensure that the interventions are delivered in a standardized way, without deviation from the core elements required for effective outcomes. This standardization promotes what is referred to as "program fidelity." Program fidelity is important because the replication of effective outcomes found in research studies is reliant on duplicating the standard intervention.

The body of research supporting standardized interventions can provide practitioners with a degree of confidence that service users will benefit if practitioners follow the manualized program in the way they have been trained to. Standardized interventions have, however, been criticized for a number of reasons. The parent educators in our fictitious Family Focus organization have reservations about the rigidity of standardized interventions, which limit the practitioners' potential to be creative and adaptable in response to the presenting issues and interests of the service users involved. Although there may be strong evidence for statistically significant improvements from standardized interventions, studies generally have a proportion of research participants who do not benefit from the intervention and a proportion who drop out altogether. This fact is important for human services professionals to keep in mind. If organizations intend to serve people with a diversity of backgrounds and characteristics, then they cannot rely solely on interventions that suit only the majority or a significant minority. Of particular concern is the potential to place minority and marginalized groups at further disadvantage.

It is possible that the population from which research participants were drawn differs in significant ways from the population that uses the services of a particular human services organization. As a result, service users may not relate well to the language or the approach of the standardized program. Consequently, they may withdraw from the program, or the intervention may not work well for them. Practitioners who are sensitive to this possibility are tempted to rely on their own assessments and draw on their professional knowledge and experience to adapt and modify the standardized program so that it is more suited to the participant group. Such decisions reduce the fidelity of the program implementation and weaken links to the evidence base. This tension between program fidelity and tailoring empirically supported interventions for service users creates professional and ethical tensions for human services workers.

Another concern associated with packaged interventions is the movement of human services interventions into the profit-making marketplace. The considerable outlays by organizations for training staff, purchasing manuals, obtaining licenses, and receiving supervision to implement empirically supported standardized interventions make an impact on tight budgets. These outlays contribute to what are often private, profit-making enterprises that market empirically supported interventions. Packaged interventions, however, are just one example of a wider, international trend that is moving the human services more into the private marketplace. Other examples of this trend include the contracting out of services previously provided by governments and the provision of individual budgets to service users to purchase services in an open market. Although the trend is not necessarily negative, it can lead to cost barriers to service access and the growth of an industry that profits from marketing packaged interventions for vulnerable groups. Critical appraisal is needed to determine whether decisions to adopt a standardized intervention are influenced by the best evidence or the best marketing.

Standardized interventions have an important contribution to make to the implementation of EIP in the human services if they carry a strong body of research evidence supporting outcomes. Empirically supported interventions do, however, have limitations in terms of applicability to particular contexts and individuals. Because of these limitations, they cannot stand alone as a way of ensuring strong links among research evidence, human services practice, and service user outcomes.

Research-Informed Clinical Decision Making

The second perspective on EIP is that it entails a well-informed clinical decision-making process. In chapter 1, the influence of evidence-based medicine on social work and human services and the five-step clinical decision-making model were introduced. This approach to EIP is in contrast to empirically supported interventions because evidence is incorporated into the practitioner's decision-making process rather than being attached to particular interventions. With training in the critical appraisal of research and access to research databases and systematic reviews of research, practitioners can make informed practice decisions about appropriate interventions for service users. According to this view of EBP, practitioners are able to draw on their professional skills in assessing the particular characteristics, desires, and needs of service users and to integrate their skills with knowledge from research on interventions that are likely to be acceptable and lead to the most desirable outcomes. This approach gives a degree of professional autonomy to practitioners, and it provides scope for service user input into decision making.

The research-informed decision-making approach to EIP also comes with limitations. Practitioners are generally limited in their capacity to locate and appraise research evidence because of time constraints, inadequate relevant research evidence, insufficient research skills, or limited access to research findings. Like the case manager in the Family

Focus organization, practitioners are interested in their direct work with service users and are generally less interested in reviewing research. Intervention choices made by practitioners are also limited by organizational parameters and resources and the policy context. Although social workers tend to support the use of research to inform practice, many social workers have expressed that they lack sufficient time and skills to adequately locate and appraise research (Gray, Joy, Plath, & Webb, 2014, 2015; Wike et al., 2014). But it is not just the time and skill of practitioners that limit use of this approach; the breadth and diversity of the field of human services practice, the diversity of human characteristics and circumstances, and the myriad of issues that present in practice, together with limits on the amount of funding for research, mean that research relating to many practice questions posed by practitioners is simply unavailable. This can be frustrating. There is, however, a growing recognition of the need for research-focused organizations that can assist practitioners with locating, synthesizing, and disseminating research findings, like the one remembered by the social worker in the Family Focus example.

The link between the dissemination of research summaries and changes to practice is a tenuous one. It is very easy to delete an e-mail in the course of a busy day, as the Family Focus social worker tended to do, and continue with the familiar interventions and practices that have become accepted practice in the organization. Although evidence-informed clinical decision making values professional knowledge, assessment of service user circumstances, and autonomous decision making, practitioners often experience the divide between research and practice as a challenge. The integration of research into practice decisions is very difficult to manage alone as a practitioner. The isolation and practical limitations experienced by individual practitioners attempting to implement an evidence-informed approach to practice can, however, be addressed with professional and organizational support. More attention is now being paid to knowledge dissemination, knowledge transfer, and knowledge mobilization, which are concepts that attend to the links among research, practice, and the processes that support and improve the uptake of relevant research findings in practice.

Best Practice Guidelines

At the instigation of the EIP process, the Family Focus manager was imagining a set of best practice guidelines as the outcome of the implementation process. Practice guidelines identify the principles and processes that guide practices within the organization, the types of programs that are offered, and the ways interventions are to be delivered. Research evidence on the effectiveness of different types of interventions and practice principles are incorporated into the guidelines. In addition to the research evidence base, best practice guidelines tend to be informed by ethical principles, statements of mission and goals, service priorities, and practice standards that are derived from social, political, economic, and professional trends in the wider context.

Family Focus has broad service types on offer, including case management, group programs, and home visiting. In developing best practice guidelines, the organization may draw on evidence that broadly demonstrates how similar programs support well-being and safety outcomes for children, strengthen parent–child attachment, and reduce known stressors and risk factors for families and children. There may also be evidence supporting the value in providing both universal programs and targeted interventions for families with specific needs. Beyond this broad evidence base for the types of programs, best practice guidelines include evidence for adopting particular practice principles, such as the role that workers take with families in the home visiting program, the goal setting and stages entailed in the case management program, and the processes for managing group dynamics and participation in the group programs.

There may be separate guidelines for the different programs within an organization, but these should correspond with the overarching guidelines for the organization and with the best practice guidelines of the external organizations responsible for standards in the sector. These external guidelines could be developed by the responsible government department, another funding body, a professional practice organization, or an advocacy organization. In such situations, there is a limit to how prescriptive best practice guidelines can be because they must be applicable in different practice settings. Guidelines tend to remain at the level of practice principles and standards rather than offering the step-by-step guides that accompany manualized interventions. Best practice guidelines provide a foundation and guide for practice, but they generally also allow for some flexibility in application.

The principles and standards included in best practice guidelines in the human services tend to be shaped by social, political, and professional norms as well as by research evidence. For example, for Family Focus, there may be principles about inclusive approaches to practice that respond to the diversity of family cultures and forms in the community. Such approaches are grounded in ethical, moral, or cultural principles but may also draw on some supportive evidence. Although the types of programs on offer in the center may be supported by evidence in the guidelines, the fact that these programs and not others are on offer could be a result of current political trends and associated funding rather than a lack of evidence. Best practice guidelines also include standards relating to current work practices that have been shaped historically in the particular professional and social context. In this way, best practice guidelines contribute to EIP but are always located contextually. They are also shaped by other forces that reflect current norms and standards.

The relationship between best practice guidelines and day-to-day practice in an organization is not an automatic one. As the Family Focus manager imagines her row of matching practice guidelines in the bookcase, she may be thinking that it will impress the board and meet the requirements of the funding body. Ensuring that the principles contained in the guidelines actually flow on in practice throughout the organization, however, requires attention to internal organizational culture, structures, and processes. The formal overt statements of an organization do not always equate with the messy reality of day-to-day practice. If an external consultant is engaged to produce the guidelines with little participation by Family Focus practitioners, the connection between paper and practice will be even more tenuous. There is much to be done in shifting the culture of an organization toward new practices and a critically reflective approach to EIP that a glossy document will not achieve. Conversely, if the guidelines are the documentation of an engaged, participatory process to which staff, service users, and other stakeholders have contributed, there is more likely to be a commitment across the organization to bring practice into line with the guidelines.

Local Practice-Based Research Activities

If the EIP process is viewed as cyclical and cumulative, the role for practice-based research within this process becomes clear. With an ongoing process of evidence gathering, intervention, review, and further evidence gathering, practices can be continuously reviewed and adjusted to suit the particular circumstances in the local practice context. Local practice-based research can have an important part to play in this cyclical process. Although local practice-based research may not stand alone as evidence, it can be used to verify whether the types of outcomes that have been reported in systematic reviews of published research are being replicated in the local context. Factors such as culture, professional skills, participant attitudes, language, logistics, resources, participant circumstances, and a range of other contextual factors can influence whether the practices with an evidence base are suited to a particular local setting and can make a difference for service users with particular characteristics. Local research into these factors can contribute to the local evidence base because it informs questions about the relevance and suitability of practices to the local context. If this information is systematically collected, it may also be reported and of use to a wider audience beyond the organization. Importantly, findings can be used as part of strategic planning and decision making in the organization to direct resources to interventions and programs that are responsive to presenting concerns in the local community.

The way in which evidence is conceptualized influences how the relationship between practice-based research and EIP is understood. Returning to the practice example, in the meeting between the consultant and Family Focus staff, differing opinions on what counts as evidence begin to emerge, and the role for practice-based research within the EIP process is teased out.

Case Study: Family Focus (Organizational Scenario 2)

The Family Focus case managers are keen to embark on some research with the service users to examine outcomes and experiences for families. During the workshop with the consultant to develop the EIP strategy, the case managers discuss their ideas. Another colleague challenges their view that practice research is part of EIP. He says that their proposal sounds like practice evaluation rather than evidence. He argues that findings from such research projects would be relevant only internally for the organization. To be classed as evidence, the colleague continues, research would need to be conducted by independent, external researchers using control groups and random allocation. Evidence, he says, is the body of knowledge that is available to the public, derived from rigorous research and systematic reviews of that research.

This practitioner's assertions lead to a debate within the group about the standing of a range of internal information gathering and research activities as evidence for practice. Every day, practitioners enter results from client feedback surveys, notes on consultation sessions, and client data into a bank of information. This information can be extracted to assist with service planning and evaluation, but is it part of EIP? The consultant offers the view of evidence as cyclical, cumulative, and contextually bound. The group discusses how practice research projects could contribute to the body of internal and external evidence for their programs.

One year on, Family Focus is implementing EIP strategies across the organization. A standardized parenting education program with strong external evidence is now being offered to families. With the assistance of an internal pre- and postintervention evaluation, they find that there are significant improvements on both parenting and child behavior measures within their client group after completion of the program, findings that correspond with published research on the program. What they also find, however, is that although there is an improvement in scores overall, single-parent families are not doing so well. In addition, single parents who are working generally drop out and do not complete the program.

This local practice-based research contributes to a process of strengthening the evidence for parenting programs at Family Focus. The locally collected information is very useful for Family Focus because it triggers critical reflection on practice and contributes to the ongoing improvement of services. The findings lead to a number of actions. A database search produces research on programs targeted to single parents and on effective delivery of services to working parents. A small qualitative study is undertaken in which participants who withdrew from the program are contacted to discuss their experiences and what might have been done differently to support them. The combination of external and internal knowledge informs the tailoring of program delivery. The process of critical reflection also leads to practitioners paying more attention in their marketing and delivery of parenting programs to inclusive language and engagement with not only single-parent families, but also the entire range of family types in the community.

The Family Focus example illustrates the value in integrating locally generated data with the body of published evidence. This book argues that in order to be relevant to the particular contextual features of a human services organization, EIP must consist of an ongoing process of evidence gathering, application to the local context, and critical review in light of local information. It requires openness to working in new ways, to gathering new information, and to critically reflecting on information and practice. Local practice-based research has an important role to play in this process.

How the Four Views Influence Organizations

The way in which EIP is conceptualized will influence how it is regarded and implemented within an organization. The four interpretations of EIP can shape different implementation strategies but also can be drawn together to inform an enhanced and comprehensive EIP implementation strategy.

How practitioners or managers conceptualize EIP can depend on their education and training, the expectations placed on them in their professional role, and the organization's approach to EIP. It is possible to incorporate a number of complementary approaches to EIP and to strengthen research–practice connections in different ways for different aspects of the organization. The organizational needs, composition, culture, and purpose will also shape the view of EIP and the implementation strategies that flow on from that. Table 2.1 offers some examples of how implementation strategies flow from different conceptualizations of EIP.

Table 2.1 The Four Views of Evidence-Informed Practice and Potential
Implementation Strategies

View on Evidence-Informed Practice	Potential Implementation Strategies
1. Empirically supported standardized interventions	Dedicate resources to investigate features of and evidence for different manualized intervention programs.
	Consult with service user and practitioner groups to inform the choice of program.
	Provide staff training to implement the selected program.
2. Research-informed clinical decision making	Recruit practitioners with strong research skills and good knowledge of evidence for practice.
	Improve access to research reviews through electronic databases and membership in research dissemination organizations.
	Allocate regular time slots for review of practice in the context of emerging research evidence.
	Include reference to evidence as an integral component of professional supervision.
3. Best practice guidelines	Develop guidelines for the provision of services in line with standards for service quality and outcomes using a managerial, top-down approach.
	Review industry standards and norms.
	Engage experts or consultants to facilitate the development of guidelines.
	Facilitate staff and service user input and participation into the development of guidelines.
	Provide information and training sessions for staff.
	Disseminate and promote guidelines to strengthen the organization's position in the economic, social, and political environment.
4. Local practice-based research	Generate outcome, process, and experiential data to guide the planning and adaptation of interventions to suit the local context.
	Recruit research staff to undertake and support practice research and evaluation projects.
	Include research use in practitioner job descriptions.

Implementation Paths

Based on these four different conceptualizations of EIP, it is easy to see how organizations can head down quite different implementation paths. Nutley, Walter, and Davies (2009) undertook a cross-sector review of the ways in which organizations were implementing

EBP and identified three different approaches: the research-based practitioner model, the embedded research model, and the organizational excellence model.

Research-Based Practitioner Model. In the research-based practitioner model, individual practitioners are reasonably autonomous and are given the responsibility of identifying and applying research findings to their day-to-day practice. This model is conceived largely as an instrumental, linear process of accessing, appraising, and applying research to presenting practice issues. The organizational role is to support practitioners by providing professional education and training and access to current research. The research-based practitioner model aligns with the research-informed clinical decision-making approach.

Embedded Research Model. In the embedded research model, the organization directs resources to the development of systems, processes, and standards that are informed by research and best practice guidelines. The responsibility for translating research into practice moves away from practitioners to specialized intermediary staff guided by national and organizational priorities. As with the research-based practitioner model, the embedded research model process is largely an instrumental, linear one. Organizational activities entail encouraging or coercing the uptake of research-informed protocols or practices. This model can incorporate aspects of both the empirically supported standardized intervention and best practice guideline approaches.

Organizational Excellence Model. In the organizational excellence model, a research-informed approach is reflected in the leadership, management, structure, and culture of the organization. There is an interactive, developmental approach to locating research, drawing practice connections, trialing applications, and evaluating outcomes throughout the organization. A partnership approach is also taken with external research organizations.

This model takes the practice-based research approach a step further by using a whole-organization approach to both the formal structures and the organizational culture. An important feature of the organizational excellence model is that it adopts an interactive, rather than a rational–linear, perspective. That is, knowledge is viewed as context dependent and evolving through a collaborative process of local adaptation, testing, and modification (Nutley, Jung, & Walter, 2008).

The chapters that follow present a framework that can be used to guide organizations in the achievement of organizational excellence in the implementation of EIP. An organizational approach to building and applying knowledge that is relevant, effective, and responsive in the local practice context is quite different from a linear, rational approach that assumes unambiguous evidence for what works. The stance taken in this book is that the application of research evidence to practice should entail critical appraisal of both context factors and research findings and that a developmental, cumulative approach to building evidence for practice should focus attention more on the outcomes for service users. When viewed in this way, the EIP process is a cyclical rather than a linear one. Monitoring and critical reflection on processes and outcomes in collaboration with service users and research partners can feed into future practice questions, evidence searching, and decision making. Although much of the EBP literature depicts a five-step linear process of clinical decision making, there is also wide recognition that the EIP process should be iterative and cyclical (Bellamy, Bledsoe, & Mullen, 2009; Straus, Richardson, Glasziou, & Haynes, 2011). New questions about the same practice issues will continue to arise, and new evidence can be gathered as practices are refined and adapted to improve service user outcomes.

WHAT IS MEANT BY "EVIDENCE"?

EIP hinges on gathering evidence, but there is much debate on what counts as evidence for practice in the human services. Chapter 5 is devoted to the process of gathering evidence. The overview in this section examines different ways in which evidence for practice can be understood.

Research findings are a fundamental form of evidence for practice. Research that can inform practice includes findings on the outcomes from particular interventions, the experiences of service users, the causes of or risk factors associated with particular social phenomena, the prevalence of certain social characteristics, and the nature and features of practice approaches. Depending on the practice question that is posed, different types of research will be relevant.

Within the social sciences, conventions have developed historically that define the different research methodologies and the features of strong methodologies. Research methods in the social sciences are influenced by both the scientific, positivist paradigm and the interpretivist, phenomenological paradigm. These paradigms are often aligned with quantitative and qualitative methods, respectively, and are sometimes presented as opposing. However, the rich complexity of social research brings such simplifications into question. This book does not delve into social science research methods in any detail, because there are many books that do. It is important to note, however, that these different methodological influences have led to tensions and divisions throughout the history of social research that are also reflected in the way evidence for human services is conceptualized.

In a broad sense, there are two positions on evidence in the human services. First, there is the view that a hierarchy of evidence exists and that there is an imperative to pursue evidence in the upper levels of that hierarchy whenever possible. Second, there is the view that contextually relevant, credible evidence is the best evidence, even if it is not as methodologically strong as other research. Each of these perspectives has strengths and is considered in turn.

Hierarchy of Evidence

In the hierarchical approach to evidence in the human services, evidence is judged according to scientific strength, with experimental design, and the randomized controlled trial (RCT) in particular, placed at the top of the hierarchy (Gambrill, 2006; Roberts, Yeager, & Regehr, 2006). The RCT is an experimental research design in which participants are randomly assigned to either a treatment or control group. Variables are then measured before and after the intervention to determine whether the treatment group has significantly different outcomes from the control group. In the strongest form of the RCT, neither the participants nor the researchers know which participants are in the treatment or control group (double blind). This study design is suited to medical research in which the nature of the treatment can be disguised, for example, in the contents of a pill.

There are, however, practical and ethical issues that limit the use of this design in many circumstances. Denying treatment to members of a matched control group can be an ethical issue. In some circumstances, this conflict can be dealt with by comparing two treatment groups that receive different types of treatment. For example, an RCT could compare the outcomes for people with depression who are randomly allocated to counseling and exercise treatment groups. Although the participants would know what treatment they are receiving, the researcher carrying out the pre- and postintervention assessments of depression could be blinded to which participants received which treatment to minimize the chance of potential bias. The RCT is a strong form of evidence and is the best research design for controlling the impact of interfering variables on the results.

Although a single RCT may produce strong findings, the hierarchy of evidence approach requires that several studies confirm findings. The RCT has strong internal validity, which means that one can be confident that the treatment intervention produced the outcomes in a controlled setting with specific participants. Studies that measure effects in well-controlled research environments are referred to as "efficacy research." However, to apply the research to other settings with some confidence, several studies must be conducted by different research groups in different settings. Research conducted in real-life human services settings is referred to as "effectiveness research" (Soydan, 2015). A meta-analysis of several studies can be undertaken to draw together the results from across studies.

The Cochrane Collaboration is a worldwide organization that gathers and summarizes evidence from research to inform decision making about health care treatment. Cochrane Collaboration reviewers typically undertake meta-analyses of all relevant research on a specified intervention. The preference for RCT studies is well established in the Cochrane Collaboration protocols; inclusion of RCTs in Cochrane Collaboration evidence reviews is mandatory "if they are feasible for the interventions and outcomes of interest" (Chandler, Churchill, Higgins, Lasserson, & Tovey, 2003, p. 2). There is, however, a growing recognition of the value in including other study designs in evidence reviews if these designs are clearly defined and suited to the research question being investigated. The Campbell Collaboration, the sister organization of the Cochrane Collaboration, is concerned with evidence reviews on the effects of social interventions in the fields of crime and justice, education, international development, and social welfare. As such, it is one source of evidence for the human services. While recognizing the value of RCT research, the Campbell Collaboration is also cognizant of the limitations, as articulated in the following extract from their guidelines:

> In many intervention areas, the circumstances under which the available RCTs have been conducted tend to be somewhat circumscribed. Those studies may be more likely to be conducted as research and demonstration projects rather than evaluating routine practice, to involve the program developer or researcher in the implementation of the intervention, to occur in atypical settings such as university clinics or especially high functioning organizations, to use participants who have been selected or screened to be especially appropriate to the intervention or who are less diverse than the general population of application, and so forth.

In those circumstances, the greater validity of RCTs comes at least partially at the expense of external validity, that is, the generalizability of the results of the research to other settings. (Campbell Collaboration, 2015, p. 9)

The contrived nature of experimental efficacy research enables the control of variables and gives strength to findings, but the conditions of the intervention can be very different from those in human services settings. Strategies to deal with this limitation include undertaking meta-analyses of RCTs in different settings and effectiveness research studies that better reflect the real world of practice.

With meta-analysis of RCTs as the gold standard within the scientific paradigm, other research designs fall in below RCTs in the hierarchy. These include quasi-experimental designs in which conditions of the RCT may be weakened in a number of ways, including using naturally occurring treatment and control groups (for example, using people on service waiting lists to create a control group), forgoing random allocation because of ethical concerns, or not blinding participants or researchers because the nature of the intervention makes it impossible to do so.

The other study designs that follow in the hierarchy are single-case designs, cohort studies, and case–control studies. Single-case design entails multiple measurements of variables for a participant both before and after the intervention to better delineate the impact of an intervention versus the impact of other variables. For example, a participant's level of depression may be measured several times before and after a therapeutic intervention in recognition of the fact that a range of environmental factors can cause depression levels to fluctuate. Cohort studies track a group of people who have had a particular experience that equates with an intervention, but this experience is not controlled under research conditions. For example, a study may track people who are retrenched when a large business closes. Data on a range of variables, such as mental health measures, are gathered over a period of time and compared with a control group or the general population. Case–control studies are similar to cohort studies in that a group of people with the same experience are selected for participation. However, data are collected retrospectively to assess exposure to particular risk factors, experiences, or interventions. For example, people who dropped out of university studies could be contacted to provide information on their financial and housing circumstances during the period of study, information that would be compared with data from a control group who continued their university studies to see whether there is an association between financial and housing circumstances and university completion.

In comparison with the RCT, quasi-experimental, single-case, cohort, and case–control studies offer less control over the range of interfering factors, reducing the strength of the findings. Although less control over variables and measurement has a negative impact on the strength of findings, these study designs can more easily be used to examine the real world of human experience and human services provision than the constructed and controlled environment of an RCT. Despite their strength, RCTs are often inappropriate for the investigation of particular research questions. For example, people would not be randomly allocated to retrenchment and continued employment groups for the purpose of tracking their outcomes.

The next level in the hierarchy of evidence comprises qualitative research designs. Such designs encompass a variety of theoretical approaches, including grounded theory and phenomenological and action research, and a range of methods, including observation, interviews, and focus groups. Qualitative research offers scope to examine meanings, explanations, and a complexity of interdependent themes, factors, and patterns in real-world settings. Such research is not limited to measuring outcomes from discretely defined interventions using predefined measures, as is the case with RCTs. However, despite the depth and breadth of explanatory and illustrative detail that qualitative research may offer, it is less definitive about the association between factors or variables and outcomes than the methodologies higher on the hierarchy. For example, qualitative research may help us understand the experiences of being retrenched, but there may still be questions about how retrenchment affects mental health outcomes in comparison to the general population.

On the lowest level in the hierarchy are practice wisdom and expert opinion on standards for effective and appropriate practice held by professionals with expertise in the field of practice. This evidence is derived from the practice experience of experts who are held in high regard in the profession. The use of practice wisdom as evidence has drawn criticism, however, because it can be used to uncritically legitimize and maintain accepted practices and avoid engagement with stronger evidence (Gambrill, 2001). Although practice wisdom and clinical observation are recognized as a source of evidence, they do not offer the strength of evidence that the higher levels of the hierarchy do. From a hierarchical perspective, evidence that is higher on the hierarchy should be considered before drawing on practice wisdom and expert opinion.

Relevant and Credible Evidence

Because of the controlled circumstances and artificial environments in which some research studies, and particularly RCTs, are conducted, questions are often raised about the transferability of findings to the real world of human services practice in which service user groups have unique characteristics and practice is constrained by resources and logistics. These concerns, together with the recognition that all research has limitations, have led to an alternative approach to evidence for human services practice. This approach emphasizes the relevance and applicability of research for the purpose of improving social work and human services practice and the credibility or quality of research regardless of research design (Mullen, 2015; Shaw, 1999).

The quality or credibility of research should be assessed before it is adopted as evidence, regardless of whether the research is an RCT or a qualitative study. The hierarchy of evidence is useful in prompting consideration of the strength of findings regarding relationships between interventions and outcomes. With greater control of interfering variables, more confident conclusions may be drawn about the relationship between a particular intervention and the outcomes for participants. There are, however, other factors apart from the research design that influence the confidence with which conclusions can be made about likely outcomes for service users.

How outcomes are measured is one aspect of quality. For example, in following up with retrenched workers, standardized tools for measuring depression may not capture the particular debilitating circumstances associated with retrenchment and may miss key concerns. Although standardized tools may offer validity and reliability for the measurement of a particular construct (for example, depression), they may not identify the issue of concern that is being researched and may not be suited to all circumstances or cultural groups. Survey tools designed specifically for the research project are necessarily better, however; home-grown survey designs do not have a bank of research supporting their validity and reliability.

Research design entails many choices and decisions and generally involves some compromises for ethical or practical reasons. Participant selection methods and the population from which participants are drawn can lead to research biases, which are another aspect of research quality and relevance.

In sum, all research has limitations, and these need to be carefully assessed in reviewing evidence for practice in a particular context. It is not the research design alone that determines the quality of the evidence. There are many types of research methodology, mixed methods, and adaptations of standard research designs. An RCT does not always offer the most credible evidence in response to a particular practice question.

Alongside quality, research needs to be relevant if it is to be used as evidence for practice. Relevant research has appropriate research questions, methods and designs that suit the particular questions, and findings that can inform practice decision making and program planning in the human services. In appraising the research, determinations are made of whether the methods and measures produce data that are relevant to the research question. For example, if a study sets out to examine well-being outcomes from a community intervention for refugee immigrants, use of a number of qualitative and standardized measures would be preferable to use of a single standardized scale of well-being. A mixed-method approach may be more relevant because it mitigates potential cultural bias in a single measure and provides opportunities to examine how immigration affects various aspects of life. To build a picture of how the program made an impact on the lives of the people involved, it is necessary to draw on different sources of information. Results from a standardized measure of well-being may contribute to that picture but would be of limited use on their own.

Relevance also relates to the transferability of findings to practice contexts. Evidence is sought in the human services to guide practice so that outcomes for service users are improved. If it is impossible to see how the type of intervention delivered as part of an RCT could be replicated in a human services organization or with a particular service user group, then the relevance of findings must also be questioned. Rather, human services professionals seek evidence on programs and interventions that can be implemented in their settings or principles for practice that they can adopt or integrate. Thus, the evidence that is relevant for one organization may not be relevant for another. An organization providing preventive health services in Indigenous communities, for example, may select a few qualitative studies as more relevant evidence because of Indigenous participation in these studies, even though RCTs that draw participants from white, middle-class communities may also be available. To assess the relevance of research, detailed information is required on the characteristics of participants, the components of programs or interventions, and the ways programs were implemented.

A risk associated with focusing too closely on the relevance of evidence is that it may limit the scope of what is considered useful evidence for practice. If evidence is sought narrowly within the parameters of what is seen to be appropriate, relevant, or practical to implement in a particular setting, consideration of alternatives may be limited, serving to sustain existing ways of providing services. An EIP approach entails openness to new and better practices and preparedness to look critically at existing practices. Because the evidence gleaned from RCTs can prompt consideration of alternative practice approaches, it may still be useful in practice even if the population group is different or the interventions cannot be exactly replicated. The important thing is to review findings critically and with an overarching focus on what can be applied to the practice setting in question. Although a mental health organization may not offer exercise programs, for example, emerging evidence on the benefits of physical exercise for people with schizophrenia could be drawn on in designing a program that includes regular physical activity. Evidence from a variety of sources can support innovation and thinking outside the box.

Systematic Reviews of Evidence

Whether a hierarchical approach to evidence is adopted or the focus is on relevant and credible research, evidence involves more than the findings from a single study. Systematic reviews of available research on a particular practice question are a key part of the evidence-gathering process. When only RCTs are included in evidence reviews, it is somewhat easier to carry out a meta-analysis of results because study design aligns. Results can be pooled to establish trends across research projects undertaken in different settings. When studies with a mixture of research methodologies are gathered together in the body of evidence, a meta-analysis is no longer standardized. A systematic, thorough, and critical approach to the review of evidence is, however, just as important. Systematic reviews of research are discussed further in chapters 5 and 6.

Knowledge and Evidence

The discussion of evidence in this section has largely been concerned with research findings, but other information may be gathered within organizations that can contribute to the body of evidence used for practice decision making. Whether information other than research findings can be regarded as evidence is, however, a matter for interpretation and debate.

Mathews and Crawford (2011) drew a distinction between evidence and knowledge that informs social work practice. They regarded *evidence* as findings resulting from a structured enquiry or research process—that is, "a formal, planned and organized process which systematically produces knowledge which can then be usefully disseminated to a wider audience" (Mathews & Crawford, 2011, p. 12) and is aligned with the values of scientific research. They regarded *knowledge* as multifaceted, broad in meaning, and having a lower level of certainty than evidence. They saw knowledge as including theory and explanations and evidence as leading to the revelation of facts and understanding through a process of hypotheses and judgments. The distinction between knowledge and evidence is, however, not clear-cut. Some degree of theory, explanation, and value judgment is involved in both knowledge and evidence. Therefore, the negotiation of knowledge and evidence occurs in interactive, relational ways.

In order for information to be regarded as evidence, the expectation is that it is the result of a systematic process of inquiry that is verifiable and robust. This process includes the description of methodology in a research report or in an internal report on service user data. In making use of evidence for practice decision making, an explanatory logic links decisions about practice to evidence. This process requires rigor, critique, and analysis. Unlike opinion, which is individual and internal, evidence is verifiable. Hard facts about the impact of interventions are, however, elusive to varying degrees in human services practice. The subjective, individualized, and context-bound nature of human experience means that associated practice and research information is generally open to some level of interpretation. Different ways of knowing are shaped by values, politics, and power relations in society. Critical reflection by decision makers and a thorough appraisal of the practice context are thus required in the process of applying evidence to practice.

For a particular organization, evidence for practice involves more than research findings. To be meaningfully applied in the human services, research must be considered in the context of the range of information about the practice setting and individual circumstances. Professional assessments of a service user's circumstances; the nature of the worker–client relationship; and service user experiences, opinions, and preferences count as evidence toward the choice of intervention in a particular situation. Information about workers' skills in carrying out certain interventions, knowledge about resource constraints, and information on policy and legislative requirements can also be used as contextual evidence. Contextual evidence informs judgments about the most suitable interventions or programs to be delivered by an organization. Such context-dependent knowledge must be considered in conjunction with research findings in building an evidence base for practice.

Evidence in the human services is rarely static or definitive because of the variation, complexity, and changes that are characteristic of human lives, relationships, and cultures. Although questions about what will work for service users are commonly attached to discussions about EBP, evidence is rarely so straightforward. There are generally provisos and limitations to the available evidence. There are also cultural variations on what counts as credible evidence. For example, what is regarded as strong evidence from a clinical research perspective may be dismissed as an example of white colonization from an indigenous perspective. For service users to engage with interventions, they need to regard them as culturally appropriate. The interventions generally need to make sense if they are to make a difference. What counts as evidence becomes a negotiated terrain among the stakeholders involved in decision making about practice. An EIP approach entails an ongoing process of seeking relevant and useful evidence that is continually reviewed, updated, and refined to suit the practice context.

From the critical realist perspective adopted in this book, *evidence* is regarded as provisional, well-informed, negotiated knowledge on what is reasonably expected to produce the best outcomes in a particular context. It draws together robust research, both qualitative and quantitative, and contextually relevant information, including service users' perspectives.

CRITICISMS AND LIMITATIONS OF EIP

Over the past 20 years, the EBP movement in social work and the human services has drawn criticism as well as support. Although the benefits and limits of EBP are now widely accepted (Gray et al., 2014), there remain some criticisms that raise concerns about an uncritical adoption of EBP in the human services.

Disputed Evidence

As discussed earlier, all research has its limitations and requires appraisal and interpretation before it can be applied to practice contexts. Because evidence is open to interpretation, it can also be disputed. Disputes over evidence can occur, for example, when quantitative, experimental research is in disagreement with qualitative, experiential findings. The dispute can hinge on which research methodology is valued over the other, but different findings can also emerge when the same research design is used. When findings are varied or disputed, the way is open for divergent positions to be argued in the name of evidence and for political forces to come into play. For example, a program promoted as having a strong evidence base may receive government funding, when other programs appearing to have evidence that is equally as strong do not. When there is political will or a strong advocate, the evidence for a particular program can be highlighted at the expense of that for other programs. In this way, evidence can be used as a political tool.

Engaging with evidence in the human services requires a preparedness to accept that definitive answers are often unavailable and to focus on building a balanced body of evidence. Research findings can be disputed and have their limitations, but this does not mean that the evidence is worthless or useful only as a political tool. An EIP approach requires that stakeholders be as astute about the political processes as about the strengths and limitations of the research, recognizing that research evidence can inform practice but is not necessarily the only basis for practice decisions. From a social justice perspective, there is an imperative to allow the voices of minority or marginalized groups to be heard. This imperative entails including diverse types of research and information as evidence and giving credence to the perspectives of researchers, advocates, practitioners, and service user groups.

Inadequate and Inconclusive Evidence

Another criticism of EBP is that there simply will never be sufficient research evidence to address the vast and changing circumstances that present in human services practice. Because of this inadequacy, evidence for practice is invariably inconclusive. Again, there is a political dimension to this criticism of EBP. Valued programs and higher profile service user groups or social concerns attract more funding for research. Research evidence, in turn, strengthens the standing of these programs and generates further expansion, research, and evidence. Meanwhile, there is less research in practice areas that are underfunded, perhaps because practice is with lower profile service user groups or social issues. For some areas of practice, there is little evidence to scrape together, not because programs are producing poor outcomes, but because there are few programs and even less research or evidence.

This criticism cautions us not to immediately associate a lot of research with stronger evidence. This caveat is particularly relevant in relation to packaged standardized interventions that use their evidence base as a key marketing tool. Getting research done and building an evidence base give the companies selling standardized interventions an advantage over their competitors. It is important to look at who has done the research, whether there is a vested interest in the outcomes of the research, and how high the quality of the research is, including potential for bias.

In response to this criticism, a degree of comfort with inconclusive evidence is required. In addition, it is important to continue to advocate for, engage in, and publish research on practice to build the body of quality research in the human services. A critical perspective on the evidence landscape is needed. One high-quality study on a particular parenting program may provide evidence that is as strong as, or stronger than, six studies on another program.

Emphasis on Research Evidence over Service Users' Perspectives

The third criticism made against EBP relates to the centrality of human relationships in achieving positive intervention outcomes. Human services are fundamentally about human relationship building, which can be viewed as operating on a different level with a different value base from that of the scientific paradigm in EBP. By focusing on evidence, attention can be diverted from the relationship building that is fundamental to human services practice. The experiences and desires of service users can be overlooked in preference for a more technical approach to practice.

Relationship building is the basis of much of effective practice in social work and human services. Gathering and applying research evidence and building trusting relationships require different processes. This does not mean, however, that research mindedness cannot be integrated with relationship building. Social work and human services practice is characterized by work on a number of levels: individual, family, group, community, organization, policy, and research. Different processes come into play in these different levels of practice, but they continue to operate in complementary ways in providing a holistic approach to human services practice. This multilevel, person-in-environment approach to practice is well established in social work and conveyed in the International Federation of Social Workers (2014) global definition of social work. As previously stated, the triad relationship among critical reflection, relationships, and evidence is a key theme in this book. It is the responsibility of human services practitioners and managers to ensure that these three elements are appropriately balanced and integrated into practice. The inter-relationship between evidence and human relationships is now looked at more closely.

RELATIONSHIPS AND EIP

The quality of the relationship between practitioner and service users is fundamental to the effectiveness of a practice or program. This assertion is not in conflict with an evidence-informed approach, and there is much evidence to support it. The therapeutic relationship and clinician skill in building relationships have been identified as the most important factors influencing effective outcomes, regardless of the type of counseling intervention (Wampold & Imel, 2015). Following a program manual without attention to relationship building and the associated processes of empathy, client engagement, and service user participation is unlikely to achieve the same level of success as when relationship dynamics are prioritized. How these relationship factors are measured and what level of influence they have on outcomes in comparison to the contents and structure of the particular intervention techniques are questions that continue to be grappled with in research. It is fair to say, however, that both the components of the intervention and the quality of the relationship influence outcomes for service users.

Empirically supported standardized interventions or off-the-shelf manuals and packaged evidence-based programs are not in themselves evidence based. Rather, it is the skillful delivery of such programs that has an evidenced link to effective outcomes. This is one of the reasons why these programs have compulsory training, licensing, and supervision requirements associated with them. This specific training is, however, limited, and EBP would not exist without professional skills and competence to implement interventions. For EIP to produce effective outcomes, it is important for practitioners to recognize the central importance of relationship building and for organizations to support professional development with appropriate training and opportunities for debriefing, reflection, feedback, and supervision. With professional expertise and critical reflection, practitioners are able to integrate relationship-building skills with evidence as they choose appropriate ways of working with service users.

Relationship building is a central component of human services interventions, but it is also part of the process of engaging people with services. Seeking help can be experienced as challenging, humiliating, or stigmatizing. A precursor to effective service provision is thus initiating relationships that will engage people with the organization through promotional, outreach, community, partnership, and intake activities. The quality of relationships will also have an impact on retention rates. Interventions will be effective only if people experience them as worthwhile and continue to engage with the process. The strongest research evidence for a program is useless if people stay away from the service. In this sense, effective engagement and retention are as important as effective outcomes.

The implementation of EIP also involves relationship building beyond the worker–client relationship. Relationships within organizations and between organizations must be attended to if the implementation process is to be successful. Chapter 3 focuses on these organizational processes and relationships.

REFLECTIVE QUESTIONS

Four Views on EIP

- From your own practice experience, identify examples of each of the four interpretations of EIP:

    1. empirically supported standardized interventions

    2. research-informed clinical decision making

    3. best practice guidelines

    4. local practice-based research activities

- What were the strengths of the practice in each of the examples you chose?
- What were the limitations or drawbacks of the practice in each of your examples?

Implementation of EIP

- What are some examples from your own experience of strategies that support an EIP approach in the organization?
- What are the conceptualizations of EIP that underlie those strategies?

Nature of Evidence for Practice

- What do you regard as the benefits and drawbacks of the two approaches to identifying evidence for practice?

   1. Hierarchy of evidence approach

   2. Relevance and credibility approach

- What is your position on these two approaches? Do you favor one or the other? Why?
- What types of information would you accept as evidence for practice? In which circumstances?

Politics of EIP

- In what ways is EIP a political process?
- In what ways are knowledge and evidence for practice negotiated? What are some examples from your own practice experience?
- In your view, what are the key strengths and limitations of adopting an EIP approach?

3

Organizational Groundwork for Evidence-Informed Practice

Whether you are a clinician striving to make well-informed practice decisions that will lead to the best outcomes for service users, a board member or manager seeking to position your organization well for future funding and recognition in a competitive environment, or a team leader asking your staff to engage more actively with research evidence for service user outcomes, you will need organizational systems and strategies to achieve your goals. To plan, implement, and engage with such organizational systems and strategies, it is helpful to have a clear rationale for taking an organizational approach to the implementation of evidence-informed practice (EIP) and a grasp of some theoretical perspectives that can guide your approach and aid your critical reflection on the process.

This chapter establishes the rationale and theoretical backing for an organizational approach to the implementation of EIP. The positive outcome to be gained from engaging with this material is a clearer, critical perspective on the implementation of EIP in organizations and an improved capacity to argue a position in the face of doubts, entrenched practices, and scarce resources. The rationale and theoretical perspectives covered in this chapter provide the groundwork for the subsequent chapters, which offer a more practical guide for human services boards, managers, and practitioners wishing to enhance EIP in their organizations.

Before launching into the rationale and theories, the chapter provides a brief overview of what is meant by an "organizational approach" to EIP. An organizational approach supports evidence-informed decision making at all levels from the practitioner–client relationship, to specific programs, to service planning across the whole organization. This approach addresses organizational leadership, structures, processes, guidelines, and protocols that help embed EIP in day-to-day operations. Among other things, it includes practitioner supervision and information technology services to support the process. An organizational approach also involves attention to organizational culture with strategies for staff engagement and training that promote commitment to and ownership of the EIP processes.

WHY TAKE AN ORGANIZATIONAL APPROACH?

Chapter 2 introduced four perspectives on EIP: empirically supported standardized intervention programs, research-informed clinical decision making, local practice-based research activities, and best practice guidelines. Each of these perspectives will have limited impact if organizational strategies are not engaged to support their implementation. To recap briefly, much of the social work literature on the topic aligns evidence-based practice (EBP) with a clinical decision-making process similar to that used in medicine, which places the onus on the practitioner to gather and appraise the best current research evidence and then to make informed decisions about practice interventions with individual clients. This is an unreasonable expectation to place on busy practitioners without also providing resources to support the process. Practice-based research, likewise, requires organizational resources and processes to ensure integration of research outcomes with practice.

Alongside these perspectives, there is pressure in the realm of human services practice to adopt particular empirically supported standardized programs, such as specific parenting education programs, which are deemed to be evidence based. Programs are sometimes adopted without critical appraisal of whether the given program is the best match to the cultural and demographic characteristics of the service user group or the skill set of the organization's practitioners. In such circumstances, practitioners may feel frustrated by the restraints placed on their clinical decision making. Best practice guidelines can also be experienced as a top-down imposition on practitioners if practitioners have not been involved with their development and the organizational culture does not readily accept new practice directions.

Regardless of the perspective on EIP, there are compelling reasons to take a wider, organizational view of implementation:

- There is more to social work and human services practice than individualized practice.
- It is unreasonable to expect practitioners to gather, generate, appraise, and apply evidence alone.
- Priority setting, resource allocation, and program implementation decisions occur at an organizational level.
- Organizational practice is an established and integral part of generalist social work practice.
- The viability of an organization may depend on taking a strategic approach to the implementation of EIP.

Each of these arguments is looked at more closely in turn.

The first argument is that social work and human services practice have wider mandates than individualized practice. It is true that many clinical practitioners in the human services have clients with whom they work through a traditional casework process of assessment and intervention. For these practitioners, like those in medical practice, the clinical decision-making model for EBP makes sense. There are, however, many social work and human services practitioners who do not work in this individualized way. To make progress toward social change goals, their practice encompasses work at different levels, including the individual, family, group, social institution, community, policy, and political realms. According to the International Federation of Social Workers (2014),

> The social change mandate is based on the premise that social work intervention takes place when the current situation, be this at the level of the person, family, small group, community or society, is deemed to be in need of change and development. (para. 5) . . . Social work practice spans a range of activities including various forms of therapy and counseling, group work, and community work; policy formulation and analysis; and advocacy and political interventions. (para. 14)

Research evidence can inform practice in all of these domains of social work and human services practice. A wider perspective that encompasses the clinical decision-making approach is needed to include these different types of human services practice.

The second argument for taking an organizational approach to EIP is that it is unreasonable to expect practitioners to gather, generate, appraise, and apply evidence. Considerable time and resources are required to gather and appraise the evidence relating to an issue presenting in practice or to plan and conduct a practice-based research project. Human service practitioners generally do not have the capacity to direct the required amount of time away from service delivery activities to do this well. Many social workers say that they lack the time, skill, or inclination to carry out the information gathering and research appraisal requirement when they need evidence for daily practice decisions (Burke & Early, 2003; Carrilio, 2008; Comino & Kemp, 2008; LaMendola, Ballantyne, & Daly, 2009; Mullen, Bledsoe, & Bellamy, 2008). It is organizationally inefficient for each individual practitioner to compile, evaluate, and apply evidence without collaborative interactions with others in their practice group or organization. An evidence-based clinical decision-making process is unlikely to be successful without additional resources provided by supervisors, teams, and organizations. Thus, even for the human services practitioners who work individually in a clinical role, the clinical decision-making model of EBP does not account for the resource and support needs for EIP implementation.

In a review of research on barriers and facilitators to the implementation of EBP, six types of barriers were found: (1) inadequate agency resources dedicated to EBP, (2) skill and knowledge needs of practitioners, (3) agency culture, (4) research environment, (5) practitioner attitudes, and (6) inadequate supervision (Gray, Joy, Plath, & Webb, 2013). Perhaps with the exception of practitioner attitudes, all of these barriers are functions of the organizational environment and need to be tackled at an organizational or interorganizational level to implement and sustain an EIP approach.

The third reason for taking an organizational perspective is that priority setting, resource allocation, and program implementation decisions occur at an organizational level. Individual practitioners face constraints in the types of interventions they are able to provide. The reality of modern human services practice is that practitioners tend to have quite specialized or defined roles within a wider, varied realm of practice. The way in which roles are defined and mandated within organizations determines the degree of power or influence that individual practitioners have over their own practice and, hence, their room for implementing different types of EIPs. Government priorities also play a significant role in shaping the types of programs that are funded and consequently provided. Practitioners take on positions and perform roles that are defined by the broader programs organizations have developed and provided resources for. Interventions and practices are also shaped by partnerships with other professionals in multidisciplinary teams that are negotiated and established over long periods of time. A complexity of social and political factors thus influence the programs and types of interventions that are provided by organizations and delivered by practitioners. Although it is expected that social and human services workers have some degree of professional autonomy in their roles, they have limited capacity to decide on interventions in the way that the clinical decision-making model of EBP suggests.

Shifting practices to align better with evidence generally requires strategic processes supported by resources and organizational policies. For example, a child and family services practitioner may be able to determine the way she works with a family within the constraints of the practice setting and timeframe that are deemed appropriate by the organization. If, however, a shift in practice from an individual worker–family intervention to a multifaceted school or community-based program is indicated by the evidence, the practitioner is unlikely to be able to provide such an intervention without taking an organizational approach to gain approval and resources. Time, resources, and collaborative partnerships would be required to establish such a new approach to working with families.

This consideration leads to the fourth reason for an organizational approach—that organizational practice is an established and integral part of generalist social work practice. The need to work strategically within organizations is nothing new for social work practitioners. Most social workers are employed in organizations and use organizational approaches to attain practice goals. The need to work strategically equally applies to the goal of building stronger relationships between research evidence and practice. A. Jones and May (1992), examining the centrality of organizational work for effective human services, presented significant reasons why organizational practice cannot be ignored in the human services that are summarized in Table 3.1.

Organizational practice provides practitioners with strategies to influence organizations. Understanding how to work effectively with organizational processes to uphold practice principles and achieve goals is a core component of Western social work education. It is therefore unsurprising that knowledge of organizational culture and change processes is also useful in understanding and implementing EIP.

The final argument for taking an organizational approach to EIP is that the viability of organizations can depend on doing so. Organizations that direct resources to EIP and demonstrate that their services produce good outcomes for service users are positioned better in the current climate of human services provision. The pressure placed by governments, the media, and the general public on organizations to have reasoned and substantiated evidence for interventions and programs has continued to grow (Broadhurst & Pithouse, 2015).

The pressure to provide evidence for the effectiveness of interventions is further highlighted by the international policy trend toward individualized budgets widely adopted in the disability and elder care sectors in Western countries. In this approach

Table 3.1 Reasons for the Centrality of Organizational Practice in Social Work

Factor	Explanation
Location	Most human services are provided in organizational settings.
Nature of the occupation	Social work is an organizational as well as a professional occupation, with professional standing and roles being negotiated in organizational settings.
Purpose	Social work aims to link people with resources, services, and opportunities. This effort involves extensive dealings with organizations, including work to improve the effective operation of human service systems and policies.
Service users	Organizations are powerful in the lives of service users, and principles of social justice, access, equity, rights, and participation guide the work of practitioners with organizations.
Personal needs of workers	Understanding how to work with organizations can help workers cope with the stresses of organizational life.

Source: Adapted from A. Jones & J. May (1992). *Working in human service organizations: A critical introduction* (Table 1.2, pp. 10–11). Melbourne, Australia: Longman Cheshire.

to service funding, service users hold budgets and draw on them to purchase services from publicly funded and private service providers (Scourfield, 2010). Organizations reliant on individualized budget holders for income operate in a marketplace in which they need to attract service users and their individual budgets. The organizations that can demonstrate that their practices, services, and programs are guided by current evidence and produce effective outcomes are better placed to attract customers and maintain long-term viability.

MANAGERIALISM, EFFECTIVENESS, AND QUALITY PRACTICE

Having presented the arguments for taking an organizational approach to EIP, it is worth addressing the concern that an organizational approach may serve managerial goals rather than the goals of quality practice and service user well-being. Notions of effectiveness are fundamental to this discussion. It is useful to consider the different value stances that shape notions of effectiveness and some of the associated tensions for EIP.

One of the criticisms leveled against the EBP movement is that it is driven by a managerial agenda that defines effectiveness in efficiency terms and rationalizes funding by directing resources to interventions that have established evidence or are more cost-effective (Webb, 2001). Although focusing attention on practices that have demonstrated outcomes has appeal, there is a risk that interventions that have not been sufficiently researched, innovative ways of practicing, and work with groups that require more complex (that is, costly) interventions will be sidelined.

Social work is centrally concerned with addressing power imbalances and promoting access and equity for socially disadvantaged and marginalized groups. Social justice principles are also present in the mission statements of many human services organizations. EIP can support this social justice mandate, but an uncritical adoption of EIP may work against social justice principles. For example, there may be strong evidence for an intervention for young people with depression gathered from research involving predominantly white, middle-class participants. Practice in an organization may suggest that young people from particular cultural groups in economically disadvantaged communities do not engage well with the intervention program, drop out, or have poorer outcomes. If so, there is a case to be made for gathering more carefully targeted evidence rather than uncritically accepting the evidence base for this program.

Critically appraising evidence is vital when choosing appropriate ways of working with service user groups. In seeking to control interfering variables as much as possible, research studies generally select participants with a single issue of concern. However, human services organizations often work with people who have complex problems. Research findings may not directly apply to these individuals. A well-evidenced parenting intervention, for example, may not be effective for parents with substance use or mental health concerns, who need more targeted or multifaceted interventions. If positive outcomes are to be achieved, interventions for people with multiple concerns may be more complex and costly. Thus, the most economical service that appears to be evidence based may not be effective for service users in greater need.

If an inclusive, social justice agenda is to be upheld, human services managers and practitioners must be vigilant in both critically appraising the relevance of evidence and in articulating challenges to narrow, efficiency-based views of EBP. A closer examination of the notion of effectiveness and the associated value perspectives is required to promote a social justice–oriented approach to evidence-informed practice.

A narrow view of effectiveness could be grounded in economic rationalism. Effectiveness could be measured, for example, in terms of the number of people who complete a parenting program, participation rates for sessions, and delivery cost per head. Focusing only on cost is not the only narrow view of effectiveness. It would also be narrow to view effectiveness only in terms of building close relationships with service users if this view results in large amounts of time spent in directionless interactions with a few service users. A narrow view of effectiveness could also entail focusing on the achievement of specifically defined objectives without respect for the wishes, personal goals, and attributed meanings of the service users involved. For example, a narrow measure of effectiveness would be the number of jobs obtained for service users if these jobs were acquired without regard for users' employment goals. When funders, managers, or practitioners hold such narrow views of effectiveness, clashes and conflicts inevitably arise. It is an ethical responsibility of the human services to provide effective services, but what actually constitutes effectiveness is contested terrain. The capacity to identify differing views on effectiveness, and the underlying values, will aid in negotiating the relevance and strength of the evidence.

These different perspectives on effectiveness all have some legitimacy. That is, cost per head, quality of relationships with service users, and achievement of defined outcomes are aspects of effective human services. Because organizations are accountable for the use of the public or philanthropic money they receive, value for money is a measure of effectiveness. From a social justice stance that incorporates equity, inclusion, and redress disadvantage, however, the cost of a service cannot stand alone as a measure of effectiveness in the human services. Quality of relationships and level of consumer satisfaction are also indicators of effectiveness. It is important for service users to be engaged with services and to feel that their goals are recognized and that appropriate support and interventions are being provided. Specific, defined outcomes are also measures of effectiveness because they can indicate social, emotional, and economic well-being. Such indicators are important at the individual, family, and social levels and provide the basis for planned and purposeful interventions. Just which outcomes are relevant and how these should be measured are generally complex questions that require investigation and negotiation.

Taking a multifaceted view of effectiveness is proposed as a better approach than adopting a single, narrow view. Figure 3.1 depicts a multifaceted approach to effectiveness that incorporates the three domains of cost-effectiveness, service user experiences, and defined outcomes. Taking this approach requires bringing several bodies of evidence together to create a holistic picture of the effectiveness of service provision. Evidence about comparative costs can inform judgments about the ethical use of limited resources. Evidence about consumer satisfaction can be used to judge effectiveness of service user engagement and relationship building as the basis for responsive, inclusive, and appropriate interventions. Evidence on specific outcomes can help measure the degree to which practices and interventions have facilitated particular desirable outcomes. Giving consideration to effectiveness from different perspectives and value positions is the starting point for negotiating wider, more inclusive understandings of effectiveness and the related role of evidence.

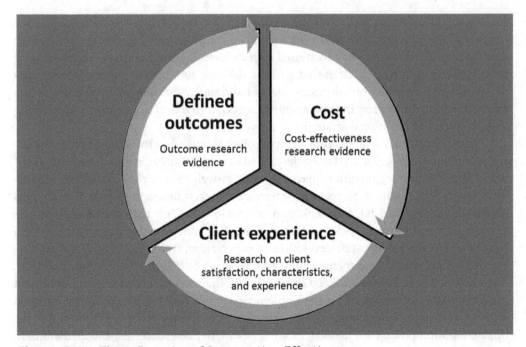

Figure 3.1 Three Domains of Intervention Effectiveness

How effectiveness is defined for services and programs can shift with changes in political priorities, social expectations, and organizational demands. Different stakeholders can also have different value perspectives. Service users' views on the types of services that would be of assistance to them can be at odds with what organizations are providing and how they do so. Opportunities for service users to influence the services provided by organizations are often quite limited. From the practitioner perspective, there may be a clear sense of what an effective service looks like for the service users they work with, but external forces such as the policy or funding framework can define effectiveness differently over time. Practitioners may be forced to defend or change their practice and may feel powerless in the face of uncompromising views on outcomes and effectiveness measures held by managers. Similarly, managers can feel powerless when faced with the same type of pressure from senior executives or funding bodies. Such scenarios are challenging. Even when evidence and rational argument are drawn on, the politics of power relationships can shape discourses and decision making about effectiveness and associated resource allocation. Proactively establishing a multifaceted and inclusive view of effectiveness, locating appropriate evidence, and presenting a well-developed argument may offer a strategic advantage for organizations.

This discussion has reinforced the need to work strategically and organizationally on the implementation of EIP. EIP is partly a technical, professional process, but it is also shaped by values and political processes. Service users, practitioners, and managers of human services organizations can take part in the approach at an organizational level in that political process.

ORGANIZATIONAL ANALYSIS FOR EIP

Having established that EIP implementation is to be approached organizationally, the next step is to determine what an organizational approach to EIP means for human services organizations. An organizational approach entails analyzing and understanding organizations and, on the basis of that analysis, devising suitable organizational strategies to support EIP. This section addresses analysis and understanding with an introduction to organizational theories; in subsequent chapters, a practical approach to identifying and planning organizational strategies is provided.

Every organization is different in terms of its historical, cultural, and social context. Implementation strategies need to be developed to suit that organizational context. What works well for one organization may not work as well for another. Although organizational analysis assists with planning strategies in each unique organization, there is always an element of trial, feedback, and adaptation through the experiential process of organizational change. There are some indicators from research that organizational factors such as leadership, staff development, supervision, systems, funding, and staffing resources support the implementation of EIP (Aarons & Palinkas, 2007; Aarons, Wells, Zagursky, Fettes, & Palinkas, 2009; Gray et al., 2013); however, further research is needed into organizational strategies for the implementation of EIP in different organizational settings. Ongoing monitoring, critical reflection, review, and planning throughout the implementation process are needed. Sharing of experiences, successes, and challenges in implementing EIP among organizations will also contribute to the body of knowledge on the topic.

Some understanding of how organizations work contributes to informed organizational strategies. A good way to gain new insight into the processes, functions, and outcomes of an organization is to apply different organizational theories. Offered in the following paragraphs is the briefest of introductions to organizational theory, which is a vast field of scholarship. The purpose is to trigger reflection on organizational processes and explore possible ways of working within organizations to promote EIP.

Several alternative theoretical perspectives have been brought to an understanding of organizations, each of which can prompt consideration of different aspects of the implementation process. A. Jones and May (1992) provided a useful overview of organizational theories and associated practice implications for the human services that forms the basis of the analysis for EIP presented here. The critical realism perspective recognizes that different systems and mechanisms—and, hence, theoretical influences—can operate concurrently in producing and understanding outcomes. Table 3.2 outlines the theoretical framework developed by A. Jones and May. For the purpose of this book, however, the practice implications have been reworked so that they specifically relate to issues in the implementation of EIP. This framework is a useful starting point for human services executives, boards, managers, and staff to analyze features of their organization and to reflect from different perspectives on how it is positioned for EIP implementation.

Being presented with so many theoretical viewpoints at once may seem a daunting starting point for organizational analysis. As presented in Table 3.2, however, each theory offers key principles for the implementation of EIP. The theories offer different perspectives on how one may go about working for change in an organization. Each theory on its own is limited, but by considering the theories in relation to an organization, a critically reflective analysis in preparation for implementation emerges.

Considering an organization from different theoretical standpoints draws attention to its particular values, principles, and mechanisms and leads to a richer understanding of its processes and discourses. Theories can also reflect the different subjective experiences and interpretations that manifest among individuals and groups in organizations. Critical postmodern and critical realist approaches offer a metatheory for considering these different discourses, recognizing that individual histories, experiences, and value systems lead to different meanings and interpretations of organizational life. Critical postmodernism promotes critical reflection and analysis rather than the rigid application of a single theoretical perspective (Fook, 2002). Like the critical realist perspective, it attends to the structural systems and dominant discourses that propagate privilege or marginalization for particular groups and examines power and influence.

Analyzing organizations from these varied theoretical viewpoints can assist managers and practitioners in identifying the formal and informal processes influencing the uptake of EIP. Although there are differences and some tensions between the key propositions and value stances of the theories listed in Table 3.2, these theories need not be conceived of as exclusive of one another. Rather, the theories offer lenses through which the coexisting complexities and contradictions in organizations can be examined. For example, the formal structures of power, authority, and decision making aligned

Table 3.2 Theories about Organizations and Their Implications for Understanding Evidence-Informed Practice Implementation

Theory	Key Proposition	Principles for Evidence-Informed Practice Implementation
Bureaucracy	Legal–rational authority is fundamental to power relations in organizations.	Determine whether there is formal authority for the adoption of evidence-informed practice (EIP), for example, in a funding agreement, organizational charter, or government policy binding on the organization.
Scientific management	Formal structures and processes are critical to organizational functioning.	Determine the structures (for example, board, policies, committees, supervision, approval processes) within the organization required to approve, endorse, and support EIP.
Human relations	Informal social, relationship, and psychological factors have an impact on organizations.	Engage employees and managers with the EIP process to promote successful implementation. Pay attention to relationship building and to the social gains and rewards of getting involved with EIP.
Systems	Different units or parts of an organization are interdependent social systems.	Assign the tasks of gathering, appraising, disseminating, applying, and generating evidence to people in different parts of the organization. Develop systems to integrate and coordinate efforts across the organization.
Ecological	External environments determine the nature of organizations.	Attend to the ways government policy, funding context, competitive markets, professional associations, practice networks, organizational partnerships, and the like shape and shift the organization's approach to EIP.
Decision making	Organizations are decision-making systems. Decision-making processes are varied and often not solely rational.	Analyze where and how decisions about practice are made in the organization (for example, individual practitioners, board, executives, teams, program managers) and how reference to evidence can support decision making.
Market	Transactions occur in organizations, as in marketplaces, between self-interested individuals.	Identify and communicate the benefits and rewards of implementing EIP for the different stakeholders and units within and outside the organization.

(continued)

Table 3.2   (Continued)

Theory	Key Proposition	Principles for Evidence-Informed Practice Implementation
Neo-Marxian	Organizations operate as a structure of capitalism. Processes of power, control, and employer–employee relations are central.	Identify structural constraints and the impact of dominant political and economic interests on efforts to promote evidence-informed interventions for marginalized groups.
Political economy	Organizations are political arenas of power, influence, and authority. Position, function, political skills, and structures determine power.	Understand the sources of power, influence, and authority in the organization that can be used to support or hinder EIP implementation. Develop political skills to influence support for EIP and to voice the interests of marginalized groups.
Feminist	Gender relations influence organizational processes. Personal experiences and politics (power) are linked.	Remain sensitive to gender relationships in EIP implementation because the human services workforce has a higher proportion of female than male practitioners, which is often not mirrored in management ranks.
Indigenous	Institutional racism operates through social arrangements in organizations. Key concepts can have different cultural meanings.	Be attentive to marginalization or exclusion of Indigenous and other cultural groups and ensure that views on effectiveness and the nature of evidence are inclusive of different cultural perspectives.

Source: These descriptions of theories are derived from the framework in A. Jones & J. May (1992), *Working in human service organizations: A critical introduction* (pp. 43–73), Melbourne, Australia: Longman Cheshire, and applied to evidence-informed practice.

with the bureaucracy and scientific management theories offer a logical structure for analysis. Such an analysis can run alongside a critique of the complex decision-making processes informed by decision theory. This examination is further enhanced by analysis of structural power imbalances identified through the application of political theories. The overt, official face of the organization exists alongside the sometimes contradictory daily interactions and varied work practices. The systems and ecological theories prompt us to look holistically at internal and external environments, whereas the Indigenous and feminist approaches alert us to privileged and marginalized discourses that need to be challenged. These theoretical perspectives will be picked up again in later chapters as different aspects of EIP implementation are discussed.

It is recommended that an organizational analysis be undertaken as the starting point for developing a strategy for EIP implementation or enhancement. Based on the theories presented in Table 3.2, the reflective questions provided at the end of this chapter are a guide to assist practitioners and managers through such an organizational analysis process.

DEALING WITH PRESSURES FROM OUTSIDE THE ORGANIZATION

Several factors in the current human services environment are influencing the adoption of EIP approaches by organizations. Although, to some degree, organizations are swept along with changing trends at the wider political, social, and economic levels, critical reflection on the features of the external environment can assist organizations in clarifying and strengthening their position, maintaining their principles, and achieving their goals. This section considers two forces at work in the external organizational environment in relation to the implementation of EIP: (1) the pressure to demonstrate value for money and (2) the impact of information technology.

The dominance of economic models in social policy and the language of cost–benefit analysis have created an overriding expectation that human services will provide value for money. This expectation is often translated into cost-cutting and efficiency measures. Value for money can also be interpreted, however, in terms of quality service outcomes. If communities and service user groups are the stakeholders for whom human services organizations are established, then positive outcomes for communities and services user groups should be the measure of value for public money. The definition of value for money is, however, a realm in which human services organizations, service user groups, and professional and advocacy bodies participate in ongoing debates.

Rather than using the language of EIP as a weapon for cost cutting, organizations with a well-developed understanding of evidence for practice are positioned to engage in political debate and argue for the role and outcomes of human services practice. There are many concerning examples of funding cuts to organizations on the grounds that the outcomes for service users could not be adequately demonstrated even when face validity was strong, such as in the provision of shelter to homeless women and children experiencing family violence. The onus is on the organizations to demonstrate that they are accountable for the use of public money, that their services are in line with what effectiveness research indicates, and that positive outcomes are optimized for service users. The capacity of organizations to successfully defend their positions is strengthened by analysis, planning, and a strategic approach to the implementation of EIP. This process offers the basis for articulating the value for money, whether public money, philanthropic money, or individual budgets, that the organization provides.

The second aspect of the external environment influencing EIP implementation is digital technology, which can facilitate implementation by providing faster, wider, and more efficient dissemination of research information. In contrast with the time and effort required at the end of the 20th century, practitioners and managers can now access research and syntheses of research relevant to practice issues without leaving their desks. Technology has also enabled connections and networks between communities of researchers and practitioners beyond the boundaries of organizations, countries, and formal roles. There is huge potential to share information that supports the research-to-practice and practice-to-research transfer of knowledge.

Supported by technology, specialized practice research clearinghouses, advocacy groups, and research centers have taken on the tasks of gathering, synthesizing, and disseminating research findings so that practitioners and organizations do not need to duplicate this work. The demands of face-to-face work, however, mean that virtual connections and access to online information are often haphazard and intermittent. Although the links among bodies of research, research synthesis, dissemination, and practice uptake are generally not strong, they are improving (Bellamy, Bledsoe, & Traube, 2006; Wike et al., 2014). Again, this situation points to the need for a planned and strategic approach by organizations in deciding on which types of information to access, which organizations or groups to connect with, how information will be gathered and disseminated, and what processes will be used to facilitate the uptake of evidence in reviewing and reshaping practices and interventions. The need to direct organizational time and resources to plan and support this process is also evident.

In summary, the environment in which human services organizations operate places pressures to comply in particular ways and to demonstrate value for money. It can also create considerable uncertainty for organizations through threats of funding withdrawal. To maintain a degree of autonomy and influence, there is an imperative that organizations take a proactive approach to reviewing, planning, implementing, and articulating their approach to EIP. In this way, arguments can be made about quality practice, positive outcomes for service users, and value for money.

The online environment offers significant opportunities and resources to support EIP. Systems and processes can be established within organizations to support evidence-gathering activities and the translation of new evidence into revised practices with better outcomes for service users. Attention also needs to be paid to how organizations communicate and promote their own approach to EIP. When negotiating in a political realm, the service that an organization delivers is not the only aspect that is important. It is also essential that there is capacity within the organization to convincingly articulate the EIP approach taken by the organization and the ways this approach enhances value.

WORKING WITH THE ORGANIZATIONAL CULTURE

Having considered the external environment, attention is now turned to examine the environment within the organization. The organizational systems, processes, and culture (that is, shared meanings, values, dominant language, and patterns of behavior) will influence how EIP is defined, approached, and implemented within an organization. It is useful to approach the implementation of EIP as a change process because there is much that can be gleaned from the organizational change literature. Subsequent chapters describe strategies for changing human services organizations so that the environment, systems, and resources support EIP. The change process approach offers a way to reconceptualize and focus management strategies and processes to better facilitate the mission of the organization through stronger links between research and practice. To achieve this, organizational culture must be attended to.

Regardless of how rationally and convincingly EIP goals and processes are presented in organizational documents, if employees throughout the organization are not engaged and on board with the process, then good intentions can easily be thwarted. The three aspects of evidence gathering, evidence dissemination, and practice modifications should be regarded as parts of one process, and strategies need to be in place to integrate these parts (Figure 3.2). There are critical links in the EIP process between evidence gathering and evidence dissemination and between evidence dissemination and modifications to practice. Strong leadership, relationship building, clear strategies, encouragement, and resources are required to support organizational change that will strengthen the links between evidence and practice in organizations. Organizational culture and processes need to be addressed so that members of the organization can believe in the EIP process.

Organizational cultures are complex and intangible because values, behaviors, and practices are enmeshed with personalities, historical patterns, and an array of internal and external factors. In large human services organizations, there are likely to be several discourses that operate concurrently within different sections or groupings in the organization. For example, some units within an organization may have a culture of discussing and using research, whereas other groups may draw on personal or collegial experiences to inform practice decisions. Cultural change in organizations tends to be slow and is generally unpredictable. Gradual shifts in aspects of the organizational culture are more likely than sudden, organizationwide cultural change. Changes to organizational culture may be instigated as a formal top-down process, but changes can also be initiated, facilitated, or thwarted by employees in different parts of the organization. It is useful to look at the roles, values, attitudes, and behaviors of management and employees across the organization and to identify how they relate to EIP strategies. In considering

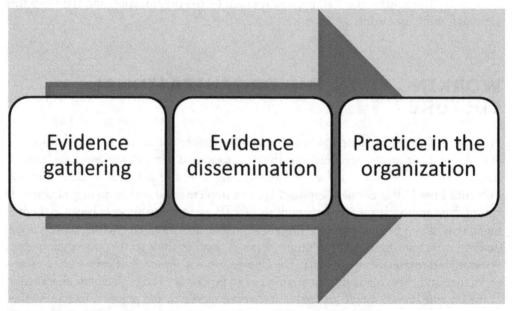

Figure 3.2 Three Elements of the Evidence-Informed Practice Process

the readiness of organizations to adopt EIP approaches, Wike et al. (2014) found that cultures of learning, critical reflection, evaluation, practice modification, and innovation were more open to EIP.

The theoretical perspectives outlined in Table 3.2 are useful for considering the different angles from which the change process can be approached. If there is a formal mandate within the organization to implement EIP, then the manager holds particular responsibilities to implement change processes (supported by the theories of bureaucracy and scientific management). From the other theoretical perspectives, attention is drawn to the need to consider human relationships, individual gains, and power politics and to plan strategies accordingly to get staff across the organization on board with the process. Strong leadership that inspires a shared vision for EIP in the organization will facilitate a cultural shift. Practitioners at different levels in the organization who value the implementation of EIP for professional or ethical reasons can also take on a variety of roles that contribute to the organizational change process.

Kirst-Ashman and Hull (2006) delineated 12 roles that the generalist human services practitioner may take on when implementing change at a macro-organizational or community level: enabler, mediator, integrater or coordinator, general manager, educator, analyst or evaluator, broker, facilitator, initiator, negotiator, mobilizer, and advocate. All of these roles can be adopted by practitioners at different levels in the organization who take on a leadership role to support the EIP implementation process. Over time, it is likely that wider support will be generated for the shifting culture in the organization. Table 3.3 shows how each of the roles proposed by Kirst-Ashman and Hull can be extended and applied to the goal of implementing EIP in organizational settings. This schema can help identify people in key positions in an organization who may be able to take on leadership roles that support EIP implementation.

Efforts to change organizational culture are invariably faced with some resistance because change often presents real or imagined threats and challenges. In dealing with resistance, it is helpful to invite, recognize, and acknowledge the different individual histories, positions, knowledge, and experience of staff. Although the social work profession has been accused of having a culture that does not engage well with research or EIP approaches, social work also has a long history of social investigation and research to inform practice (LaMendola et al., 2009; Murphy & McDonald, 2004; Webber & Carr, 2015). Practitioners may experience barriers to engaging with research and may view the implementation of EIP as a threat to the way they have been working, a challenge to their own professional autonomy, or a dismissal of the practitioner–service user relationship and their insight into service users' unique circumstances. These areas of practice knowledge, however, can also play a significant part in implementing an EIP approach that is relevant and responsive to service user circumstances.

Finding ways to engage with practitioners and integrate their valuable practice knowledge with research evidence is important for effective implementation. Some degree of resistance is to be expected, but there is also considerable support for evidence-informed approaches to practice and growing recognition among practitioners of the benefits in building stronger links between research and human services practice. For example, in a survey of 364 Australian social workers in a variety of fields of practice, more than 80 percent regarded EBP as useful for social work and as a means to improve practice with service users (Gray et al., 2014).

Table 3.3 Leadership Roles that Support Organizational Implementation of Evidence-Informed Practice

Role	Support Provided
Enabler	Provides encouragement and suggestions to help staff understand and implement evidence-informed practice (EIP) more easily and successfully
	Reduces resistance and ambivalence to EIP by recognizing feelings of concern, identifying strengths in staff, and conveying optimism about the potential for EIP
Mediator	Resolves arguments and objections to EIP by taking a neutral role to facilitate communication and clarify misconceptions
Integrator or coordinator	Initiates contacts with other parts of the organization that have a role to play in EIP implementation
	Identifies ways to effectively share information and coordinate activities
General manager	Holds administrative responsibility for the planning, implementation, and monitoring of EIP, demonstrating technical skills in the EIP process, people skills in leading and motivating staff, and conceptual skills in understanding how EIP improves the quality of services to service users and meets macroenvironmental requirements
Educator	Establishes a strong knowledge base of relevant evidence and the EIP process and educates others in the organization in both formal and informal ways
Analyst or evaluator	Monitors and evaluates the effectiveness of the EIP implementation process by maintaining process and outcome data and providing feedback to others in the organization
Broker	Identifies potential external resources, linkages, and partnerships to support the EIP process and facilitates connections (for example, university partnerships, research clearinghouses)
Facilitator	Brings colleagues together to promote EIP by pooling ideas and resources, identifying strategies, and providing ongoing updates on outcomes and information (for example, setting up a journal club in which members locate, appraise, and apply relevant research)
Initiator	Alerts management and decision makers in the organization to the reasons an organizational EIP strategy is needed for the organization to respond appropriately to expectations in the external environment and promote quality service provision
Negotiator	Resolves conflict regarding the relative merits of EIP by articulating its value and strengths

(continued)

Table 3.3 (Continued)

Role	Support Provided
Mobilizer	Identifies key people and resources and convenes forums to initiate and develop the EIP process (for example, by forming a community of practice that draws together practitioners and researchers to implement an EIP approach for a particular field of practice)
Advocate	Speaks out and activates strategies to increase awareness among decision makers of the links between evidence and outcomes for service users and the need for organizational planning, policies, and resources to implement the EIP process

Source: This list of roles (applied to evidence-informed practice implementation) was derived from K. K. Kirst-Ashman, G. H. Hull (2006). *Generalist practice with organizations and communities* (pp. 21–26). Belmont, CA: Thomson.

Preparing an organization for changes that result in better use of research to inform practice will have resource implications. Dedication of staff time is required to develop and implement new processes and, importantly, to get staff across the organization on board with the goals and processes of EIP. The concern with directing resources to organizational change is that most human services organizations are overwhelmingly stretched with the demands of direct service provision. For publicly funded services, managers are accountable for the appropriate use of funds. If resources are directed away from service provision, then management has an ethical responsibility to ensure that the implementation of EIP processes will lead to better services and improved well-being for service users. The reflective exercises at the end of this chapter give an indication of the scope of potential organizational change and can be used to prompt reflection about whether implementing EIP will strengthen the viability of the organization into the future.

The model presented in this book, with the associated strategies and processes for implementation, is not intended as an all-or-none solution. Careful thought should be given to the type of change that is likely to lead to improved service user outcomes for any particular organization. Strategies provided throughout the book can be selected if they appeal as suitable for the organization. In the unique and complex circumstances faced by each individual organization, there is no guarantee that strategies will be easy to implement or that intended outcomes will be achieved. A preparedness to engage in an ongoing process of analysis, reflection, planning, trial, feedback, adaptation, and further analysis is also part of the organizational implementation process and can contribute to building the knowledge base on the effectiveness of EIP implementation strategies. It is, however, important to realize that the implementation of EIP must involve much more than an official change in organizational policy and public statements. It is also about orienting the culture of the organization to support solid research-to-practice links. This orientation requires strong leadership by an individual or a leadership team that is able to devote the time, thought, and energy to engaging with stakeholders across the organization and planning implementation strategies that respond to organizational circumstances.

ORGANIZATIONAL MODEL FOR THE IMPLEMENTATION OF EIP

Figure 3.3 depicts EIP implementation in organizations as a five-phase, cyclical process. As discussed in chapter 2, presenting the EIP process as a cyclical one supports the cumulative nature of evidence gathering and application to practice as learning develops in an organization. Information obtained from practice monitoring and evaluation continues to be fed back into question formulation and evidence gathering. By presenting EIP implementation in phases, the model offers a way to order thinking and guide strategies in organizations. The phases are not, however, discrete. The phases interact in dynamic and recursive ways. For the purpose of planning and implementation, progress through the phases and associated strategies can be monitored and evaluated.

Features of the model are explained and illustrated in chapters 4 through 8 of the book. Each phase in the cycle is addressed in a separate chapter, along with the associated organizational strategies. Reflective questions are provided for each phase to guide application to unique organizational settings.

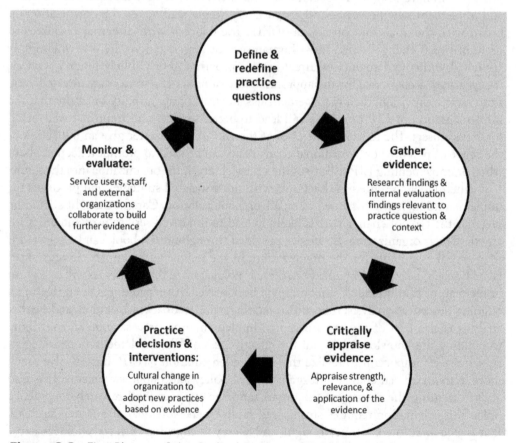

Figure 3.3 Five Phases of the Cyclical Process of Evidence-Informed Practice Implementation

This model for the implementation of EIP in organizations is derived from the five-step EBP clinical decision-making model discussed in chapter 2 (Gibbs & Gambrill, 2002). It is also informed by an organizational case study of the conceptualization and implementation of EIP in which each of the five steps in the decision-making model was found to be present in the organization (Plath, 2014). The case study revealed a complexity of activities connected with the life and culture of the organization that could be related to each of the five steps in evidence-based decision making. The descriptive model that emerged reflects much more than a clinical decision-making process, although clinical decision making remains a part of the EIP approach in an organization. Knowledge building and practice development can be cumulative within organizations. Practitioners across the organization can contribute to this knowledge building in different ways. The process of using evidence to shape practice is ongoing and cyclical.

The model presented in this book draws on research into the implementation of EIP and is designed to support strategic planning for organizational learning and evidence-informed processes. Rather than being an alternative to the five-step clinical decision-making model introduced in chapter 1, the four perspectives of empirically supported standardized interventions, research-informed clinical decision making, local practice-based research activities, and best practice guidelines have been incorporated into the model. The model is intended to be adaptable to the complex and varied types of organizations in the human services. In the subsequent chapters, the reader is guided through a reflective process of considering how aspects of the approach could be applied to their organization and the plans and strategies that could flow from this application. The model is not prescriptive but rather offers a structure to assist in conceptualizing and managing the complex process of EIP implementation.

The framework in this book is offered as a resource to organizations embarking on the organizational change process required for enhancing EIP and, consequently, the quality of practice and outcomes for service users. Before embarking on the implementation model, it is suggested that a leadership and coordinating team be established. The reflective questions can be used within the leadership group to analyze and prepare the organization for an EIP strategy.

REFLECTIVE QUESTIONS

Defining Effectiveness

- Select a program or type of intervention provided by your organization. How do you think effectiveness is defined by each of the following: service users, practitioners, managers, funders, and the wider community?
- What values underlie these views on effectiveness?
- What different types of evidence could be obtained to assess the effectiveness of the program or intervention from these different perspectives?
- Are there other ways in which effectiveness could be defined for this program or intervention?

Key Questions for Analyzing Your Organization

The following questions are a useful starting point in planning for an EIP implementation strategy:

- Where does the formal authority for the adoption of EIP lie? Are there funding agreements, an organizational charter, or policies that require or support EIP?

- Are there leaders in the organization who can champion and drive the implementation of EIP?

- What are the organizational structures (for example, policies, decision-making bodies, approval processes) that would authorize and support EIP? What are the associated processes required for approval?

- What are employees' views on EIP? What social and relational benefits could there be for employees engaging with EIP?

- What are the likely benefits and rewards of implementing EIP for different stakeholders, individuals, and units in the organization?

- Which units or practitioners in the organization are already adopting an EIP approach?

- How is, or could, evidence gathering, appraisal, dissemination, application, and generation be performed by different parts of the organization? How would integration and coordination among the different parts of the organization be achieved?

- How are decisions about interventions actually made at different levels in the organization, including individual practitioners, teams, program planning and development, resource allocation, and priority setting? How is evidence identified and used in this decision making?

- What are the structural constraints and the impact of dominant political and economic interests on efforts to promote quality and effective services for service user groups? How can the efficiency agenda be challenged?

- What are the sources of power, influence, and authority in the organization that could be used to support or hinder EIP implementation? How might political skills be enhanced by key players to influence EIP support?

- What processes would support the inclusion of racial and ethnic, gendered, and other cultural views on the definitions of effectiveness, evidence, and EIP within the organization?

External Environmental Influences on EIP Implementation

- What external influences are there on how EIP is approached in the organization (for example, government policy, funding context, markets, professional associations, practice networks, service user groups, and organizational partnerships)?

- What opportunities are there for connections or partnerships with other organizations or groups (actual or online) to support EIP in the organization (for example, in relation to gathering, appraising, and applying research evidence or conducting practice-based research)?
- Where can information, research, and other evidence be obtained externally that could inform practice within your organization?
- What capacities does the organization have for articulating the EIP approach it takes? How effectively is this done? How could this be strengthened?

Building Capacities to Support an EIP Organizational Culture

- Review the roles outlined in Table 3.3. Are there people in your organization who are already taking on these roles?
- Are there others who could be supported to take on roles to champion and facilitate EIP?
- In what ways could leadership roles be strengthened or supported within the organization?
- Where could resistance to EIP emerge in the organization?
- What practice knowledge and experience do practitioners and others in the organization have to contribute to EIP?
- How could the value of this practice knowledge and experience be recognized in the organization?
- In what ways could staff be supported or encouraged to engage with the EIP implementation process?

4

Phase 1: Defining Practice Questions

Practice questions are the reference point for the evidence-informed practice (EIP) process and guide what evidence is sought. Defining practice questions is presented here as the first phase in the implementation cycle. Because practitioners can draw on their experience to ground practice questions in the key practice concerns for the organization, they have a central role to play in this phase.

Clearly defined practice questions support evidence gathering that is more efficient, focused, and goal directed than research into general areas of practice. Careful consideration is needed to select and shape practice questions that reflect the key service provision issues in the organization and focus decisions about the most appropriate interventions for current and future service users. An abundance of questions about practice could be asked within any human services organization. Although there are generally no right or wrong practice questions in EIP, the capacity to investigate practice questions is limited. It is beneficial to select questions that will be most useful for the organization to investigate. Canvassing and consulting within and beyond the organization about the appropriate practice questions to ask will help enhance the relevance and applicability of findings and engage staff in the EIP process. Construction of clearly focused practice questions provides the foundation for the subsequent phases of evidence gathering and practice implementation.

Straus, Richardson, Glasziou, and Haynes (2011) gave seven reasons why it is worth putting time and effort into well-formulated practice questions. Such questions

1. help the organization focus resources on evidence that is directly relevant to practice and service user requirements;
2. help focus resources on evidence that directly addresses the organization's particular knowledge needs;

3. focus and guide evidence search strategies;

4. suggest the forms useful answers might take;

5. can help the organization communicate more clearly with service users and other stakeholders;

6. help stakeholders critically reflect on practice and better understand the nature of practice in the organization; and

7. by facilitating answers to important questions, increase stakeholders' knowledge and learning, which in turn strengthens the competence and confidence of practitioners.

Although defining practice questions is discussed here as the first phase in the EIP cycle, practice questions can emerge at any point in service planning and delivery and can relate to any aspect of practice, whether at the start of a new program or in the course of existing practices or projects. Well-formulated practice questions are as relevant for managers making program funding and policy decisions as they are for practitioners working directly with individuals and families. In this chapter, the components of a practice question are examined, along with the steps and strategies that can support a planned and coordinated approach to the development of practice questions in human services organizations.

The generation of practice questions is of limited use if there are no opportunities to gather evidence or use findings to influence and improve practice. An organizational approach to EIP entails identifying how the organization can support the generation of key practice questions and plan strategies to move from questions to evidence, interventions, and outcomes.

As explained in earlier chapters, the approach taken to EIP in this book incorporates critical analysis, relationship building, and attention to evidence. This is the case with regard to each of the phases of EIP implementation, including designing practice questions. This chapter therefore includes some critical analysis of the ways different stakeholders, roles, and perspectives can shape practice questions and the implications of excluding stakeholders from the process. The chapter also looks at how leadership and social relationships can support the design of relevant and well-formulated practice questions.

WHAT A PRACTICE QUESTION LOOKS LIKE

A practice question is used to focus evidence-gathering activities and can take a variety of forms. The circumstances, resources, and service user groups in each human services organization are unique, and therefore practice questions should be designed to reflect the distinctive context, knowledge needs, and organizational goals. This section provides a guide for formulating different types of practice questions. The organizational and relational processes required to generate these questions are discussed later in the chapter.

Rubin and Bellamy (2012) offered six broad categories of practice questions that can be asked as the starting point for an evidence-informed enquiry:

1. What factors best predict desirable or undesirable outcomes?

2. What can I learn about service users, service delivery, and targets of intervention from the experiences of others?

3. What assessment tools should be used?

4. What intervention, program, or policy has the best effects?

5. What are the costs of interventions, policies, and tools?

6. What are the potential harmful effects of interventions, policies, and tools? (Rubin & Bellamy, 2012, p. 7).

The following sections provide some pointers on structuring and refining practice questions in relation to

- interventions and outcomes,
- assessment and risk factors,
- engagement of service users,
- targeting and tailoring in response to service user characteristics,
- experiences of service users,
- unintended outcomes, and
- explanations of practice.

Interventions-to-Outcomes Questions

The work undertaken by Sackett, Richardson, Rosenberg, and Haynes (1997) in evidence-based medicine has established a widely accepted framework for shaping practice questions about the outcomes of medical interventions, commonly referred to as the PICO approach. The letters represent the four components of a practice question and are a useful starting point for designing practice questions relating to the outcomes of human services interventions:

1. *Population or Patient and Problem:* In the human services context, this component may also be referred to as the "client," "service user group," "client group," or "community" and the "issue" they are facing.

2. *Intervention:* Human services terms for this component include "service," "program," "treatment," or "practice"—that is, what could be done in relation to the presenting concern.

3. *Comparison:* The intervention may be compared with doing nothing or with an alternative course of action, practice, or intervention.

4. *Outcome:* This component addresses what the practitioner and the service user aim to achieve.

A practice concern in a child health clinic is described here to illustrate these four components of practice questions.

Case Study: Child Health Clinic

A child health clinic sees a large number of children around 10 to 12 years of age who are referred by schools for disruptive, aggressive, and defiant behaviors. The clinic has been offering family counseling to assist with parenting, relationship issues, and other stressors that the families face. The practitioner team is aware that there are some group programs designed to address child conduct problems, but to date, the clinic works only with individual families. The clinic leader encourages the practitioner team to identify practice questions as part of an organizational EIP strategy.

Using the PICO framework, the team comes up with six practice questions:

- Practice Question 1: What is the effectiveness of family counseling (I) compared with group programs (C) in reducing the incidence of disruptive, aggressive, and defiant behaviors (O) among children ages 10 to 12 years (P)?

This practice question contains each of the four components: The population (P) is children ages 10 to 12 with disruptive, aggressive, or defiant behaviors. The intervention (I) is family counseling. The comparison (C) is group programs, and the outcome (O) is reduction in the incidence of particular behaviors. Practice Question 1 would be useful as a starting point for gathering evidence if the clinic is considering offering group programs for families and there is the potential to shift service provision in this direction.

The expertise of the practitioners may, however, be with individual and family counseling, and there may already be organizations that offer parenting programs. In such circumstances, the team may want to ensure that they are taking the best approach to family counseling, in which case an alternative practice question may be more appropriate:

- Practice Question 2: What is the effectiveness of different models of family counseling (I and C) in reducing the incidence of disruptive, aggressive, and defiant behaviors (O) among children ages 10 to 12 years (P)?

The P, I, and O components are the same as in Practice Question 1 for this practice question, but the C (comparison) is between different models of family counseling. As a starting point for an evidence inquiry, Practice Question 2 would facilitate closer examination of the features of different models and components of family counseling for child behavior concerns. Similarly, a practice question could focus on a comparison between different group programs.

Alternatively, the clinic may be shifting focus toward early intervention for children. Under these circumstances, the practice question could be constructed differently again:

- Practice Question 3: What are effective interventions (I) for the early reduction of emerging aggressive, disruptive, and defiant behaviors (O) in children up to 10 years of age (P)?

In this question, the population (P) has changed to younger children with emerging problems in response to the interest in early intervention. As is often the case with new areas of practice, the question does not have a stated comparison (C) between different interventions, so the comparison being made is to not offering interventions. The purpose is to canvass a range of interventions (I) and to see whether there are more effective benefits to offering interventions than not offering interventions. The outcome (O) remains a reduction in specific behaviors. A subsequent inquiry may produce a comparison between specific interventions.

For an organization considering a shift to early intervention, another important practice question is whether early intervention is more effective than later intervention. Another practice question is required:

- Practice Question 4: How effective are early intervention measures (I) in reducing aggressive, disruptive, and defiant behaviors (O) in children up to 10 years of age (P) compared with later intervention (C)?

Because the focus of the comparison is on the point of intervention, this question leaves the type of early intervention measures open. The inquiry is likely to reveal a range of different types of interventions, information that can be used to guide future inquiry and comparisons.

It is possible for the intervention component to relate not just to the type of intervention, but also to where it is provided. Consideration may, for example, be given to interventions in clinic, home, or school settings. A corresponding practice question could be formulated:

- Practice Question 5: What is the comparative effectiveness of family counseling provided in clinic, home, and school settings (I and C) in reducing aggressive, disruptive, and defiant behaviors (O) in children up to 10 years of age (P)?

In this question, the interventions that are compared relate to the different settings in which they are provided. The investigation may reveal, however, that the nature of family counseling varies with the setting; this possibility could also become a part of the investigation and inform future program development.

The organization may also be interested in investigating the value for money of different intervention options. As a result, an additional practice question would emerge:

- Practice Question 6: What are the costs and benefits (O) of group parenting programs (I) for families of children with emerging aggressive, disruptive, and defiant behaviors (P) compared with individual family counseling (C)?

Such a practice question leads into the realm of cost–benefit and other forms of economic analysis, in which outcomes and benefits are translated into monetary terms. As discussed earlier, this focus can contribute to a holistic view of effectiveness.

The PICO framework is a useful starting point for developing practice questions because it helps focus thinking and clarify specific information needs. By working through options within each of the four components of the question, consideration can be given to how answers to the question could inform practice decision making. Reflections on the particular organizational policies and circumstances may also help focus and clarify the most relevant practice question for the organization or team. In the previous examples, this reflection led to the proposed policy shift to early intervention and a review of the skill level of the staff, which influences the type of interventions considered as feasible and worthy of investigation in the organization.

The PICO framework is well suited to medical and health contexts in which patients present with particular conditions, the desirable outcomes are reasonably clear, and the intervention options are well defined. The framework is also helpful in the human services context, but there are many other relevant practice questions that emerge in the human services that do not easily fit this schema. These are considered in the following sections.

Assessment and Risk Factor Questions

Returning to the earlier child health clinic practice example, questions about assessment practices and risk factors may include the following:

- How can emerging aggressive, defiant, and disruptive behaviors be assessed in young children?
- What are the risk factors associated with aggressive, defiant, and disruptive behaviors in childhood?

In this practice example, as in many other areas of practice, a better understanding of the needs, strengths, and opportunities associated with the service user target group will help the organization select appropriate services, interventions, and programs for those who are likely to benefit. Practice questions about assessment can address comparison of different assessment tools for reliability, validity, brevity, cost, and compatibility with the target service user group. Questions could also relate to the time frame or manner in which the assessment is conducted. Practice questions about risk assessment and associated tools, as in the second of the two questions above, could be used to inform inquiries about population-based preventive and early intervention measures.

Engagement Questions

Practice questions about service user engagement are concerned with how best to spark the interest of people who would benefit from particular interventions, how to motivate them to contact a service provider, and how to counter the negative images and stigma that can be associated with some human services. Early engagement is particularly important when there is evidence for greater effectiveness of interventions before problems become too severe. Engagement may, however, be harder at this time because potential service users may not recognize emerging concerns as a problem worthy of intervention. Service user engagement is also concerned with how to keep service users engaged and motivated to continue with an intervention or program. For our practice example, a suitable practice question could be as follows:

- What strategies have been successful in engaging families of children with emerging aggressive, defiant, and disruptive behaviors in early intervention programs?

Targeting and Tailoring Questions

Practice questions can be designed to gather information that will assist in targeting and tailoring services better to different service user groups. Identifying the characteristics of service users who withdraw from services and the links between particular service user characteristics and intervention outcomes could help in the selection of relevant service models and interventions, such as in the following sample questions:

- What family characteristics (for example, cultural, demographic) are associated with early withdrawal from counseling?
- What family characteristics are associated with better outcomes in group programs versus family counseling intervention options (for example, coexisting social, psychological, and health problems; age of child; family structure)?

Questions about Experiences

Practice questions that lead to a better understanding of service users' and service providers' experiences help build a picture of the impact of programs and services. Human services are concerned with improving well-being. Therefore, questions about subjective experiences are as useful as questions about measurable outcomes. It is important to recognize that the lived experiences of service users can offer valuable insights into the aspects of services that are effective or require improvement. This information can also help inform service user engagement strategies. Similarly, practice questions could be asked about the experiences of service providers to offer a professional perspective on the nature and impact of interventions. Practice questions about experiences can elicit descriptive information about programs and practices that is useful in building a better understanding of the principles, approaches, and details of practice models. Typical types of questions about service users' experiences include the following:

- What are families' experiences of the aspects of counseling that made a difference for them?
- What was unhelpful?
- How could counseling be improved?

Questions about Unintended Outcomes

Questions may be posed about the range of intended and unintended outcomes from programs and interventions. Although the PICO framework requires a question with a predetermined desirable outcome, asking open questions about intervention outcomes promotes a wider examination of the impact of interventions. For example, in addition to improving child behavior, school-based group parenting programs may or may not have the additional benefits of strengthening social support networks and improving communication between schools and families. Weighing the range of potential outcomes, intended and unintended, positive and negative, is part of informed decision making about appropriate interventions. Asking practice questions that can generate this information, such as the following one from the practice example, will assist the decision-making process:

- What is the range of potential outcomes (positive and negative) for families who participate in parenting group programs for child behavior concerns?

Explanatory Questions

Attention to the different components of interventions and how these work together with external factors and service user characteristics to produce desirable outcomes can produce more complex explanatory questions. Explanatory questions rely on generally untestable theoretical explanations as well as information generated in response to each of the preceding types of questions. An example of an explanatory question is as follows:

- How can a school-based parenting program engage families of young children with emerging behavior problems in early interventions that have a positive impact on parenting practices and child behavior in the short and long term?

Developing a response to this question would draw on knowledge generated from all of the preceding types of practice questions. It requires attention to multifaceted processes and a sophisticated compilation of knowledge and theoretical, value-based explanations. Such explanatory questions are context bound and addressed through a cumulative process of integrating knowledge into explanatory models of program effectiveness. This process is discussed further in relation to program logic and explanatory models in chapter 8.

PRACTICE QUESTIONS IN CONTEXT

The preceding section portrays the design of practice questions as a rather technical process. The techniques and guides for the formulation of practice questions are certainly useful. However, it is also important to recognize the contexts in which practice questions are generated and the associated personal, social, economic, and political factors that can come into play. Selecting practice questions involves making decisions about the aspects of service provision that are regarded as priorities in the organization or program and therefore worthy of further investigation and resources. Practice questions can be shaped in a variety of different ways that can emphasize particular outcomes, experiences, processes, principles, or explanations. The way in which a practice question is designed reflects values and perspectives about what is relevant and important.

Every human services organization works with the interests of different stakeholders, including service users, practitioners, management, funding bodies, and communities. The theories of organizations presented in chapter 3 include Indigenous, feminist, neo-Marxist, and political economy theories. These theories depict organizations as arenas of power, influence, and authority in which the voices and interests of certain groups can dominate over others. The design and selection of practice questions is one way in which this dominance can be established. It is possible for the perspectives and priorities of some stakeholders to be valued over others. When the views of service users or practitioners are not sought or are ignored, useful information about relevant practice issues for the organization may be lost. Without consultation and engagement of stakeholder groups in this process, the selection of practice questions and the consequent focus for evidence gathering and service development can become narrow and biased. The bias may, for example, be toward managerial needs, funding priorities, or particular service provision fads at the expense of other key practice issues being faced within the organization. Similarly, even when assessment and targeting questions may be more useful for service development, the bias may be toward intervention–outcome questions.

An organizational approach to the implementation of EIP is supported when the methods used to facilitate and design practice questions aim for wide engagement and lateral, creative thinking about practice opportunities. This engagement may be across the organization, within a program area, or within a new funding program opportunity. One challenge is to find ways to jolt people out of the accepted ways of thinking and acting and to consider alternatives. Another challenge is to interest and engage stakeholders in meaningful ways in the identification of key practice questions for the organization. Constraints on meeting these challenges include economic constraints on funding for new services, logistical constraints on staff time, the skill set of staff, the interests and confidence of workers, and the organizational culture. Some strategies for working with these challenges are presented later in this chapter.

Another tension in the design of practice questions relates to the ways in which outcomes are defined. Chapter 3 considered the variety of ways in which effectiveness can be defined. Certain views on effectiveness can be reflected in the design of practice questions that focus on particular outcomes at the expense of others. Returning to the practice example used to illustrate the PICO framework for the design of practice questions, outcomes were consistently defined in terms of reduction in aggressive, defiant, and disruptive behaviors in children. There is a risk that such outcomes could be conceptualized very narrowly because of cultural or class biases regarding appropriate child behaviors. The focus on behaviors could also overshadow other outcome goals for children and families, such as community connections, school achievement, attainment of personal goals, and strengthening of family relationships. It is easy for a particular service outcome to be adopted as the goal toward which an organization is driven. If other outcomes valued as important by service users or practitioners are ignored, these stakeholders can become unmotivated and disengaged from the EIP process. Similarly, if practice questions ignore the cost-effectiveness dimension of interventions, management may be unsupportive of EIP initiatives.

Because practice questions are the starting point for the EIP process, it is worth putting the effort into identifying where the power and influence lie in decision making and priority setting in relation to practice questions for EIP investigation. Finding ways to engage service users, practitioners, partner organizations, and communities in the practice question design phase will facilitate a broader perspective on the key issues for service provision in the organization. The design of practice questions, on which the EIP process hinges, can then be more clearly focused on improving services and outcomes for service users and potential service users. Those who are engaged from the start with the design of practice questions are more likely to be motivated to support the EIP process as it unfolds.

LEADERSHIP AND ENGAGEMENT

This book emphasizes building relationships and facilitating engagement as key elements in the effective implementation of an organizational approach to EIP. One of the roles of a leader or champion of EIP can be to focus on engagement and relationship building within the organization. The leadership function may take the form of a leadership team or group that is responsible for different roles and responsibilities in relation to the implementation of EIP. For legitimacy within the organization, the leader or leadership group requires both formal authority and respect among the stakeholders engaged to participate in the process. Leaders need to believe in the potential benefits of implementing an EIP approach and to recognize that meaningful engagement with the process across the organization or program will strengthen it. Strong leadership is the starting point for engaging people across the organization with the process.

Some of the roles that leaders take on in the practice question design phase include mobilizer, educator, facilitator, enabler, and coordinator. Table 4.1 outlines some features of these roles. Strategies presented in the following section suggest how these roles may be carried out.

Table 4.1 Leadership Roles in Designing Practice Questions

Leadership Role	Features of Role
Mobilizer	Starts conversations with stakeholder groups on the role of evidence-informed practice in addressing key practice issues
	Mobilizes interest by identifying the relevance and benefits of evidence-informed practice to stakeholders
	Convenes forums to generate practice questions that correspond to real concerns and are derived from everyday practice
Facilitator	Facilitates forums with stakeholders that encourage lateral and creative thinking, sharing of ideas, and consideration of alternative viewpoints in identifying key practice issues and designing practice questions
Educator	Educates stakeholders on the nature of evidence-informed practice, where and how to find evidence, and the role of practice questions
Enabler	Provides encouragement and suggestions to participants as they engage with an evidence-informed practice approach and design practice questions
Coordinator	Initiates contacts, both within and outside the organization, with those who have a role to play in evidence-informed practice

STRATEGIES FOR DESIGNING PRACTICE QUESTIONS

Every organization is different, and organizational implementation strategies need to be selected or adapted to suit the particular organizational context. Two useful questions to ask in selecting or adapting strategies for a particular organization are as follows:

1. How can this strategy be incorporated into existing structures and processes within the organization or program?
2. How can this strategy build on existing strengths within the organization?

Consideration of these two questions will help with selecting strategies that are in tune with the current organizational culture and therefore more likely to be accepted by key players. By building on existing strengths and structures, the implementation strategies will place less demand on resources.

Set Parameters

The first step is to set parameters for the practice question design phase. The scope could be wide or may focus on one program or type of service. This step could include a trial process in preparation for wider implementation across the organization. A service stream may be selected because it is facing changes or challenges due to other factors and it is an appropriate time to consider new approaches. Interest in taking a more evidence-informed approach may exist among practitioners in a particular program who are already taking initiative in this area. Capitalizing on existing interest helps mobilize stakeholders, so focusing on this program may be a good place to start. The parameters of the practice design phase could be even narrower than the program level. There may, for example, be a new funding program that the organization is considering applying for to expand service provision. A process could be embarked on to design practice questions within the parameters of that funding program.

An interorganizational approach may also be taken. In such an approach, the parameters for the practice question design phase could be set beyond a single organization but within a specific field or practice. This approach would be appropriate, for example, if the organization initiating the process has a research synthesis and dissemination role and wants to ensure that the evidence being disseminated is responsive to the main practice issues that are emerging in the sector. Alternatively, there may be collaboration by several organizations providing similar services that see the benefit in sharing the resources and knowledge generated from an EIP process.

A common scenario is that staff return from a conference or presentation inspired to implement a new practice. This type of inspiration can lead to a haphazard approach to practice decision making and implementation. Enthusiasm about a new practice can, alternatively, be used as the impetus to design practice questions and to engage in a more considered, reflective approach to the evidence and applicability of the new practice model to the organization. For example, staff may be enthused about a program showcased at a conference that supports families in which a parent has a mental illness.

Generating practice questions related to families and mental illness that are derived from current experiences in the organization could support a measured and informed approach to evidence gathering and decision making that incorporates knowledge gained from the conference but does not rely on this alone.

Economic factors also require consideration in setting the parameters for practice questions. If additional funding is available, practice questions can be framed around new practices that could complement existing practices. If there is no new funding, practice questions may be shaped in terms of realigning or adjusting existing practices or shifting resources from one type of practice to another. Although the design of practice questions provides the invitation to think broadly about the possibilities for service provision, at some point the financial constraints must be acknowledged.

If the organization has dedicated resources to the EIP implementation process and has undertaken trials in different parts of the organization, an organizationwide process could then be embarked on to generate new practice questions. This process would become a major organizational project that requires the appropriate allocation of resources. An organizationwide process to generate practice questions is best integrated with other strategic planning activities within the organization to ensure that the scope of practice questions aligns with the mission and service priorities of the organization as a whole.

Decide Whom to Involve with the Design of Practice Questions

Various groups of stakeholders could be invited to participate in designing practice questions for the organization, including executives, board members, managers, practitioners, staff in other roles in the organization, service users, the community (for example, geographic area, potential service users, interested parties), partner organizations (for example, referral organizations, member or service user organizations, research organizations), and experts in the field of practice or evidence. How wide the net is cast can be guided by the size and scope of the exercise. If the EIP process is focused on a particular program and is a trial run for the organization, it is probably better to keep the group small and familiar; for example, practitioners working within the program or stakeholder representatives who already have a good working relationship with the organization.

Staying within the confines of the known and safe can, however, limit the range of practice questions and ignore alternative viewpoints. Challenging accepted ways of thinking about practice is one of the intentions of EIP. For this reason, it is worth including some participants who can offer new ways of thinking about service provisions. Selecting a group facilitator who is familiar with the design of practice questions and who is prepared to identify and challenge assumptions can also help expand and clarify thinking. The larger and more diverse the group of participants, the greater the need for skilled facilitation to manage group dynamics and work toward the goal of designing practice questions to guide evidence gathering.

Engage Interest

Social workers and human services managers generally acknowledge that there are benefits to be gained from adopting an EIP approach but struggle to formulate strategies to support and sustain implementation (Gray, Joy, Plath, & Webb, 2014; Mosson, Hasson, Wallin, & von Thiele Schwarz, 2017). Social workers have indicated that organizational support is a requirement for the implementation of EIP (Gray, Joy, Plath, & Webb, 2015). Leadership in initiating a strategy to design practice questions for an EIP strategy is a demonstration of that support. Participants are more likely to be engaged with the process, and the design of practice questions in particular, if they can identify the direct relevance, helpfulness, and practical application for them.

To foster support and involvement by practitioners and other stakeholders, it is important to commence with and give value to the concerns and questions arising from the daily practice and everyday experiences of participants. This is an effective engagement strategy and a perfect starting point for shaping practice questions. Involving people in this first phase of defining practice questions allows them to influence the foci of the EIP process in a way that is relevant to them and is seen as leading to useful, practical knowledge and greater confidence in practice in the future.

An engaging speaker who can talk about the benefits for practitioners, organizations, and service users of engaging with EIP can also inspire interest. This speaker could be a practitioner or manager from another organization who can speak about his or her own experiences with EIP implementation. Participants also need to know what the whole process will involve and to negotiate what their ongoing involvement will entail. Describing the cyclical model presented in chapter 3 is a concise way to convey the process.

Practice Question Design Process

Decisions concerning well-formulated practice questions are likely to take some time to contemplate and review. Ideas need to be developed through a collaborative team process to get the practice questions sufficiently focused and suited to an evidence search strategy. Once the evidence-gathering activities, discussed in chapter 5, get under way, it may also be appropriate to revisit and reshape the practice questions. There are three steps in the practice question design process:

1. Canvass ideas about practice issues and concerns that could be aided by the availability of evidence.
2. Formulate practice questions based on the issues and concerns, using the guide provided earlier in this chapter.
3. Reflect, review, and fine-tune the practice questions.

These three steps can be approached in a number of ways. If the steps can be incorporated into existing structures and processes in the organization, the logistics of bringing people together will be less demanding. For example, time could be allocated to the process during program meetings over a number of weeks, or the process could be incorporated into an organization's annual consultation, review, and planning forum.

In the first step, canvassing ideas about practice issues and concerns, it is important to establish the parameters and purpose of the exercise with participants. Within these parameters, participants can be engaged in exercises to interact and brainstorm issues. Spending time designing suitable open questions that will trigger thinking will assist the process. Because the purpose is to consider the evidence that will inform practice, such questions should focus on the need for new knowledge—for example, "What do we need to know to improve services to families in which a parent has a mental illness?" This process may be preceded or followed by practitioners individually keeping a log of ideas about potential practice questions as they emerge in practice. Participants could also be asked to record any ideas they have over a period of a couple of weeks, either individually or within professional supervision or team contexts.

If the parameters set for the exercise are wide (for example, work with families generally), some work will be needed to collate all responses and group similar issues together. A process to get agreement on priorities for the program or organization may need to be facilitated if there is wide diversity in responses. If the parameters are narrower (for example, work with families in which a parent has a mental illness), then it may be possible to work with all of the generated issues in the next step.

The second step involves moving from a list of similarly grouped issues to formulate a number of practice questions. Before wording the questions, it is useful to use an interactive process to consider the contextual factors affecting each issue or group of issues. This process could be done in small groups using mind maps to note the range of external and internal factors that affect the identified issue. For example, the practice concern may be the carer–dependent role reversal that can occur in families in which a parent has a mental illness. Participants would be encouraged to identify the range of contextual factors, including the relevant systems in which the issues emerge (school, home, services) and the social and economic implications. This process broadens thinking about an issue so that the practice questions are more likely to reflect the complexity of issues being faced in practice. Groups can then formulate practice questions that are in line with key concerns for the service users. If participants are unfamiliar with the design of practice questions or evidence search questions, the guidance earlier in this chapter can be used to educate them.

The third step entails reflection, review, and fine tuning. Potential practice questions are grouped and recorded so that participants can reconsider whether the practice questions capture the key concerns of the organization or program and address the goals of an EIP process within the parameters set out in the first step. The following questions derived from Straus et al. (2011) can be used to review the question design process and decide whether the process of fine-tuning needs to continue:

- How is this question relevant to practice and service users?
- How will this question address our knowledge needs?
- How will this question guide evidence gathering?
- How could this question help us communicate with service users and colleagues?
- How has the design of this question helped us think critically about practice?
- How will knowledge provided by answering this question strengthen the confidence of practitioners?

Following this review process, questions are selected for the next phase of evidence gathering. If all of the practice questions cannot be handled at the same time, a time frame for addressing the questions or groups of questions can be developed.

Because the development of practice questions takes place over a period of time, it is important to ensure that the questions are kept alive and that the process does not drag on for too long. Prolonging the development of practice questions can lead to diminishing interest and increasing skepticism about the worth of the process. It is important to have someone be responsible for facilitating the process, updating stakeholders, and highlighting its relevance and utility.

CHALLENGES AND PITFALLS IN THE DESIGN OF PRACTICE QUESTIONS

This section discusses potential challenges and pitfalls that can be encountered when designing practice questions and provides suggestions for navigating them. One barrier to designing practice questions is that the availability of evidence relating to the questions may be unknown. If participants have reservations about whether evidence can be obtained, they may curtail the scope of the practice questions they generate. Although lack of available evidence can be a disheartening outcome from an evidence-gathering venture, this outcome is nonetheless educative and part of the reality-testing process involved in implementing an EIP process in the human services. Conversely, participants may be unrealistically optimistic about the ability of research to answer the practice questions. Apart from the end goal of gathering evidence to guide practice, the design of practice questions is also concerned with developing a critical, reflective approach to practice and an awareness of how research evidence can inform practice. Part of the process entails questioning accepted practices, considering alternative ways of practicing, and identifying knowledge requirements. Engaging participants with the design of practice questions contributes to this process goal, even if the outcome goal of identifying evidence is achieved only in a very limited way or not at all.

It is also important to keep in mind that the EIP process is a cyclical one. As seen in Figure 3.3, the generation and review of practice questions are returned to with each cycle. The knowledge gained from each of the other phases in the EIP process will further inform the design of practice questions for the future. If evidence is not available and the organization has the capacity to undertake research, the organization could contribute to knowledge building in its field of practice.

A possible barrier to embarking on the design of practice questions is that the organization may not have the resources to implement new practices. Concern for the future resource implications among managers has been identified as a reason for reluctance to implement evidence-based practice (Aarons, Wells, Zagursky, Fettes, & Palinkas, 2009). It is therefore important to consider available resources at the outset of the practice design phase and to ensure that those who make decisions about the allocation of resources are involved with the process. Negotiating resources was identified as a component in the first step of setting parameters for the design of practice questions. When no additional resources for service provision are available, development of practice questions needs to be approached in terms of generating new knowledge to assist with reshaping existing practices or shifting practices from one type to another. Such practice questions might involve a comparison between current practice and an alternative course of action or generate information on how to enhance, tailor, or target existing practices.

A potential pitfall is that practice questions may be too broad or too narrow, and consequently, the search for evidence can produce too much material to manage or too little to be of much use. For example, if the population group in the practice question is "children," the search may yield too much evidence to work through, but if the population is "children up to 10 years of age" or "preschool-age children," the evidence search may be more manageable. It is useful to record various practice question options because in many cases it is not known if the practice question needs refining until the evidence search begins. Again, this is part of the awareness raising and learning process. This issue is discussed further in chapter 5, which focuses on the evidence-gathering phase.

Sometimes evidence is presented before practice questions are designed. There may, for example, be a sectorwide drive to adopt early intervention strategies with children because there is strong evidence for the benefits. Human services practitioners and managers at times are presented with strong evidence that challenges accepted ways of practicing. In such circumstances, it may not be necessary to go back and begin designing practice questions. It will nonetheless be important to review the evidence and reflect on how the evidence relates to the key practices and practice issues in the organization.

Another potential drawback in embarking on a process to design practice questions is that participants may not be motivated to participate if they do not see the benefit for them or their practice. It can take time for the culture and practices of the organization to shift and for people to witness any benefits from engaging with the EIP model. Although all may be invited and informed about the process, only a small number may take part. It is important not only that those who do participate are informed and engaged, but also that those who do not take part are kept up to date with progress and have opportunities to be involved in the future.

Finally, a possible pitfall is that the EIP leadership group may become exclusive and narrow. This pitfall has two likely negative consequences. First, it can limit the breadth of ideas generated about practice and information needs. Second, if people feel excluded and disengaged from the process, they are less likely to support the implementation of new or modified practices in the future. It is important to keep opportunities to become involved open and to continue to promote exchange among practitioners, service users, managers, and relevant external people about practice questions and the EIP process. This openness will promote a better understanding of the EIP process and of the different views and perspectives present within the organization. It is useful to stop and review the makeup of the leadership group and other participants in terms of positions, histories, gender, and culture to see where biases may lie. Strategies can then be considered for getting others involved. It is important to integrate processes for the design of practice questions with other strategic planning, service development, and practice review activities in the organization because EIP should be integral to, and not marginalized from, mainstream activities and decision making in the organization.

LOCATING PRACTICE QUESTIONS WITHIN THE EIP APPROACH

The EIP approach presented in this book is a cyclical, iterative five-stage process that logically starts with the design of practice questions. Depending on events and practices in the organization, however, the model could be implemented beginning at another point in the cycle. It is also likely that the process may be at different points and move at varying rates in different parts of the organization. The model is not a rigid, staged process but rather a framework for thinking about and planning the phases to be addressed in developing an evidence-informed culture and approach to practice in the organization. Oversight and monitoring of the process as it is initiated and rolls out across the organization will support a coordinated approach and help identify opportunities to build on growing knowledge and experience in the organization.

Four views of EIP were presented in chapter 2: empirically supported standardized interventions, research-informed clinical decision making, local practice-based research activities, and best practice guidelines. The design of practice questions requires that participants take a step back to examine the key practice issues and associated knowledge needs they face. This process is relevant to each of the four approaches to EIP.

First, the reflection and consideration involved in designing practice questions can inform the selection of standardized interventions by guiding the comparison of claims and evidence for the intervention with the key concerns of the organization. Second, practice questions remain central to evidence-informed clinical decision making. When practice questions are designed collaboratively with practitioners and service users, they will have greater confidence that evidence-seeking activities are in tune with their key concerns and the knowledge needs that are presenting in practice. Engaging in such a process as a team promotes the potential to share and build knowledge in a collaborative way so that it is of benefit to the program and service as a whole.

Third, practice questions are also a useful starting point for the design of best practice guidelines. Practice questions can point to the particular areas in which specific guidance is required in the organization. If the practice principles, procedures, and associated evidence offered in guidelines respond to these questions, the guidelines will be a useful resource for practice in the organization.

Finally, practice questions are also closely connected with practice research. A review of practice questions can identify knowledge gaps related to the local context and lead to the identification of research questions for practice-based research in the organization. A well-designed practice-based research project can produce knowledge in response to these questions. The knowledge produced can be used with other external evidence to inform practice and local service planning.

As the first phase in the EIP process, the design of practice questions plays an important role in anchoring activities to the real questions and knowledge needs presenting in the human services provided by the organization. The EIP leader or leadership group has the responsibility to ensure that a system is in place to keep track of the practice questions and to address these questions through the subsequent phases of the process. A record of the practice issues, practice questions, next steps, responsibilities, and time frames is needed as the organization or program moves to the next phase, evidence gathering, which is the topic of the next chapter.

REFLECTIVE QUESTIONS

Designing Practice Questions

- Choose an aspect of your own practice or an issue of concern for service provision in your organization for which decision making would be aided by additional knowledge. Construct a practice question on your practice issue using the PICO framework:

- P (People or Population, Problem)
- I (Intervention)
- C (Comparison)
- O (Outcome)

- Try some different options for each of the four components in shaping a few questions that would be useful to guide evidence gathering. Refer to the examples of practice questions provided in this chapter for guidance if required.

- Formulate some additional practice questions that address the following dimensions of practice as they relate to your chosen issue:
  - assessment and risk factors
  - engagement of service users
  - targeting and tailoring in response to service user characteristics
  - experiences of service users
  - unintended outcomes
  - explanations of practice
  - practice questions in context

- Revisit the practice questions you formulated. In what ways have the foci, elements, and wording of these questions been influenced by the following factors?
  - historical experiences in the organization
  - your personal and professional background
  - values regarding what "effectiveness" looks like
  - power, authority, and influences within the organization
  - economic factors

PLANNING A PROCESS FOR THE DESIGN OF PRACTICE QUESTIONS

Imagine you are planning a process for the design of practice questions in your own organization:

- At this stage in your organization's engagement with an EIP approach, what parameters would be appropriate for the practice question design phase? For example, would the whole organization, a service stream, a program, or an aspect of practice be an appropriate focus?

- Which strategic priorities would benefit from considered development of practice questions and implementation of EIP processes?

- What external pressures and factors need to be managed through the practice question development process?

- Which individuals, or representatives of which groups and organizations, would be able to contribute knowledge, skills, ideas, and experience to the design of practice questions?

- Who could coordinate and facilitate the process?
- What messages would engage participants with the process? How could these messages be conveyed?
- What strategies could be implemented in your organization to
    - canvass ideas about practice issues and concerns that need evidence?
    - formulate practice questions?
    - reflect, review, and fine-tune the practice questions?
- How could these strategies be incorporated into existing structures and processes within the organization (for example, meetings, forums, information-gathering processes, supervision sessions)?
- What existing strengths in the organization could be used to enhance the practice question design process?

CHALLENGES AND PITFALLS

- How could the practice question design initiative be integrated with other initiatives, processes, or organizational change activities underway in the organization?
- What challenges and pitfalls to engaging participants and designing practice questions are likely to be encountered in your organization or program?
- What strategies or approaches could minimize or address these potential barriers and pitfalls?

5

Phase 2: Gathering Evidence

Gathering evidence is the discovery phase of evidence-informed practice (EIP). Motivated by the practice questions designed in Phase 1 and a curiosity to discover information that can shed light on these questions, practitioners can gather evidence from a number of different sources. The knowledge needs captured in the practice questions will be addressed if relevant and credible information is found. Of course, it is not the case that any evidence will do. The EIP approach requires a balanced, critical appraisal of the range of evidence relevant to the practice question and to the practice context. Even when programs or training courses are marketed as evidence based, an appreciation of the body of evidence is required so that informed decisions can be made about whether a particular program should be adopted. This chapter provides some guidance on where and how to gather evidence; chapter 6 tackles the critical appraisal of that gathered evidence.

It should be acknowledged at the outset that the task of gathering evidence can be time consuming and even daunting. Locating primary evidence involves conducting searches for research on library databases, extracting findings, synthesizing these findings across a range of studies, and drawing out implications for practice. This process requires time and advanced skills that are not always available to human services practitioners or in human services organizations. There are, however, other ways organizations can access evidence for practice. An organizational approach to evidence gathering supports a clear connection between priority practice questions and evidence-gathering strategies. Once the evidence is gathered, the organization can support a coordinated approach to the critical appraisal and use of evidence to inform practice decisions.

Organizational strategies are needed so that evidence-gathering tasks are appropriately supported through funding and other resources, manageable, and carried out as efficiently as possible. Evidence gathering may involve undertaking primary evidence searches internally, building partnerships with external organizations to undertake this work, or working collaboratively with others. Finding ways to promote the uptake of information from knowledge dissemination organizations and training staff to access and use online evidence resources are also part of an organizational approach. The material in this chapter is intended to assist with decisions about who should be tasked with gathering evidence, where to obtain evidence, how to gather information, and how to ensure relevance to the organization through the engagement of stakeholders.

MAPPING SOURCES AND TYPES OF EVIDENCE RELEVANT TO THE PRACTICE QUESTION

Chapter 2 considered the meaning of evidence in the human services and the tension that can exist between strong evidence and relevant evidence. The realist position adopted in this book asserts that evidence is provisional, well-informed, negotiated knowledge about what is reasonably expected to produce the best outcomes in a particular context. It draws together robust research, both qualitative and quantitative, and contextually relevant information, including service users' perspectives, practitioner wisdom, and local practice-based research. Evidence is thus a complex mix of information from a number of sources. Evidence is context bound and not static. Evidence accumulates from an ongoing process of consideration and review in the context of new information and changing circumstances. It may be unrealistic to expect to collect all of the evidence relating to a practice or outcome. Therefore, strategic decisions need to be made about what evidence will be valid, reliable, and possible to collect.

The practice questions designed in Phase 1 are the starting point. The types of evidence gathered should match the knowledge needs defined in the practice questions. Certain sources of information are more suited to particular types of practice questions than others. Pawson, Boaz, Grayson, Long, and Barnes (2003) proposed five sources of knowledge for the social or human services:

1. organizational knowledge
2. practitioner knowledge
3. policy knowledge
4. service user knowledge from lived experience
5. research knowledge

Knowledge from all of these sources could be brought into play in building a body of evidence in response to a particular practice question.

It is research knowledge, however, that has dominated as a source of information in EIP discourse because it is publicly available, controlled by standards, and open to public scrutiny. For research knowledge, there are systems and standards for regulating and publishing findings. Findings are generally accessible to the wider community for inspection and use through libraries, online databases, and journal publications. Policy knowledge is also largely in the public realm but is not as systematically catalogued and accessible as research knowledge. Organizational, practitioner, and service user sources of knowledge are more tacit and difficult to access systematically.

For each of the sources of knowledge, information must be drawn out and synthesized so that it can be used as evidence for practice in particular practice contexts. Knowledge from each of the sources is also open to interpretation and dispute. Hence, a process of reflection and negotiation is required to determine the evidence that is credible and relevant to inform practice questions.

A practice scenario helps illustrate how each of these five sources of knowledge can be drawn on in response to a practice question. A community health organization in a rural town, in response to raised awareness about suicide and suicide attempts in the area, begins an evidence-gathering exercise in response to the practice question, "What interventions are effective in reducing suicide attempts?" In response to this question, the research team develops a knowledge map to identify the types of information they will seek within the five broad areas of knowledge:

1. Potential organizational knowledge includes codes of practice, protocols, risk assessment tools, safety planning tools within the organization, and client data.

2. Potential practitioner knowledge includes therapeutic models and approaches, theoretical frameworks for understanding suicide, and experiential knowledge from work with suicidal people and their families.

3. Potential policy knowledge includes best practice guidelines for the management of people at risk of suicide or who have attempted suicide, guidelines for reporting suicide in the media, legislation and standards to reduce access to particular means of suicide, and strategic plans and policies for suicide management and reduction.

4. Potential knowledge from lived experience includes experiences of crisis care, aftercare, safety planning, and support and service gaps among people who have attempted suicide and their loved ones.

5. Potential research knowledge includes research on the effectiveness of interventions to prevent suicide, research on suicide risk factors and risk assessment tools, and research into the incidence of suicidal behaviors and associated trends.

Thinking about evidence in this way helps the team map out potential sources and types of knowledge in response to practice questions and plan out the evidence-gathering process. Like all fields of human services practice, suicide prevention is a complex issue, and it is unlikely that definitive, directive evidence will emerge. An open-minded, critical, and reflective approach is required at the outset of the process and as the organization builds a body of knowledge that will inform decisions about the best practice responses. The benefit in considering all of these different sources of evidence is that the information gathered will be contextualized in relation to existing organizational, practitioner, and service user perspectives. Local knowledge is valued alongside knowledge gathered from the wider body of research and policy evidence. The following sections present ideas for accessing the respective bodies of knowledge.

Organizational Knowledge

Formal internal organizational knowledge should be reasonably easy to access for someone working within the organization. Gathering organizational knowledge involves asking key people for organizational information and locating relevant documents, such as policy and procedure documents, practice guidelines, forms, and data reports. Evidence gathered from other sources may, however, identify the need to revise documents or develop new organizational systems. The development of new EIP guidelines and a more useful data collection system could be outcomes from the evidence-gathering process.

Practitioner Knowledge

Practitioner knowledge is also available within organizations, but it is generally not in a form that can be compiled easily or systematically. Practitioner knowledge is embedded within practice details and theoretical knowledge that is built up over time through formal professional education, continuing professional development, and practice experience. Some of this knowledge may be recorded in project and case reports, but mostly it is tacit individual knowledge or a common knowledge and understanding developed in a team over time. Small and Kupisk (2015) referred to the "practical wisdom" of practitioners, which they defined as "the ability to take thoughtful, practical and ethical action in response to important, difficult and uncertain situations. Practical wisdom entails a mix of ethics, creativity and problem solving" (p. 18). The practical wisdom of practitioners incorporates theoretical frameworks, ethical standpoints, and professional knowledge that are grounded in the reality of the local practice context.

Consultation forums with practitioners, involving facilitated and recorded discussions on experiences and learning in relation to the practice questions, can be used as a way to elicit tacit knowledge in a more systematic way. To prepare for such forums, practitioners could be provided with a list of reflective questions that relate to the practice questions generated in Phase 1. Questions that prompt practitioners' reflections include "Which models or approaches to practice in relation to this issue have you found most effective?" and "What are the features of your practice that contribute to effectiveness?" Similar questions could then be used to guide the group discussion. Alternatively, a survey questionnaire could be used to gather information on practitioner knowledge.

The gathering of practitioner knowledge could also go beyond the experiences of practitioners within the organization. Consultation sessions may include practitioners from a range of organizations so that information can be shared and pooled. A systematic way of recording the information generated from these discussions is needed so that it can be presented as evidence alongside material from other sources. Such a system might involve grouping written records into themes or recording and transcribing material and analyzing it systematically and thematically as qualitative data. Such work could be conducted as a qualitative research project, written up, and made available to a wider audience. Other, similar work may be available in the public realm on practitioner experiences of implementing different models and approaches to practice. Published descriptive articles and qualitative research on practice models in other contexts could also be accessed to further build the body of evidence based on practitioner knowledge.

Gathering practitioner knowledge is important for the implementation of EIP for a number of reasons. It helps identify where and how new knowledge could build on existing knowledge. It also values the contextualized knowledge and experience of practitioners and their insights into the nature of practice and issues faced by client groups, which are too detailed to be conveyed in a research report. Engagement with practitioners is also important because recommendations for changes to practice that emerge from the EIP process will rely on the support of practitioners to be implemented and sustained in the organization.

Policy Knowledge

Historical, social, economic, and situational factors shape policies that in turn shape practice in human services contexts. Policies are specific to the systems of government and the regulation of human services in each country, state, and city. Policy knowledge provides direction regarding what is valued, allowable, and supported through funding and other resources within particular jurisdictions. Policies govern how services and organizations can be structured and place constraints on how services may be provided. Knowledge gained from policy statements can therefore assist in making decisions about what is feasible and practical for service provision in particular fields of practice.

Such policy knowledge is important to include in evidence-gathering exercises because policy and legislation can shape whether and how practices can be adopted. For example, eldercare policy may instigate a shift from organizational funding to provision of individual budgets to older people to purchase community support services. The latter funding model affects the nature of services that organizations are able to provide; it limits the potential to develop community-based programs while facilitating individualized interventions. Policies may not fully determine the services organizations provide; there are often opportunities for alternative funding sources and creative models of care. However, policy knowledge must be considered in conjunction with other sources of evidence when making practice decisions.

Knowledge of the policy context is also relevant when examining research conducted in other jurisdictions. For example, for a practice question about suicide prevention, there may be strong research evidence for a city-based, multisectorial suicide prevention program involving mental health providers, schools, police, and other relevant services. If this program is considered for a city in another country where these service sectors are administered differently at a state level, rather than by city administration, the evidence and transferability of that intervention will be tempered by knowledge of that policy context.

Policy knowledge is obtained from legislation and publications produced by government departments. Often, this information can be found by searching department Web sites for legislation, policy documents, and guidelines but not always reliably so. Because policies are constantly revised with changes in government and shifting national and international trends, it may be difficult to ensure that material located through online searches is current and comprehensive. Policies are also influenced by independent reports, reviews, and other published research findings. In this way, there is an interrelationship between policy knowledge and research knowledge.

Service User Knowledge from Lived Experiences

Service users hold knowledge from their own experiences about the impact of service provision. This experiential knowledge can shed light on the aspects of services that make an impact and can motivate changes and improvements for service users. Experiential knowledge aids an understanding of how the process of change works and what is helpful and facilitative for positive change from the individual's perspective. Service user knowledge also informs organizations on ways to engage effectively in a partnership approach to service provision.

Service user knowledge is not just an adjunct to service provider knowledge. The experiences of service users can offer alternative perspectives that challenge dominant knowledge and views on evidence. For example, Rowe, Baldry, and Earles (2015) advocated for recognition of Indigenous perspectives in social work because social workers are often unaware of racist assumptions and ongoing colonizing practices that are detrimental to Indigenous people. They offered a guide for non-Indigenous social work researchers seeking to challenge privilege, racism, and power relationships that incorporates Indigenous perspectives challenging approaches to individualism, self-determination, and the production of knowledge. In this way, remaining open to alternative viewpoints can shift notions of service effectiveness to a higher level that embraces social justice principles.

Although client satisfaction and feedback surveys may offer some insights into service user experiences, the information that is gathered is generally constrained within a predetermined framework of what service providers regard as worthwhile information and the reporting requirements of managers and funders. Engagement and relationship building with service users are needed to elicit richer and more detailed insights into experiences as service recipients. Consultation with service users adds an important dimension to evidence gathering at the local level. Information provided by service users contributes knowledge about the local context and the ways services and interventions are received and experienced. Such knowledge can inform decisions about what new practices might be useful and how these are likely to be received by the service user community and integrated with existing practices.

In planning consultation forums or gathering individual feedback from service users, power imbalances between providers and users of services should be acknowledged and confronted. All organizational structures and cultures are different, but it is generally the case that service users do not have formal authority or much power in human services organizations. Perceptions that expert knowledge is held only by service providers can also present a barrier to participation by service users. Effort, therefore, needs to be made to create a welcoming environment, engage with service users, build relationships, and invite input. A genuine desire to understand service users' experiences of service provision is important if knowledge is to be gained on how services could contribute more effectively to positive outcomes.

Information-gathering exercises with service users should be focused around the practice questions designed in Phase 1 to ensure that they contribute to the evidence-gathering process. If a forum is organized for service users or comments from individuals are sought, input into the design of practice questions and the associated gathering of experiential evidence in Phase 2 could be combined into one session. An example of a question asked of service users in the practice question design phase might be "What do we need to know to improve services to women in violent relationships?" An evidence-gathering question that flows on from this could be "From your own experience, what would contribute to better services for women in violent relationships?"

In gathering service user knowledge, it should also be recognized that service users are not a homogenous group. Views and experiences will vary in accordance with individual, subjective experiences. Pack (2015) described gathering clients' perspectives as a process of balancing multiple discourses with competing claims as to what is regarded as evidence for practice. Service user perspectives can offer valuable insights and new directions but are often difficult to synthesize in a systematic way. A practice research project could be implemented as a methodical way to gather and present service user perspectives. Practice research offers the potential to move from informal knowledge to knowledge that is more systematically collected, reported, and open to public scrutiny. The organization may have the resources to conduct such a research project, or it could be undertaken in collaboration with another organization. When the study is completed and a report available, there may be opportunities to disseminate this service user knowledge to a wider audience beyond the organization. Alternatively, published work on service users' experiences and perspectives relevant to the practice question may already be available. It is important, however, to examine the characteristics of the service user group in the published research to make judgments about comparability and applicability of the findings.

Service user perspectives, experiences, and explanations can be gathered through forums, individual sessions, surveys, and published research. Systems to collect and review service user complaints are another source of information. Formal and informal observations and client data or records can also shed light on service users' experiences, which in turn can contribute to the knowledge base for answering practice questions.

Research Knowledge

Published research provides an enormous bank of knowledge that can be a rich and varied source of evidence to assist in answering practice questions. As indicated earlier, published research and commentary are also a secondary source of information on service users' lived experience, practitioner knowledge, and policy information. Published research is the main source of evidence for practice because it enables access to information on human services practice experiences and outcomes from around the world.

There is so much published research that specialized databases, search techniques, library support services, and research dissemination organizations are used to bridge the gap between the abundance of research papers and potential users of this research. Despite these tools and systems, locating research that is relevant to a practice question requires time, effort, and skill. Knowledge gleaned from published research should not stand alone; consideration of research in the context of knowledge obtained from the other four sources discussed earlier informs decisions on what evidence is relevant to the local context. The subsequent sections focus on different organizational approaches to accessing published research knowledge for human services.

ORGANIZATIONAL APPROACHES TO GATHERING RESEARCH EVIDENCE

Taking an organizational approach to gathering knowledge from published research makes sense for a number of reasons: Specialized skills are required to search for research evidence, there are resource implications in terms of staff time and technical resources, and the research that is gathered needs to be relevant to the key practice issues for the organization. A planned, organizational approach includes providing additional training for staff, directing resources to evidence-gathering activities, identifying knowledge gaps and priority areas, and avoiding duplication and inefficiency in research-gathering activities.

Organizations can take one or more different approaches to gathering research evidence, including the following:

- conducting primary literature searches
- locating systematic reviews of research
- contracting out evidence gathering
- using repositories of research-informed programs
- linking with knowledge dissemination organizations

The staff time, skills, and other resources that an organization can direct toward evidence gathering will influence the choice of approaches. In addition, certain types of practice questions are more suited to particular research-gathering approaches. In many situations, however, a combination of approaches to gathering research evidence is required to obtain satisfactory coverage of research evidence relevant to the practice questions under investigation.

The five approaches to gathering research evidence are discussed in the following sections. From an organizational perspective, the concern is not only with what each approach entails, but also with who should be involved and how to promote relationships across the organization to ensure that relevant participants engage with the evidence and take it forward to shape future practice.

Conducting Primary Literature Searches

To locate primary research publications that relate to practice questions, access to publication databases is needed. Subscriptions to such databases are costly, but membership in a major library at a university or research institute generally provides access to online databases and to library resources and support staff who can provide assistance and guidance in making best use of the resources. Library membership should also provide access to electronic journals and the full text of identified research articles. An Internet search may locate some relevant research and literature, but if a primary literature search is to be relied on in answering the practice question, it is imperative that the sources are credible and the search is thorough. An Internet search using a free search engine is insufficient to achieve the EIP goal of locating and appraising current best evidence.

Because the body of published research is vast, systems and methodologies have been developed to handle searching for literature related to specific questions. Most professionals learn how to search research databases during their university training. It cannot be assumed, however, that professionals have maintained these skills in the workplace. Some larger organizations may employ designated staff for library search and research synthesis roles to support the work of the organization or even have research and evaluation unit staff with specialized skills. Professional staff can also be trained to undertake library searches alongside their other practice roles. The benefit of having designated staff conduct evidence searches is that they can take a focused and efficient approach to the searches; the drawback is that there can be a disconnect between the evidence gatherers and practitioners. Strategies are needed to promote communication between practitioners and evidence gatherers and to ensure that the gathered research is relevant to the practice questions being asked. For example, there may be potential for the designated evidence gatherers to work to build capacity in practitioners in evidence-searching techniques. The benefit to be gained from practitioners carrying out the searches is that they have a detailed understanding of the practice issues, which can be helpful when undertaking literature searches and making decisions about which research may be relevant and useful. The drawback can be that immediate practice demands often take precedence over evidence-gathering tasks, which are more easily postponed. The particular circumstances in each organization will influence decisions on who should carry out literature searches and how to facilitate communication and exchange across the organization.

Literature searches can also be conducted as a collaborative group or team project. A team may be encouraged to identify a practice question of common concern and work together to carry out a primary literature search, supported by the organization with training and library resources. The search results can then become the focus of journal discussion meetings within the team as they critically appraise articles and draw out implications for practice.

If the organization does not have staff with the appropriate skill set and access to online databases required to conduct primary searches of research literature, one or more other approaches to gathering research evidence should be adopted. Even if the organization does have the skills and resources to conduct primary literature searches, it is worthwhile to review other options as well. The hard work of gathering and reviewing research may already be done, and there is no need to duplicate this. For organizations with the capacity to undertake primary searches and the need to do so, guidance is provided in the paragraphs that follow.

The practice questions generated in Phase 1 are the starting point for conducting a literature search. A search question is needed to locate relevant research in databases, and this search question should be aligned with the practice question. Designing a database search question is, however, an iterative process. Generating too many or too few publication items from a particular search question suggests that a modification to the question is needed to make the review of research manageable. The initial practice questions may also need to be refined or revised on the basis of insights gleaned from a cursory review of items generated by the initial literature search, which may or may not be adequately focused on the particular knowledge needs.

An example from my own work in supporting human services organizations to implement EIP will help illustrate the search process. Our research team at the University of Newcastle in Australia was interested in the practice question "What supports and impedes the implementation of EIP in human services organizations?" (Gray, Joy, Plath, & Webb, 2013). There were no published reviews of literature on this new research area, so a review of primary literature was appropriate.

First, we needed to select the appropriate databases to search and then identify relevant search terms for the electronic search. We selected several databases related to social work, social sciences, psychology, and medicine because human services publications appear in journals in a range of discipline areas. As a group, we brainstormed key words and terms that might be used in research related to our practice question about EIP (for example, "evidence-based practice," "best practice"), implementation (for example, "dissemination," "application"), and human services (for example, "social work," "community services," "social care," "social services").

Boolean logic is the technical name given to the words and symbols, or "operators," used in database searches to find publications that contain particular key words and combinations of key words. The words AND, NOT, and OR (often written in capital letters) between key words define and limit the search. Exact terms can be searched by putting single quotation marks around the term; otherwise, the search identifies publications with different spellings of the same term. All key words with different extensions of a root term can be searched by using an asterisk; for example, a search on the term "implement*" will identify articles containing the words "implementing," "implementation," and "implemented." Familiarity with Boolean conventions is useful for getting a comprehensive coverage of the field and for expanding on an initial search that generates too few items.

Generally, a couple of trial searches are needed to see what types of publications different search terms and combinations of terms generate. The first searches are preliminary ones used to refine the search methodology and key words. A reference group is useful to brainstorm ways to generate and modify the search terms so that unwanted publications from unrelated contexts can be excluded. It is best to start broad, review what is generated, and decide how the search can be refined. The initial searches are also useful to get ideas on other key words to use. A record of the search terms and the number of items generated will help the group keep track of options before making the final decision on search terms.

Despite the care and precision taken in conducting electronic searches of databases, some items that are generated will not be useful. Some will be clearly irrelevant to the practice question, perhaps because the same key words relate to research in very different fields. For others, it may be initially unclear as to whether they are relevant or not, so it is important to establish criteria for including items in the final search results. Again, a reference group that includes practitioners will be useful to negotiate criteria for including or excluding particular research papers. These criteria can relate to the definition of key terms, research questions addressed, interventions investigated, research methodologies used, participant groups studied, language or country restrictions, and publication date ranges. Table 5.1 lists the inclusion criteria and their rationale for our search for research on the implementation of EIP in the human services.

The hierarchy of evidence discussed in chapter 2 is a schema for judging the strength of research methodologies used to investigate the effects of interventions. Randomized controlled trials (RCTs) are at the top of the hierarchy for methodological strength. In

Table 5.1 Criteria for Inclusion of Articles in an Evidence Search for the Practice Question "What Supports and Impedes the Implementation of Evidence-Informed Practice in Human Services Organizations?"

Criterion	Requirement for Inclusion	Rationale
Definition of key terms	The article defines evidence-informed practice as a clinical decision-making process.	This definition is the most commonly used in social work.
Research question	The research question is worded to include investigation of barriers and facilitators to the implementation of evidence-informed practice in the human services. Practitioner perception is one of the domains in which barriers and facilitators can be located.	A wide scope of research questions are included because of limited research in this area.
Participant groups	Data collection took place in human services contexts where there was some representation of social care professionals (social workers, welfare workers, or community workers) in the participant group.	This criterion captures variability in human services professionals and settings in different countries.
Research methodology	The article reports results from original empirical research.	No restrictions are placed on methodology or research design because this is a new and exploratory area of research with limited research publications.
Language and country	The article was published in English.	No resources are available for translations.
Time frame	The article was published in 2000 or later.	Evidence-based practice began to be discussed in social work literature in about 2000.

conducting a search of primary research, the reference group needs to decide what types of research methodology will produce useful evidence to inform the particular practice question, which will, in turn, influence the type of studies that will be included in the evidence search. If effectiveness is being examined in terms of measurable outcomes (for example, level of alcohol consumption, number of violent incidents), then experimental or quasi-experimental designs, including RCTs, may be best suited. If, however, the organization is looking for a suitable assessment tool, then correlational studies examining validity, reliability, and sensitivity may be more suitable. An understanding of service users' experiences is best gained from qualitative studies.

The goal of evidence searches is to obtain credible evidence from reliable sources that is relevant to the practice question. Identifying appropriate research methodology is an important part of achieving this goal. The team may decide to include only RCTs in the search. Alternatively, they may be interested in including research conducted only in a particular country because of the contextual factors that influence practice. They may decide to exclude publications on the basis of population group if interventions only for a particular age group (for example, preschool children) are of interest to the organization. The team should articulate a clear rationale for each inclusion and exclusion criterion and recognize any biases.

Once the search terms and inclusion criteria are finalized, the search should be conducted and recorded systematically for each database to monitor the scope and extent of the search. Documentation of the search process is required so the search methods can be reported (for example, in the methodology section of an evidence review report) and the search can be replicated and updated in the future, if required. The record of the search should include the following:

- names of databases searched
- dates of the searches
- search terms and Boolean operators
- inclusion and exclusion criteria
- number of items found
- number of items that met inclusion criteria.

Even several database searches may fail to locate all relevant research on a topic. Databases may miss unpublished research and government reports, referred to as "gray literature"; doctoral theses; reports from independent researchers; and other research. Follow-up individual searches of reference lists in located publications, general Internet searches, government department Web sites, and content searches of relevant journals are avenues for supplementing the results generated from database searches.

All items are reviewed in accordance with the inclusion criteria to establish a final list of research documents relevant to the practice question. It is generally the case that many research articles identified in a database search turn out to be irrelevant on review of the title or abstract or the full text. Our search for research on the implementation of EIP initially generated 586 items on the basis of key terms. After reviewing these articles in light of the inclusion criteria, we included only 12 articles, two of which were related to the same study; thus, the final evidence review included 11 studies. We quickly eliminated some articles in the original group after reading the title or abstract. Others required careful consideration and discussion before we decided whether they met the inclusion criteria. A reference group is useful for ensuring that the search process remains grounded in the original practice question.

If one does not conduct database searches regularly, it can be hard to maintain competence and confidence in one's search techniques. Librarians generally can provide helpful advice because they have expert knowledge and are up-to-date with new databases and system modifications, which are always changing and developing. Further guidance on conducting searches and finding primary research evidence in social work can be found in publications by Cargill (2015) and Ross (2015). Both offer practical guidance on systematically conducting and recording a literature search, with templates to support the process.

Whether the primary search for evidence was carried out by specialist staff in the organization or practitioners, it is important that the generated material is relevant to practice in the organization and disseminated to those who can integrate new knowledge into practice. Otherwise, the time and resources that have gone into the process will have been wasted. Finding ways to keep relevant people informed about and engaged with evidence gathering will assist with future uptake of the knowledge generated. There are, however, other ways that human services organizations can access research evidence apart from conducting a primary search of the research literature, including locating systematic reviews of research, contracting out evidence gathering, using repositories of research-informed programs, and linking with knowledge dissemination organizations.

Locating Systematic Reviews of Research

The demanding task of undertaking a primary review of research literature may be avoided if there is an existing review of research that addresses the practice question of interest. Research synopses, systematic reviews of research, and meta-analyses are conducted by teams in universities and other organizations who have expertise in gathering and critically appraising research. Such reviews have become important sources of information for busy practitioners and human services organizations that do not have the resources to undertake such work. A systematic review of research requires considerable time and resources, so it is wise to make use of existing reviews. Such reviews could then be supplemented with a primary search on specific aspects of the practice question if required.

A systematic review aims to report on the findings of all research literature relating to a designated practice question, within the bounds of specified search criteria (for example, databases, dates, search terms, research participants, research methodology). A systematic review follows and reports a rigorous primary search process, as described earlier. However, given the complexity and variety of research publications in the human services, the quality and rigor of reviews vary (Crisp, 2015). A critical eye is needed when using systematic reviews to assess how included research items were selected for the review and why others were excluded. Some systematic reviews, for example, include only RCTs and may consequently exclude useful information for practice in an organization. Other reviews of research highlight some themes and issues from the body of research but are not as thorough as a systematic review. Although such narrative reviews can be useful, one should be mindful of the limited scope of these reviews if the search and inclusion strategies are not reported.

Systematic reviews aim to report patterns of findings across the located research studies, including contradictory findings. A *meta-analysis* is a systematic review that uses statistical techniques to pool findings from a number of different studies, generally RCTs, and report combined statistical trends. Systematic reviews may identify differences in outcomes associated with participant characteristics, practice context, or research methodology, but this is not always possible because of differences in the data collected and reported on in different studies.

Because several research groups and research-involved organizations conduct systematic reviews and meta-analyses of research for use by human services organizations, results are found in a number of places. Good networking within the service sector and some investigative skills are generally required to track down relevant systematic reviews.

Advocacy organizations within a field of practice can generally provide useful suggestions. They also may have undertaken systematic reviews that they make available to service providers. Collections of reviews relating to different practice questions are also published as books, such as the collection for social work edited by Vaughn, Howard, and Thyer (2009). Systematic reviews may be published in journal articles, which can be located by searching databases as described earlier but limiting the search to systematic reviews as an inclusion criterion.

Online libraries are also an easily accessible option for human services organizations to locate systematic reviews. The Cochrane Database of Systematic Reviews focuses on health-related issues and is freely accessible online (http://www.cochranelibrary.com). The benefit of accessing the Cochrane Database is that systematic review reports are monitored and scrutinized for quality before being made available to the public. A recent inclusion in the Cochrane Database, for example, reviewed group-based parent training programs for improving emotional and behavioral adjustment in young children (Barlow, Bergman, Kornør, Wei, & Bennett, 2016). The Campbell Collaboration takes a similar approach to the Cochrane Database but is concerned with the domain of social programs, policies, and practices (http://www. campbellcollaboration.org). A recent Campbell review, for example, concerned school-based education programs for the prevention of child sexual abuse (Walsh, Zwi, Woolfenden, & Shlonsky, 2015).

Social Care Online is another place where systematic reviews can be found (http://www.scie-socialcareonline.org.uk). Delivered by the Social Care Institute for Excellence (SCIE) in the United Kingdom, Social Care Online allows registered users to search by topic area or key word to generate publications and resources relevant to practice. Unlike the Cochrane and Campbell databases, Social Care Online resources are not all systematic reviews, and only some of the reviews are conducted under the SCIE auspice. Social Care Online draws together a range of resources from different sources that can be useful for practice, including systematic reviews. For example, a search of the phrase "suicide prevention" generated a list of resources that included systematic reviews of suicide-related issues and descriptions of suicide prevention programs, strategies, and plans.

Frustratingly, systematic reviews often conclude that more research is needed and that findings on outcomes are inconclusive at the time of the review. If systematic reviews or meta-analyses offer strong evidence for a certain intervention, this is useful information for practice decision making. If, however, the findings are inconclusive, alternative sources of knowledge need to be relied on, such as individual research reports, service user knowledge, practitioner knowledge, policy knowledge, and local practice-based research studies.

Although one rigorous study with strong conclusions provides some evidence for practice, a systematic review that synthesizes findings from a range of studies conducted in varying contexts with diverse clients is likely to provide more detailed insights into a practice question. The usefulness of the insights is, however, reliant on the quality of the original research studies and the quality of the systematic review process. When building a body of evidence for practice, findings from smaller studies can contribute useful information and explanations of practice interventions that inform decision making, particularly if the studies align with the characteristics of the organization's practice context and client group being served. Although a systematic review may be a great help in deciding whether to adopt a particular intervention, evidence from a range of sources is generally required when making plans for developments and improvements in practice.

Contracting Out Evidence Gathering

Systematic reviews and primary searches of research evidence are valuable, but the organization may not have the capacity to undertake these tasks. An organization's capacity to find evidence can be limited by lack of access to library databases or lack of skills and experience in conducting literature searches, and the systematic reviews that are easily accessible from online libraries may not align with or shed light on the particular practice questions of concern to the organization. In such cases, contracting a research institute, university, or research consultant with expertise in gathering research evidence for human services practice could be an option.

The benefit in contracting out this work is that the research evidence gathering can be done more efficiently and comprehensively if the right expert is engaged. It is, however, important to ensure that the external expert is clear on the nature of the practice question as it relates to the organizational setting and the purpose of the evidence-gathering exercise. The external expert works from the focused practice questions and knowledge base provided by practitioners, service users, and organizational policy.

However, engaging an external person can make staff feel disengaged from the process. Communication, updates, and opportunities for input remain important. Cost is another potential drawback. The cost will depend on the scope of the project, which is often unknown until the evidence-gathering process gets under way. Partnerships with universities can be a low-cost or no-cost alternative to a paid consultant. Student projects or research reviews undertaken as preparatory work for a funded research partnership could be attractive opportunities for the relevant departments of local universities.

Using Repositories of Research-Informed Programs

If the practice question of concern in an organization involves a choice among interventions or programs, repositories of research-informed programs can offer a more focused source of research evidence than the preceding research-gathering options. For example, after locating a systematic review that provided support for group-based parenting programs for emotional and behavioral adjustment in children (Barlow et al., 2016), the subsequent practice question may be, "Which group program would suit our organization best?" A compilation of evidence for different program options is useful in response to a practice question such as this. There are several resources in different fields of practice that provide information on interventions and programs along with supporting evidence. One example is the Suicide Prevention Resource Center, which has a repository of resources and programs (sprc.org/resources-programs). Repositories are mostly online resources, but because this platform is constantly changing, information on web addresses can become out-of-date quickly. In addition, the relevance of resources may vary among countries. Some online investigation is therefore needed to locate current, relevant repositories of evidence-informed programs.

The most basic form that such repositories take is a list of approved evidence-based programs. Such lists may be established by advocacy organizations, professional associations, government departments, or other groups in specific fields of practice that endorse the programs on the list as having sufficient empirical research evidence to warrant being labeled as evidence based. Empirically supported standardized interventions, discussed in chapter 2, are typically found on such lists. The level of rigor in appraising the evidence can vary, however, and the evidence assessment procedures may not even be stated. Although practitioners and human services organizations can be reassured that an independent body has made some appraisal of the evidence for the programs, the strength and nature of the evidence and the applicability of the program to a particular service provision context are left to the organization to ascertain. The repositories generally give a broad description of the program and some guidance on where to access further information.

More sophisticated and useful variants of such repositories pay closer attention to the nature of evidence and the methods used to appraise evidence for programs. Information on and ratings of the strength of evidence allow comparisons between programs to be made. A recent example is a published review of programs undertaken by a U.K. charity, the Early Intervention Foundation, titled *Foundations for Life: What Works to Support Parent Child Interaction in the Early Years* (Asmussen, Feinstein, Martin, & Chowdry, 2016). This review described and compared programs in some detail and provided evidence and cost ratings. The body of evidence for each program was assessed for strength and rated at one of four levels.

The California Evidence-Based Clearinghouse for Child Welfare (CEBC) (http://www.cebc4cw.org) provides an online facility with lists of programs and practices linked to nearly 50 practice topic areas. The programs and practices include broader approaches to practice (for example, models for casework) as well as standardized programs. The online selection options make this a user-friendly facility. Information includes details on the components of programs and practice models, an overview of evidence with a scientific rating at one of six levels, and guidelines for implementation. A useful feature is the capacity to select and compare the components of a number of programs in parallel on one screen, which makes selection of a program in line with organizational criteria much easier. The National Registry of Evidence-based Programs and Practices (https://www.samhsa.gov/nrepp) is another valuable online repository that rates evidence strength for programs in the substance abuse and mental health fields and provides links for users to examine the nature of evidence.

Online facilities are also available for searching best practice guidelines informed by research evidence. The National Guideline Clearinghouse (https://www.guideline.gov), offered by the U.S. Department of Health and Human Services, provides a searchable online repository of practice guidelines in a wide range of practice fields, predominantly within health and medicine. Supporting evidence for practices included in the guidelines is detailed, along with rankings of the strength of the evidence. Organizations can submit guidelines to the repository if they meet the required standards. Although most of the guidelines are medicine rather than human services oriented, there are useful resources for human services organizations developing practice guidelines. For example, there are guidelines for best practice with older people with depression and in suicide prevention. The clearinghouse also includes syntheses of guidelines within specific practice areas so that areas of agreement and difference among guidelines developed in different places can be identified.

The National Institute for Health and Care Excellence (http://www.nice.org.uk) in the United Kingdom also provides online access to guidelines informed by research evidence and stakeholder consultation. Again, the focus of the guidelines is largely health-related practice, but guidelines relevant to the human services include, for example, the transition from inpatient to community mental health settings and the delivery of home care services to older people.

Linking with Knowledge Dissemination Organizations

With the increased attention given to evidence in the human services, many organizations have emerged with a charter to gather evidence and disseminate knowledge to direct practice organizations. There are opportunities for human services organizations to become members; subscribe to online research networks; and receive regular news alerts of evidence reviews, new research, and practice resources. Australian examples are the Australian Research Alliance for Children and Youth and Child Family Community Australia. The United Kingdom offers the National Elf Service and Research in Practice for Adults. The landscape of groups and networks engaged in such activities is dynamic and varies among cities, states, countries, and fields of practice. U.S. examples are the CEBC and the Substance Abuse and Mental Health Services Administration (SAMHSA).

Online searches and inquiries within practice networks are likely to reveal a number of relevant networks and organizations providing knowledge dissemination services that suit particular human services providers. Organizations that manage repositories of evidence-based programs, such as SCIE, CEBC, and SAMHSA, also have a range of knowledge dissemination activities that are worthwhile for practitioners to connect with.

Knowledge dissemination organizations can also be the focus of a virtual community of practitioners and human services organizations operating in the same practice field with similar practice issues. There are opportunities for networking and interaction with other organizations involved with the implementation of EIP.

Within a human services organization, decisions need to be made about how best to link with knowledge dissemination organizations so that relevant information is captured and incorporated into practice decision making. Such decisions include which individuals are responsible for linking with the organization and how information will be passed along.

EVIDENCE FIT FOR PURPOSE

This chapter has considered a range of ways to gather evidence. Because different evidence-gathering strategies suit different purposes, decisions need to be made on the most appropriate approach for the organization's needs. In chapter 2, four common perspectives on EIP were presented: empirically supported standardized interventions, research-informed clinical decision making, best practice guidelines, and local practice-based research activities. Each of these perspectives on EIP requires a different approach to evidence gathering.

Repositories of research-informed programs are likely to be of more use when selecting empirically supported interventions or developing best practice guidelines. When research-informed clinical decision making is being strengthened in an organization, links with knowledge dissemination organizations are likely to be of assistance in keeping up-to-date with current trends and new research. Systematic reviews and searches of primary research are useful for practice decision making both at the individual practitioner level and when making decisions about establishing or redesigning programs and services. Local knowledge from practitioners, service users, and organizations is particularly useful in practice-based research but also provides background local knowledge for all approaches to EIP.

Practice questions are the focus for evidence gathering. Curiosity, openness to new knowledge, and a preparedness to rethink practice can fuel the evidence-gathering process. The material in this chapter can help guide the development of a plan for gathering evidence from one or more sources. However, plans need to be flexible because one doesn't know what evidence one will find until one begins to look. A critical questioning approach to practice is required when examining sources of knowledge and evidence.

LEADERSHIP TO ENGAGE STAFF WITH EVIDENCE

Strong leadership is required to oversee and guide the evidence-gathering phase in a number of ways. First, a coordination role is required for the variety of evidence-gathering activities that can occur concurrently in an organization. This role includes planning and monitoring evidence-gathering efforts, offering support and resources as required, and facilitating linkages. The coordination role entails promoting a collaborative approach to evidence gathering that incorporates a range of evidence sources, makes connections between parts of the organization with similar interests, and minimizes gaps and duplications.

Second, leadership is needed to ensure that evidence-gathering activities align with the priorities and strategic directions of the organization. Ensuring this alignment involves reflecting back to the original practice questions, and encouraging others to do so, to avoid unnecessary information gathering on topics irrelevant to the practice questions. There may also be a need to revisit and revise practice questions if, through the course of the evidence-gathering process, thinking about practice knowledge shifts or is refined. Leadership is necessary to build confidence in the role that evidence gathering can play in strategic planning and service development within the organization and to establish expectations about the use of evidence in decision making.

Third, leadership is required to ensure that practitioners, managers, and others are informed about the evidence-gathering activities and the progress being made toward answering the practice questions. Keeping relevant people engaged with the EIP process and knowledge as it comes to light supports the integration of new knowledge into practice in the organization. This integration can happen through a variety of ways that suit the organization, including using existing staff forums. An organizational approach promotes reference to research and evidence in everyday practice and decision making. To achieve everyday use of evidence, staff should be encouraged to think of evidence gathering as everyone's responsibility, rather than just the role of designated people in the organization. Instead of viewing evidence as a resource for practice, practitioners might feel that they are being told what to do (Plath, 2013a).

One way to keep staff engaged with evidence is for practitioners to keep an evidence log in which they record relevant sources of information, research papers, reviews, reports, and other evidence; these logs may be for individual use or may be used in group discussion (Hart, 2015). Keeping an evidence log encourages everyone to keep alert to evidence that may be useful for practice in the organization. Evidence logs could be entered onto a shared network and contribute to other evidence-gathering activities.

Finally, leadership is needed to ensure that people are familiar with and skilled in accessing online facilities for evidence gathering or in conducting database searches. Staff training sessions on evidence gathering could be delivered to support professional development. In summary, leadership is required to

- coordinate evidence-gathering activities to facilitate cooperation and avoid duplication;
- facilitate reflection back to practice questions and knowledge needs;
- facilitate communication about and engagement with evidence-gathering activities across the organization; and
- provide resources for and support evidence-gathering activities, including training in locating evidence.

CHALLENGES AND PITFALLS IN GATHERING EVIDENCE

One potential pitfall in searching for evidence is that shortcuts can be tempting. Picking evidence-based programs from a list in a repository may be part of an evidence-informed approach in the organization, but it is important to resist accepting all so-called evidence-based programs as equal without examining the evidence base. An EIP approach requires that the evidence for programs is considered in relation to the practice questions that have been generated, within the context of local knowledge and other sources of evidence. Ongoing monitoring and evaluation of programs also provide further knowledge on local suitability.

A barrier encountered often in the evidence-gathering phase is finding little evidence that is directly applicable to the practice questions. Evidence found may be limited because of the complex and varied nature of human services interventions and the difficulty of available evidence in keeping pace with practice developments. The experience of not finding relevant evidence can be frustrating but must be acknowledged as a normal part of the EIP process. There are no quick fixes in human services interventions. Rather than expecting to find definitive answers to the "What works?" question, success can alternatively be framed in terms of "what we now understand better." Searching the range of sources of evidence presented in this chapter will produce some new evidence. Critical appraisal of this evidence will generate new insights to inform practice. The critical appraisal of evidence, which is the focus of chapter 6, entails making inferences and interpretations from often limited evidence to suit the setting, population characteristics, and other relevant contextual factors. The lack of evidence can also be the motivator to conduct local practice research projects.

A final pitfall to be mindful of in the evidence-gathering phase is assuming that there is one right way and one source of knowledge to answer practice questions. A range of evidence sources and types has been presented in this chapter. An open-minded approach to evidence gathering is encouraged because there are different ways of perceiving practice issues. The impact of value orientations and power differentials can lead to certain knowledge being valued over other knowledge. The active pursuit of different cultural and gender perspectives on best practice, as well as insights from service users, can support a more balanced approach to the evidence-gathering process.

REFLECTIVE QUESTIONS

Five Sources of Knowledge for EIP

- Choose a practice question of current relevance for your team, program, or service (refer to chapter 4 on the design of practice questions, if necessary). List the types of evidence that could inform a response to this practice question in line with the five sources of knowledge:

  1. organizational knowledge

  2. practitioner knowledge

  3. policy knowledge

  4. service user knowledge

  5. research knowledge

- How could you obtain this information in ways that suit your organizational setting?

Organizational Approaches to Gathering Research Evidence

- Consider each of the five approaches to gathering research evidence:

  1. conducting primary literature searches

  2. locating systematic reviews of research

  3. contracting out to experts

  4. using repositories of research-informed programs

  5. linking with knowledge dissemination organizations

- What are the positive aspects and the potential barriers or limitations of each approach for your organization, program, or team?
- Which approach, or combination of approaches, would best suit your setting?
- What strategies could be implemented to overcome the barriers and limitations?

Challenges and Pitfalls

- What challenges and pitfalls are likely to be encountered in gathering evidence in your organization or program?
- What strategies or approaches could minimize or address these potential barriers and pitfalls?

6

Phase 3: Critically Appraising the Evidence

The critical appraisal phase of the evidence-informed practice (EIP) cycle judges how convincing and useful gathered evidence is in responding to practice questions. Critical appraisal is required to integrate the gathered evidence; assess the quality, relevance, and applicability of this evidence; and draw some conclusions about practice implications. Conclusions will, however, be tentative and open to reconsideration as new evidence emerges in the future.

There are two broad questions guiding what is sought from the critical appraisal process:

1. How convincing is the gathered evidence?
2. How useful could the evidence be in shaping future practice in this organization?

Within the organization, there are additional questions about how the critical appraisal process is undertaken and who should appraise the evidence.

A range of strengths, skills, and perspectives can usefully be brought to the appraisal of evidence. These will vary from one organization to the next. Valuable contributions include research expertise, practice knowledge, consumer experiences, policy knowledge, and financial knowledge. From these different perspectives, evidence can be appraised for quality, applicability, and viability in the organization. An organizational approach is intended to facilitate contributions to the critical appraisal process from across the organization, program, or team and to keep key people engaged with the EIP process.

This chapter offers suggestions for mobilizing skills and interest to engage in the critical appraisal of evidence. Practical and technical guidance is provided on critical appraisal procedures, and a process for mapping and integrating knowledge from a range of sources is outlined.

WHAT CRITICAL APPRAISAL ENTAILS

Critical appraisal does not necessarily stand as a discrete stage that temporally follows evidence gathering. Critical appraisal of evidence can occur at any time, including when the evidence is gathered. As evidence is gathered, each item is appraised to some degree for relevance and applicability to the practice context. The critical appraisal phase does, however, bring focused attention to the strengths and limitations of the evidence. Understanding gained from the critical appraisal of evidence informs decision making at the organizational, program, and practitioner levels. Rather than uncritical adoption of a practice or program as evidence based, critical reflection and analysis can lead to informed decision making about the suitability of interventions for the practice context and ways to improve current practices for the future.

Three dimensions of the critical appraisal phase can be delineated for organizational implementation:

1. *Process dimension:* engagement of the organization with critical appraisal of research and evidence for practice
2. *Technical dimension:* assessment of the credibility of research findings and other information
3. *Contextual dimension:* integration of local contextual information with research findings

These dimensions are considered in turn in the following sections.

ORGANIZATIONAL ENGAGEMENT WITH THE CRITICAL APPRAISAL OF EVIDENCE: PROCESS DIMENSION

The critical appraisal of evidence is relevant to daily practice decisions as well as to decision making about new programs, policies, or service directions. Organizational engagement entails keeping the critical awareness of evidence on the agenda across the organization. Engagement ensures that research and other evidence is discussed, shared, reviewed, and recorded as it contributes to the cumulative knowledge for practice in the organization. It also encourages a sense of ownership over the research knowledge within the organization and prevents research evidence from being regarded as something imposed on the organization by external experts.

Research evidence sits with a range of other factors that influence practice decision making, including skills, values, norms, training, expectations, theories, ethics, politics, and relationships. Human services decision making is a complex, tacit process. Although critical reflection can shed some light on the factors influencing decisions, decision making remains an elusive process. Organizational strategies that focus greater attention on the critical appraisal of evidence are intended to raise the profile of evidence in decision making and promote a critical approach to evidence. Increasing the focus on evidence involves a shift in culture and practices in organizations. In appraising evidence in the context of the range of other factors influencing decision making, recognition needs to be given to the value that can be gained from critically reflecting on evidence. Time and resources need to be allocated to the process to achieve this value.

If stakeholders have already participated in the design of practice questions and the evidence-gathering phase, their engagement in the critical appraisal process should be easy to foster. If they have not been involved in the earlier phases, then some additional effort will be required to explain the links to practice questions and knowledge needs. Useful questions for organizations in this phase are as follows:

- Who should be involved in the critical appraisal of evidence?
- What do practitioners, team leaders, managers, service users, and researchers have to offer in the process?
- What is the leadership role in this phase?
- What organizational structures and processes support engagement with evidence and a critical, research-minded approach by practitioners?
- Who should be involved, and why?

To ensure that the appraisal of evidence is connected with decision making at the front line of practice, it is appropriate to engage a range of stakeholders in different roles and at all levels in the organization in the appraisal of evidence. This range can be illustrated using the organizational scenario, first presented in chapter 2, involving the fictitious Family Focus clinic that provides case management, group programs, and home visiting services for families with young children.

Case managers and home support workers at Family Focus make clinical decisions about how best to respond to families' emerging issues and concerns. These decisions could be better informed by an understanding of the evidence for different practice alternatives. By engaging with the critical appraisal of evidence, practitioners build their knowledge and confidence to make judgments about the most appropriate ways to work. Parent educators who deliver parenting programs at Family Focus are also important to involve in the appraisal of evidence. Even though they are delivering standardized programs that have been selected for their evidence base, an appreciation of the evidence is expected to strengthen delivery of the critical components of the programs and inform decisions about local adaptations if required. It is important to engage team leaders in the critical appraisal process because they provide professional supervision to practitioners. This involvement will guide team leaders to think critically and reflectively about the practice judgments that are being made.

Family Focus managers ensure that decisions about new program directions, services, policies, and guidelines are also informed by evidence. Board members assess the quality and robustness of evidence that could be used to inform their decisions about strategic priorities, organizational change, resources, and budget allocations. Service users are involved so that their personal experiences of services can be considered when appraising the relevance of evidence for the local context. Finally, internal and external researchers provide specialized input and knowledge on particular fields of research and on the process of critically appraising research.

Leadership Role

As with the other phases in the EIP process, leadership is important in the critical appraisal stage. Leaders take on a mobilizing role by identifying the people who have skills to offer in the critical appraisal of evidence and forums in which this activity could take place. The leader acts as a facilitator who brings colleagues together to pool knowledge and resources and to engage collaboratively to critically review the body of evidence. Critical appraisal of evidence could occur in a variety of forums across the organization. Monitoring and coordinating these activities is part of the leadership role. The leader must also act as an enabler, ensuring that resources, time, and encouragement are given to staff who engage in critical reflection and appraisal of evidence.

Education on how to go about or to appreciate the critical appraisal of evidence may be needed if participants are not confident or competent in the appraisal of research. Providing education could involve brokering research experts from outside the organization to provide instruction through workshops, seminars, or hands-on guidance. Techniques for the critical appraisal of research studies are presented later in this chapter.

Organizational Processes and Structures to Support Critical Appraisal of Evidence

There are no hard-and-fast rules for shifting human services organizations toward a more research-minded approach to practice and fostering the critical appreciation of practice evidence by staff. This section offers suggestions on the processes and structures that can be helpful in supporting the critical appraisal of evidence. Culture, staff composition, and formal structures vary among organizations, as do capacity and readiness to engage with research and evidence. A unique strategy that suits the individual context is needed for each organization. Six principles, discussed in the following sections, can be helpful in guiding the approach taken:

1. Build on existing strengths to develop capacities.
2. Use existing forums.
3. Build internal and external relationships that support a collaborative approach.
4. Foster critical reflection.
5. Draw on expertise when required.
6. Maintain the focus on improved practice and service user outcomes.

Build on Strengths. Strengths and skills that are useful in the critical appraisal process include the ability to ask critical questions that draw attention to assumptions and highlight alternative perspectives, practice knowledge, competence in research design, and the ability to facilitate groups and engage people in collaborative work. At Family Focus, for example, the team leaders are trained in a model of questioning for use in supervision sessions that encourages supervisees to examine their own values and motivations for actions in practice. To build on this strength, team leaders are asked to see how reference to evidence and research can be incorporated into the questioning model. Another strength that has been identified at Family Focus is the multidisciplinary team approach to practice and the potential to draw on the knowledge base from a range of disciplines in applying evidence to practice. An expression of interest process is implemented in the organization so that people with a particular interest or training in the appraisal of research studies can be nominated to participate in a working group. Participation in this group will allow them access to professional development training and advice on critical appraisal techniques. When the strengths of individuals and teams are identified at the outset, participants feel valued and can be assisted to draw connections between practices they are currently doing well and the process of critically appraising evidence. Critical appraisal capacity is developed in the organization through training and guidance.

Use Existing Forums. Through use of existing forums, the critical appraisal of evidence can be more efficiently integrated into organizational processes and checked for relevance to current practice issues. For example, a regular case discussion forum or team meeting could be a suitable forum to incorporate the review of evidence and application to practice issues. Professional supervision is also a key forum in which time can be taken to appraise evidence in a way that is integrated with practice issues of concern as they emerge. Critical appraisal of evidence is also relevant at the executive decision-making level. It may be appropriate to engage critically with research evidence at executive planning meetings and board meetings.

The benefit in all of these examples is that opportunities are provided for reflection and follow-up in a number of sessions with a group of people over a period of time. In this way, the critical appraisal of evidence can feed into a developing understanding of the body of evidence relating to a practice issue or decision-making process. An evidence log, as discussed in chapter 5, can be used as a resource for the discussions in these forums and is yet another strategy for building on the ongoing work of practitioners.

More specialized forums may be required to run alongside existing forums to prepare for and provide resources to support the process. Specialized forums could include targeted workshops and training sessions for participants and professional development and guidance for supervisors. If practitioners have been engaged with the design of practice questions in Phase 1 and their practice knowledge has been valued and sought as part of the evidence-gathering phase, then incorporating the critical appraisal of evidence into existing forums should follow quite readily.

Build Collaboration. Internal and external partnerships can be a way to access specialized knowledge and expertise in the critical appraisal process and ensure that there is sufficient interest and participation to keep the process buoyant. Establishing such partnerships could entail facilitating collaboration between different parts of the organization or fostering relationships with external organizations. For example, Family Focus could set up a journal discussion group to review articles on family support interventions for families in which a parent has mental health concerns. Practitioners working in different organizations could also be invited to participate so that a range of different perspectives and experiences are brought to the critical analysis of evidence. By sharing and building knowledge together, collaborations can develop into communities of practice.

Partnerships with universities that can offer specialized skills in research design and critical appraisal can be another useful collaboration. Greater interest is likely to be generated within universities if the critical appraisal process feeds into a publication, research project, or grant application. A collaborative partnership with a university to undertake a Campbell review, a Cochrane review, or other review of research literature, for example, could be an attractive prospect if it leads to a publication and is directly related to a practice question of concern to the organization.

Collaboration internally within the organization is another way to generate interest in and commitment to the critical appraisal process. Lawler and Bilson (2005) argued that the professional team is a change agent in organizations and that sharing learning and research-to-practice experiences within teams promotes cultural change toward more evidence-oriented approaches. If the team is resistant to such change, opportunities to reflect on practice, current strengths, and the benefits of attending to evidence may be helpful. A collaborative approach between teams can be effective, particularly if one team is able to share the ways in which engaging with research evidence has been helpful for their practice and for building the confidence of practitioners.

Foster Critical Reflection. Theory, values, knowledge, and practice are integrated in social work and the human services. Thus, the critical analysis of evidence is best undertaken as part of a holistic analysis of how knowledge informs practice. This type of analysis has been referred to as the "interrogation of knowledge" (Mathews & Crawford, 2011). Reflective practice models can assist efforts to bring about cultural shifts within teams and organizations and to draw attention to research evidence as a factor to consider in practice decisions. There are several models to guide critical reflection. These models are essentially concerned with moving people beyond blind acceptance of information or situations and encouraging them to examine the range of factors that shape their under-standing, including personal, relational, historical, social, and political factors. In particu-lar, critical reflection is concerned with finding and challenging values and assumptions that influence understanding. A critically reflective approach is useful in relation to the critical appraisal of evidence because it can be used to prompt consideration of research evidence as one of several factors that have an impact on practice decisions. Critical reflection also challenges assumptions about accepted ways of practicing and in turn can foster preparedness to consider alternative ways of working.

A useful guide to critical reflection in the human services is the approach developed by Fook and Gardner (2007). This staged model was designed primarily for use in small groups to creatively deal with uncertainty in practice and question the imposition of limiting structures and systems. The model uses critical, reflective questioning to unset-tle fundamental assumptions, relying on the group facilitator as well as the involved, participatory dialogue of group members. Drawing connections to concrete practice examples is also a central feature of the model. Although the model does not focus directly on research–practice connections, it has the potential to do so. For example, the critical questioning of assumptions can prompt examination of the evidence for these assumptions. A critically reflective approach is also useful in appraising the application of research designs and methods (Fook & Gardner, 2007).

The critically reflective model can be used in a number of ways to support the implementation of EIP in an organization. It can be used by managers and leaders in helping to understand the approach to EIP that best suits the organization. The critically reflective model can also be used as a framework to guide professional supervision sessions. Critical reflection groups could also be established to reflect on practice, but with the added emphasis on the current and potential impact of research evidence. In reflecting on the tacit professional practice knowledge of participants, opportunities can emerge for new knowledge to be appraised and incorporated. Critical reflection models can be useful as a way to expand participants' thinking about practice options and possibilities, which is fundamental for an evidence-informed approach to practice. It can also help participants move beyond the acceptance of research findings at face value and engage with the critical appraisal of research findings.

Draw on Expertise. People with particular expertise may need to be brought in at times to assist organizations, or units within organizations, with the critical appraisal phase. Expertise may be required to facilitate critical reflection groups, deliver training sessions on critical appraisal techniques, carry out the critical appraisal of research studies, provide supervision that incorporates the critical appraisal of evidence, and train supervisors to integrate the critical appraisal of research into supervision sessions. The capacity of staff to understand research methods and engage in the critical appraisal of research has been identified as a key factor influencing the implementation of EIP in human services organizations (Austin & Claassen, 2008; Gray, Joy, Plath, & Webb, 2013). In larger organizations, there may be a dedicated department tasked with evidence gathering and appraisal to support practice and strategic decision making that can provide this expertise. Although the critical appraisal of research studies requires a more advanced understanding of research methods, training in how to understand and interpret research reports can be useful for practitioners with a range of skill levels.

When bringing in experts to assist with the critical appraisal of research or to deliver staff training, it is important to keep in mind that practitioners often lack confidence in working with research. Instruction on how to interpret findings or techniques for the critical appraisal of research is inadequate without attention to confidence and capacity building that supports engagement with the topic. Confidence can be built by drawing attention to participants' existing strengths and practice knowledge and ensuring that clear links are made to practice questions.

Participants need to be guided to identify the relevance of the critical appraisal of evidence to their daily practice. Being aware of the interplay between professional judgment and research findings is part of implementing EIP. For this reason, it is important that the critical appraisal process is not reduced to research appraisal techniques alone. Conceptual and practical links are needed between the practice domain and the research domain. Expertise is also brought by service users who can offer their consumer perspectives. Service users could participate in critical reflection groups or as a reference group in the critical appraisal process.

Practitioners may not have the time, knowledge, skills, or inclination to undertake the critical appraisal of research and may have to rely on the expertise of others. As discussed in chapter 5, accessing systematic reviews and using research summaries provided by knowledge dissemination organizations are ways that busy practitioners and human services organizations without internal resources can draw on the research knowledge and critical appraisal work of others. Repositories of evidence-based programs often include ratings of the strength of evidence for interventions derived from the critical appraisal of that research. When a primary search for evidence is undertaken, an organization may need to engage an external expert to assist with the critical appraisal, such as a statistician to interpret statistical analysis in quantitative studies. Such assistance is sometimes available through universities. If informed judgments are to be made on the basis of the critical appraisal of others, however, some level of understanding of research methods and the critical appraisal process is still required.

Focus on Improving Service User Outcomes. The final principle for supporting the critical appraisal of evidence is to maintain a focus on improving practice and service user outcomes. Providing avenues for service user input and maintaining openness to service user perspectives will help the organization stay grounded in this fundamental purpose. Keeping sight of the goal of improving outcomes should ensure that the processes to support the critical appraisal of evidence are not ends in themselves, but also feed into practice decision making.

ASSESSMENT OF THE CREDIBILITY OF EVIDENCE: TECHNIQUES DIMENSION

The technical dimension of the critical appraisal process deals with the techniques and frameworks for assessing the credibility of research findings. The primary literature search was discussed in chapter 5 as one of the ways to gather evidence. A primary search entails locating studies that could inform practice questions. Decisions are made on the inclusion or exclusion of these studies based on their content, context, population group, time frame, and methodology. Selecting and defining each of the inclusion criteria is part of the critical appraisal process, but the important next step is to assess the quality of the study, the credibility of the findings, and the relevance of these findings to the practice question as it is conceptualized within the organizational setting. Locating systematic reviews of research is another way to gather research evidence, but, as previously mentioned, there is work to be done in appraising the quality and relevance of these reviews. Even when programs or interventions are selected from repositories of evidence-based interventions, critical appraisal of this evidence base is needed to check the strength of outcome claims and to assess alignment between the context in which the research evidence was gathered and the local organizational context and practice goals.

A level of knowledge and expertise in research design, methods, and techniques is required to undertake the critical appraisal of research. As discussed earlier, staff with this expertise may need to be identified within the organization, employed, or contracted for specific research appraisal projects or to conduct staff training. There are substantial bodies of literature on social research methodology and research appraisal. It is beyond the scope of this book to tackle the appraisal of research methods in detail. Rather, some general principles for critical appraisal are presented, together with suggested resources for further information and guidance. Sheppard (2004) provided a practical text on the appraisal and use of social research that is specifically geared toward social work and the human services. Additional resources are suggested in the sections that follow.

Critical Appraisal of Individual Studies

Each research design, such as the randomized controlled trial or qualitative case study, offers a framework and methods for gathering data to answer particular types of research or practice questions. There is, however, wide variation in how research designs are implemented across different contexts. This individual and contextual variation means that interpretations must be made about the quality of studies. There are many useful resources available to assist with the critical appraisal of research studies. For example, Rubin and Bellamy (2012) provided a reader-friendly, practitioner-oriented guide to appraising different types of research designs, including experimental, quasi-experimental, survey, and qualitative. Carr and Bostock (2015) reviewed a number of research appraisal frameworks, extracting the key criteria for research assessment.

Critical appraisal of research entails examining features such as how the population group for the study was defined, what sampling techniques were used, whether random allocation was used, whether a control group was used and how comparable the research group and control group were, how key concepts were measured, whether any measurement biases were likely, and how data were analyzed. It would be misguided and potentially dangerous to use research findings in the planning of services if these findings lacked integrity because of poor research design. For example, if the study participants were not representative of the target population, the measurement of outcomes were not valid or reliable, or the qualitative data lacked detail or depth. Human services practitioners may not feel that they have the expertise to query the findings of researchers, but with the support of some training and critical appraisal resources, they can certainly develop a better understanding of the limitations of research so that they can question irrelevant or inadequate research.

Practitioners have knowledge about the relevance and applicability of research to their specific practice setting. For EIP, it is important that this expertise is brought together with the technical knowledge required to critique research design, choice of methods, and strength of findings. Judgment about the relevance of the research to the practice context and the potential to apply findings to the improvement of practice is important if critical appraisal is to translate into EIP. This type of critical appraisal is context bound. There are three components to the critical appraisal of evidence for practice: quality, relevance, and applicability (Figure 6.1).

As discussed earlier, experts with specialist research knowledge may be enlisted to assist with the critical appraisal of research. A collaborative relationship between research experts and frontline practitioners supports a stronger interplay between research evidence and practice than one or the other alone. Training in and understanding of critical appraisal tools can support the integration of research and practice across the organization. Although some critical appraisal tools are specific to particular research designs (for example, random allocation to control groups is used in experimental research designs but generally not in qualitative studies), other guides apply across a range of different

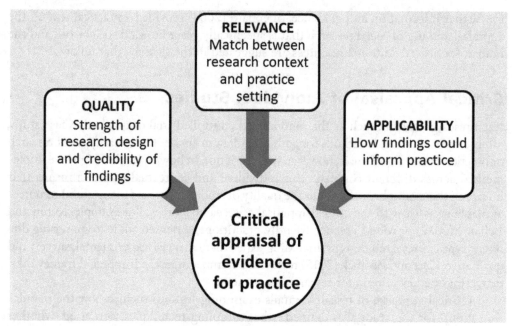

Figure 6.1 Components of the Critical Appraisal of Evidence for Practice

research designs. Carr and Bostock (2015) provided the following list of assessment criteria for use in appraising research studies:

- Are the aims and objectives of the research clearly stated?

- Is the design appropriate to the aims and objectives of the research and methods clearly explained?

- Have research ethics been considered?

- Is there a clear explanation of the outcome measures? For example, what outcomes have been defined and by whom?

- Is the method of analysis appropriate and adequately explained?

- Do the researchers discuss their interpretations and conclusions?

- Has the study captured service user and carer perspectives? (p. 52)

This list of questions is useful for reviewing the quality of the research design and the strength of findings, but it does not address consideration of relevance and applicability to service provision context in a human services organization.

The quality standards framework developed by Pawson, Boaz, Grayson, Long, and Barnes (2003) is another useful schema for guiding the critical appraisal of research and other knowledge for use as evidence for practice. This schema has seven criterion for assessing evidence for practice that address both the intrinsic quality of the study and the wider utility of the research:

1. *Transparency:* Is it open to scrutiny?
2. *Accuracy:* Is it well grounded?
3. *Purposivity:* Is it fit for purpose?
4. *Utility:* Is it fit for use?
5. *Propriety:* Is it legal and ethical?
6. *Accessibility:* Is it intelligible?
7. *Specificity:* Does it meet source-specific standards?

Together, these two schemas are convenient guides for appraising research in the context of organizational and practice needs.

To make judgments about the quality of the research and the accuracy of findings, however, a more detailed analysis of the research study is required. The ability to undertake a detailed analysis relies on adequate reporting of research methods in the research report. At times, the quality of the study design and the strength of findings are simply not known because the methods were not fully reported in the research publication. A number of online tools provide guidance for the detailed analysis of studies using different research designs:

- The Critical Appraisal Skills Programme (http://www.casp-uk.net) provides critical appraisal resources, tools, and checklists designed for varying research designs.
- The Cochrane Handbook for Systematic Reviews of Interventions (http://handbook.cochrane.org) provides guidance to authors on the preparation of Cochrane systematic reviews, with detailed guidance on the appraisal of studies.
- The Social Care Institute for Excellence (http://www.scie.org.uk) makes available resources for the review and use of research.

These are also suitable guides for designing and writing up research. Users of these tools are assumed to have social research knowledge.

Many aspects of research design and reporting can be assessed using these research tools. Sources of bias and threats to validity are two such aspects of quality. Rutter, Francis, Coren, and Fisher (2010, p. 51) outlined four types of bias that affect the quality of studies and the credibility of findings:

1. *Selection bias:* inappropriate or unjustified selection of participants in qualitative studies or systematic differences in allocation to groups in quantitative, experimental designs
2. *Performance bias:* systematic differences in the conditions experienced by the intervention and control groups beyond the intervention that is being researched
3. *Attrition bias:* systematic differences between participants who drop out or withdraw from studies and those who remain

4. *Detection bias:* systematic differences between intervention and control groups in how outcomes are measured, including whether participants or assessors knew which intervention, if any, was received.

Qualitative studies use different methods from quantitative or experimental designs; therefore, different aspects of the research design demand scrutiny. Rutter et al. (2010) noted some factors that reduce the value of qualitative research studies:

- inadequate description of the sample
- failure to ask or follow up on focused questions that generate in-depth responses
- failure to search for examples, cases, or alternative viewpoints that challenge the dominant themes or experiences among participants
- selective use of data
- lack of variation in theories or explanations
- interpretations and conclusions that do not fit with the data

Assessment of validity is another angle from which the quality of research can be appraised. The concept of validity is particularly relevant to quantitative, experimental designs. Soydan (2009) outlined the four types of validity relevant to social work research:

1. *Internal validity:* inference about whether a correlation between intervention and outcome variables reflects a causal relationship (for example, whether the suicide prevention intervention caused the outcome of a reduction in suicidal behaviors)
2. *Construct validity:* degree to which a measure (for example, questionnaire, patient records) reflects the construct that is being measured (for example, depression, suicidal behavior)
3. *Statistical conclusion validity:* use of statistical tests to make inferences about the covariation between intervention and outcomes (for example, whether a significant reduction in suicidal behavior was associated with the implementation of suicide prevention interventions)
4. *External validity:* inference about whether a causal relationship found in one research setting can be generalized to infer a causal relationship in other settings (for example, whether findings in relation to a suicide prevention intervention in Germany can be used to infer anything about the likely impact of the intervention in Australia).

Soydan (2009) identified nine threats to internal validity that can cloud conclusions about causal relationships in social work research if not adequately addressed and controlled. Some of the threats align with the biases listed earlier. Although these threats to validity are not relevant to all research designs, they are worth considering when appraising research that is used as evidence to support the effectiveness of an intervention. The threats to internal validity are as follows:

1. *Temporal precedence:* It is unclear which variable changed first and thus what the direction of impact is, if any.

2. *Selection:* There are systematic differences between the intervention and control groups in the characteristics of research participants, leading to comparison of groups that are not really comparable.

3. *History:* Other events that occurred at the same time as the intervention can account for changes attributed to the intervention.

4. *Maturation:* Natural changes occurred in the research participants over time that are inappropriately attributed to the intervention.

5. *Regression:* Scores do not reflect the typical spread of scores on variables because of the impact of unusual or extreme conditions relating to another variable.

6. *Attrition:* Data on the characteristics of participants who dropped out of the research are not included in the analysis of findings.

7. *Testing:* The same measure was used repeatedly, and there is the potential for this repeated exposure to influence the scores.

8. *Instrumentation:* The tool used to measure a construct (see construct validity earlier) or the tool's component parts may be interpreted differently by participants over time.

9. *Additive and interactive effects:* Several threats to internal validity occur at the same time, producing a cumulative effect.

Although these threats are important to consider when appraising the quality of research studies, a study that has strong internal validity will not necessarily contribute much to the body of evidence for adopting a practice in a particular human services organization if the external validity is brought into question. External validity relates to how generalizable the findings are to populations and settings beyond those involved in the research study. To assess external validity, the characteristics of the population from which research study participants were selected need to be examined along with the context dependency of the intervention. For example, the controlled, closely monitored, and intensively resourced nature of interventions examined in research studies often does not parallel the real world of practice. The critical appraisal of such studies requires judgments about the comparability of the study population with the local client population and the compatibility of the study intervention with what could be offered by the organization in the local context. If interventions are implemented in the local setting, local research that monitors outcomes could contribute evidence on external validity. The generalizability of findings about interventions to different contexts can also be informed by qualitative research that examines the circumstances under which the intervention is effective and the critical factors that influence its impact and effectiveness.

Economic analysis is a particular category of study that contributes to decisions about the implementation of interventions and programs in the human services. Such studies also require critical appraisal as part of the body of evidence. Comparative costs and benefits of different interventions in the longer term (cost–benefit analyses) and the costs involved in attaining particular outcomes (cost-effectiveness analyses) add to the body of evidence and can inform decision making about the viability of interventions. However, there can be controversy associated with how monetary values are attached to services and human behavior outcomes and with the uncertainties involved in extrapolating anticipated costs and benefits over time. Straus, Richardson, Glasziou, and Haynes (2011) provided a list of questions to consider when appraising the validity of an economic analysis:

- Are all well-defined courses of action compared?

- Does it provide a specified view from which the costs and consequences are being viewed?

- Does it cite comprehensive evidence on the efficacy of alternatives?

- Does it identify all relevant costs and consequences and are credible and accurate measures of these selected?

- Was the type of analysis appropriate for the question posed? (p. 120)

Critical Appraisal of Systematic Reviews

As discussed in chapter 5, locating systematic reviews, meta-analyses, or thematic reviews of research is an alternative for organizations that do not have the research expertise and staff resources to conduct a primary review of research. Research reviews also need to be critically appraised and should not be accepted at face value.

First, the systematic review process should be examined to identify the organizations or individuals that carried out the review, the procedures used, and the methods of ensuring the quality of the review process. For example, Cochrane reviews need to adhere to strict guidelines for the critical appraisal of studies, and a quality control process is used to ensure that standards are met before publication of the review. The systematic review should detail how the studies were appraised; otherwise, there is a risk of false conclusions being drawn on the basis of results from poorly designed, executed, or reported studies. It is also important to know whether the review was conducted by an independent group or by an individual or group with a vested interest, such as an organization that has developed and is marketing an intervention. With an understanding of who conducted the review, a judgment can be made about the possibility that the results are biased.

Second, the search methodology needs to be examined to determine how comprehensive the review is. The description of the methodology for the systematic review should detail the searches undertaken, including the databases, key words, publication time periods, languages, and types of publication (for example, journal articles, reports or gray literature, research dissertations, conference papers). Because of the size of the body of published and unpublished international research, including studies that were not published because they had no significant findings, it is probably unrealistic to expect any systematic review to be complete. In critically appraising a systematic review, however, clarity needs to be sought on the types of research that were included. Consideration can then be given to how comprehensive, useful, and relevant the studies will be for the organization. For example, if a child protection service is examining social pedagogy as an approach to working with children and families, restricting research searches to articles in English will miss the bulk of research from Scandinavia and Germany, where the approach has the strongest presence.

Third, it is important to examine the criteria for the inclusion of studies in the review and whether studies were excluded on the basis of methodology, practice or research context, or characteristics of study participants. This examination can lead to questions about the types of studies and findings that may have been missed by the search and about the transferability of findings to the practice context in the organization. Reviews that are restricted to randomized controlled trials, although they allow stronger conclusions to be drawn about causes and significant relationships, may exclude a substantial body of useful research that could offer insights, if not definitive findings. For example, if an organization sets out to gain knowledge on how the circumstances and features of the delivery of interventions for substance abuse contribute to effectiveness, then a meta-analysis of randomized controlled trials will not offer a complete picture. A thematic review that casts a wider net in terms of types of studies included is likely to produce more useful information.

The following list of questions to ask when critically appraising systematic reviews is adapted from the list developed by Rubin and Bellamy (2012, p. 191):

- Was a narrow and well-defined practice question specified?
- Was there transparency regarding search procedures, criteria for inclusion and exclusion of studies, and entities who sponsored, funded, and conducted the review?
- Were search criteria and inclusion criteria sufficiently comprehensive?
- Were there any vested interests in the conclusions among those who sponsored, funded, or conducted the review?
- Were included studies critically appraised for quality?
- Were findings sorted according to study quality?
- Were findings sorted according to client characteristics? How comparable are the client characteristics to those of your organization?
- Were the findings clinically significant? That is, are the measured outcomes meaningful and valuable in practice?
- Were there at least two independent review authors who assessed the quality of studies and extracted findings?
- Was there agreement among the authors? If there were disagreements, how were they resolved?
- Were strategies for dealing with missing data in meta-analyses described?
- Were steps taken to prevent bias in the review process?
- Were clear and practical implications for practice articulated?

Critical Appraisal of Evidence for Empirically Supported Interventions and Programs

The selection of programs from repositories of empirically supported interventions is an efficient way for organizations to benefit from the critical appraisal efforts of others.

However, it is not always easy to decide which program has the best evidence or is the most appropriate, particularly when faced with the enticements of marketing campaigns.

Human services practitioners draw on practice knowledge, theory, experience, and assessment of service users' circumstances in making professional decisions about suitable interventions. Knowledge gained from the critical appraisal of evidence for interventions is another source of information to inform these practice decisions. Engagement of practitioners with the review of evidence for standardized interventions and the selection of suitable programs promotes integration of empirically supported interventions with the professional clinical decision-making skills of practitioners. There are many factors that warrant consideration when selecting standardized, evidence-based programs. Small, Cooney, Eastman, and O'Connor (2007) identified a range of factors that they grouped into questions of program quality, program match, and organizational resources (Table 6.1). The questions can help in making decisions between programs in light of organizational and professional priorities.

INTEGRATION OF LOCAL CONTEXTUAL KNOWLEDGE WITH RESEARCH FINDINGS: CONTEXT DIMENSION

The context dimension of the critical appraisal process involves judging the weight of evidential content drawn from a range of sources. The goal is to contextualize the critically appraised evidence that has been gathered across the organization so that there is a more informed and coordinated approach to applying evidence to the practice context. A range of types of evidence may have been appraised. In relation to a particular practice issue, for example, research articles may have been reviewed in a journal club, a review of literature undertaken by a team, an evidence-based program selected from an online repository, and a systematic review located online. The value of the evidence for practice in the organization will be enhanced if effort is also made to contextualize the pieces of evidence in relation to each other and in relation to the specific practice questions and the contextual knowledge held by managers, practitioners, and service users in the organization. This effort involves moving beyond general "What works?" questions toward questions about "What would work best in our setting?" and "How could our practices work better?"

A collaborative evidence-mapping exercise is suggested as a way to coordinate and contextualize the gathered evidence. Building on the organizational engagement, relationship building, and collaborative activities that were promoted through the earlier phases of the implementation model, interest in an evidence-mapping exercise can be sought among potential participants. The practice questions designed in the first phase of the implementation process ensure that the discussion of evidence is linked to original practice concerns. Referencing the practice questions also helps prevent discussions about evidence from straying too far off on tangents. For example, a question like "How will this evidence help our understanding of how to deliver effective family counseling in our organization?" can help focus discussions about the gathered evidence.

Table 6.1 Questions to Ask When Appraising Evidence for Evidence-Based Programs

Area of Appraisal	Questions
Program quality	• Has the program been found to be effective? What is the quality of the evidence for effectiveness? If the program is listed in a repository of evidence-based programs, how respected is the organization hosting the repository? How have programs included in the repository been appraised for evidence? Is there an evidence rating system? What rating did this program receive? • For which audiences or participants has this program been found to work? • Is there information available regarding the type of program adaptations that are acceptable? Is guidance in program adaptation available if required? • What are the extent and quality of training available to support the delivery of the program? What are the charges? • Is technical assistance available to support program delivery? What are the charges? • What are the opinions and experiences of others who have used the program?
Program match	• How well do the program goals and objectives match with what the organization hopes to achieve? • How well do the program goals match those of intended participants? • Is the program of sufficient length and intensity to be effective with the potential participants? • Are the potential participants willing and able to make the time commitment required by the program? • Has the program been found to be effective with a target population similar to the intended participants? • To what extent might the program be adapted to fit the needs of the community? Does the program allow for adaptation? How might the adaptations affect the effectiveness of the program? • How well does the program complement existing programs and services in the organization and the community?
Organizational resources	• What are the training, curriculum, and implementation costs of the program? • Can the organization afford to implement the program now? in the long term? • Are staff members in the organization capable of delivering the program? Do they have the required qualifications and skills? • Are staff enthusiastic about a program of this kind, and are they willing to make the required time commitment? • Can the program be implemented within the required time frame? • What is the likelihood that the program will be sustained in the future? • Are community partners supportive of the program?

Source: Adapted from S. A., Small, S. M., Cooney, G., Eastman, & C. O'Connor (2007). *Guidelines for selecting an evidence-based program: Balancing community needs, program quality and organizational resources* (What Works, Wisconsin Research to Practice Series, Issue 3). Madison: University of Wisconsin.

Gough (2007) promoted an evidence-mapping process that functions as a "systematic synthesis" of evidence. Evaluative judgments are made about the quality and relevance of evidence. Through the contribution of theoretical and empirical understanding, arguments are formulated to support the "weight of evidence" for a particular practice standpoint. This process entails "examining and making explicit the plurality of what we know and can know" in relation to the practice question (Gough, 2007, p. 214). The notion of the weight of evidence is useful. It recognizes the limitations in research evidence and provides a place for the other bodies of knowledge that come into play in practice decision making, such as practice expertise, theoretical knowledge, policy knowledge, service user experiences, ethics, and organizational capacities and priorities. Similarly, Mullen (2015) advocated for the use of "evidential arguments" that bring information from a range of sources together to justify arguments for practice decisions in organizational settings rather than treating findings from outcome studies as evidence in themselves.

Evidence-mapping exercises are different from one organization to the next because of varying practice questions, evidential types, and organizational cultures. Depending on the scope of the evidence-gathering exercise, preparatory work may need to be undertaken in synthesizing the information that has been gathered (for example, summaries of the range of findings, trends in findings, limitations, gaps, overall conclusions). The following list of questions can be referred to in developing a suitable process for an organizational evidence-mapping exercise:

- What can be synthesized from the following bodies of knowledge in relation to the practice questions?
  - critical appraisal of research (primary research, research reviews, repositories)
  - organizational knowledge
  - practitioner knowledge
  - policy knowledge
  - lived experiences of service users
- Where is there consensus within the body of evidence? Where is there divergence?
- What holds particular weight (for example, in terms of quality, relevance, or practical applicability of evidence), and why?
- What are the limitations of each of these bodies of knowledge in answering the practice question?
- What other contextual knowledge can be gathered to inform the practice question?
- Can additional expertise be sought elsewhere?
- What theoretical, cultural, ethical, professional, personal, or value perspectives can inform how the organization or practitioners respond to the practice question?
- What practice responses are possible?
- What evidential arguments can be mounted to support particular practice responses in different circumstances?
- What evidential arguments can be mounted to oppose particular practice responses in different circumstances?

CHALLENGES AND PITFALLS IN THE CRITICAL APPRAISAL OF EVIDENCE

A barrier to embarking on the critical appraisal phase may be that the skills, time, resources, and commitment required seem too vast and too great a shift from the normal practices or approaches in the organization. The proposed processes are intended as the end result of a shift in organizational approach, capacity, and readiness that takes place over time. Initial changes may be small and fragmented across the organization. One of the aims of this book is to assist organizations in embarking on a planned approach to the implementation of EIP, with realistic expectations of what can be achieved. This approach does not, however, constitute an all-or-none process. A range of options for critical appraisal of evidence have been put forward in this chapter so that organizations can select what suits their circumstances best. Leaders are responsible for planning a manageable process within the resources of their organization and for using collaborative partnerships with external organizations that support the dissemination of evidence. Critical appraisal processes contribute over time to learning about what works best in the organization and how effective practice can be explained and developed.

In addition, practitioners may be resistant to engaging with the critical appraisal of evidence. Although efforts are made to engage with practitioners and to relate the process to practice knowledge needs, the implementation of EIP can be stymied by strong team cultures that are resistant to change. Teams can strongly resist efforts that are seen to challenge practice, and when they do so, the incorporation of critically reflective processes will not necessarily lead to the questioning of assumptions or to engagement with research evidence and its appraisal. As Lawler and Bilson (2005) noted, "these cultures and the practice that is supported by them are based on tacitly held assumptions that are difficult to challenge as they are taken for granted as truths" (p. 199). The professional identities of practitioners can also be tied up with these accepted truths.

How to shift these tacit assumptions without threatening professional identity becomes a key challenge. Engaging with service providers in trusting relationships that value their practice knowledge, strengths, and experiences is the starting point for effecting change. Attitudinal change can also occur in critical reflection groups and supervision sessions, but in the face of resistance, change is likely to be slow. There is a need to start where people are currently situated—that is, to start with their perspectives on what good practice looks like. Leadership is important in guiding people through the change process with support and encouragement. This theme of organizational and team culture is picked up again in chapter 7.

LEARNING ORGANIZATIONS

The type of organizational culture that supports evidence-informed approaches values learning and critical reflection and also directs time and resources to knowledge development and exchange. Such cultures acknowledge and support the benefits of integrating research appraisal into various organizational forums in which practice decisions are made. Organizations oriented toward knowledge development have been referred to as *learning organizations*, a concept that is returned to in the chapters that follow.

In a learning organization, individuals take personal responsibility for learning in collaborative ways to build an accumulation of shared knowledge within the organization. An interdisciplinary approach is also valued in learning organizations. A variety of professionals are employed by human services organizations from a range of health, education, and social science disciplines. There is much to be gained from critical, reflective approaches that draw on the different perspectives, knowledge, research, and practice insights that these disciplines offer. Likewise, research evidence for the human services is generated by a range of disciplines that contribute to a field of practice. The perspectives offered by different professional disciplines can assist with interrogating evidence and drawing out insights and implications for practice.

By strengthening the skills, capacity, and confidence to engage with the critical appraisal of evidence, organizations develop a competent workforce that can explain the research evidence base for interventions and respond confidently to external pressures to produce evidence for the legitimacy of practice and interventions. Engagement with the critical appraisal of evidence heightens the focus of an organization on quality outcomes for service users and on ways practice could be improved. A culture of learning creates an environment that supports EIP decision making and interventions, which are the focus of chapter 7.

REFLECTIVE QUESTIONS

Organizational Engagement with the Critical Appraisal of Evidence

- Consider your own organization, program, or team.
  - Which individuals and groups have skills, resources, and perspectives to offer the critical appraisal of evidence?
  - What value would each of these individuals and groups bring to the critical appraisal process?
  - What leadership roles and functions would support the critical appraisal process?

Organizational Processes to Support the Critical Appraisal of Evidence

- Consider your own organization, program, or team. What are the existing strengths that could support the critical appraisal of evidence?
  - How could these strengths be enhanced to support the critical appraisal of evidence?

- What forums currently exist in the organization into which the critical appraisal of evidence could be incorporated? How might this be done?
- What opportunities are there to collaborate on the critical appraisal of evidence within the organization and with external groups?
- How can critical reflection processes be strengthened within the organization? How could the critical appraisal of evidence be incorporated into these critical reflection processes?
- What type of expertise is needed to support the critical appraisal of evidence? How can this expertise be accessed?
- What can be done to ensure the integration of practice knowledge and critical appraisal of research?
- How can a focus on improved practice and service user outcomes be upheld?

Working with Resistance

- What obstacles to engaging with the critical appraisal of evidence are likely to be encountered in your organization or program?
- In what ways could this resistance be effectively managed?
- What are some manageable steps or strategies to engage staff with the critical appraisal of evidence in the organization?

Challenges and Pitfalls

- What challenges and pitfalls are likely to be encountered in promoting the critical appraisal of evidence and becoming a learning organization?
- What strategies or approaches could minimize or address these potential barriers and pitfalls?

7

Phase 4: Integrating Knowledge into Practice Decisions and Interventions

*P*ractice decision making is the process by which evidence is translated into practices and interventions. This fourth phase in the evidence-informed practice (EIP) process involves more than drawing rational conclusions about practice from the evidence. Decisions about practice draw on complex information that is intertwined with professional judgments and organizational culture and processes. The ways in which formal decisions are made in organizations, and the ways in which practitioners at the front line of practice decide how they can and will work, mediate the translation of evidence into practice.

Paying attention to decision-making processes and practice culture in organizations is critical for the implementation of EIP. The efforts put into designing practice questions, gathering evidence, and critically appraising evidence will be wasted if close attention is not paid to how the evidence is to be translated into practice implications, how decision makers and practitioners will use knowledge on these practice implications, and how understanding will flow on to improved practices.

As with the first three phases, engagement across the organization or program is important. Engagement is promoted by disseminating evidence, involving staff in a critically reflective approach to practice decision making, facilitating an organizational culture that values inquiry and learning, and supporting staff to implement and monitor new or modified practices. If decision makers and practitioners have been engaged in the earlier phases of question design, evidence gathering, and evidence appraisal, they are better positioned to make judgments about appropriate practice responses because they have

- clarity about key practice questions;
- contextual knowledge about organizational policies, priorities, resources and capacities, and service user characteristics, values, and preferences;

- awareness of the landscape of evidence relating to the practice questions; and
- insights from critical reflection on practice that incorporates reference to evidence, values, ethics, theories, and skills.

If practitioners at the frontline feel involved in and have a sense of ownership over the EIP processes and subsequent decisions about interventions, there is a solid grounding for the adoption of new EIPs and approaches.

The practice decision-making phase is, however, where the forces of inertia can hinder evidence-informed plans for change. This chapter examines the nature and types of practice decision making in human services organizations and the links between decision making and practice. The implementation of EIP is considered from an organizational change perspective. Strategies that can help support this change process are discussed.

PRACTICE DECISION MAKING IN THE HUMAN SERVICES

After evidence has been gathered and critically appraised, decisions about human services interventions and practices do not necessarily flow on in rational and timely ways. Although rationality plays a role in human services decision making, interpretations and judgments generally need to be made on the basis of a disparate and incomplete body of evidence in the context of competing organizational and practice demands. As Dore (2015) stated, "From the swirling milieu that constitutes the practice context, social workers do battle not just with competing evidence or attitudes toward such evidence but with a plethora of tensions which exist within themselves, their agency and a society" (p. 69).

The organizational decision-making literature suggests that although managers and practitioners seek to make rational, goal-oriented decisions, random or bargained decisions are often made in the face of organizational constraints, personal interests, and uncertainty (A. Jones & May, 1992). Closer attention to how decisions are being made by organizations, programs, teams, and individual practitioners can help identify opportunities to influence the culture and premises of decision making so that evidence takes on a higher profile.

Decision-making processes in social work have been the subject of research, particularly in the emotionally charged, high-stakes field of child protection. Research findings on the risk factors associated with child abuse and neglect have led to the creation of risk assessment tools and decision aids. There are, however, debates about the appropriateness of such tools. These debates stem from polarized positions on the value of rational–analytical versus intuitive–naturalistic models of decision making (De Bortoli & Dolan, 2015; O'Connor & Leonard, 2014; van de Luitgaarden, 2009).

Social work and the human services are not engaged in purely rational activities. Contextual and negotiated knowledge develop with experience over time and through information-gathering activities that rely on relationships with service users and other professionals. Decisions about appropriate practice responses in any given practice scenario are influenced by the client circumstances, ethical issues, value stances, existing intervention choices, practitioner skills, time and resources available, assessments of risk, and past experiences. Although rational decision-making models have been aligned with evidence-based and risk-adverse stances, they have limitations in complex, changing practice settings where decisions must be made in the face of incomplete information and evidence.

In the demanding world of daily human services practice, feelings and intuition can play as much a part in decision making as rationality, information, and evidence, particularly if the discussions about evidence and associated decisions occurred in a time, place, and setting that are remote from the front line of practice or policy decision making. Child protection practitioners, for example, need to negotiate evidence, knowledge of clients' circumstances and history, their own feelings, ethical principles, theoretical frameworks, and risk analysis in making professional judgments. This negotiation is done in the context of organizational systems within which time may be insufficient to systematically work through all of this information, guidance from experienced supervisors may be unavailable, and opportunities to reflect and gain feedback on practice are limited.

Intuitive–naturalistic models of decision making recognize the complex, dynamic contexts in which professional decisions must be made. These models place value on the capacity of practitioners to recognize patterns, relevant information, and plausible goals based on prior professional experiences and theoretical understanding. The term "intuition" is used to convey how experience-based knowledge is drawn on, often subconsciously, to guide practice. These models of decision making capture how social workers actually make decisions in practice (O'Connor & Leonard, 2014; van de Luitgaarden, 2009), but they do not rule out the potential to incorporate and strengthen rationality and evidence in decision making.

The danger in the overreliance on an intuitive approach is that assumptions can be made too quickly about a current case on the basis of past experiences and, as a result, disconfirming information or alternative perspectives may be overlooked. Certain pieces of information can be weighted more heavily and personal biases can come into play, particularly with a vast amount of presenting information. When families have had a long history with child protection agencies, the task of organizing and making judgments on the basis of the historical records in a large case file can be overwhelming.

Rational thinking and intuitive or experience-based knowledge need not, however, be regarded as contradictory. Decision-making models that incorporate both rational–analytic and intuitive–naturalistic elements offer a balanced approach. Such models recognize that rational, evidence-informed assessment is important and can be incorporated along with the other aspects guiding professional judgment. De Bortoli and Dolan (2015) proposed a decision-making aid called Structured Professional Judgement (SPJ) that incorporates intuitive and analytical elements as complementary processes and provides useful guidance for decision making in the human services. Features of this approach are as follows:

- Intuition and analysis are considered mutually beneficial in practice decision making.
- Decision making is a flexible process that relies on the practitioner's judgment, which is informed by practice experience and wisdom.

- A minimum set of empirically determined factors to be considered in decision making is established to suit the practice context (for example, use of an evidence-informed risk assessment tool).
- Evidence-informed assessment of different intervention options is one type of information that is integrated into overall professional judgment.
- Transparency is increased by recording which decisions are made and how.
- Uncertainty and incomplete information are not ignored but are managed by recording gaps in knowledge as part of the decision-making process.
- Emotions of practitioners are recorded and included as data in the decision-making process so that possible emotion-based biases can be examined.
- Storytelling, within theoretical and value frameworks, is used to explain practice scenarios and decisions.

An evidence-informed approach to practice decision making must allow and work with uncertainty, complexity, and incomplete evidence and recognize the strengths and limitations of both rationality and experience-based knowledge. While incorporating feelings, past experiences, theoretical frameworks, values, and intuition, an EIP approach seeks to ensure that judgments and decisions are also informed by a balanced understanding of the evidence that is available.

TYPES OF PRACTICE DECISIONS IN THE HUMAN SERVICES

Much of the decision-making literature in social work focuses on the decisions made by frontline practitioners. An organizational approach to EIP points to the need to examine practice decision making at all levels in the organization. Decisions made at the board, management, and team levels guide the systems, procedures, and resources that also influence practice decisions, actions, and service provision. Evidence may be sought to inform decisions about organizational policies, resource allocation, the adoption of an intervention model or program, and day-to-day practice. The types of decisions in human services practice that can be evidence based include the following:

- organizational statements about practice principles and procedures as embodied in practice guidelines, policies, and other organizational documents (for example, principles and procedures guiding the placement of children in out-of-home care)
- management decisions about resource allocation to services, practices and programs, and the systems and structures required to support programs for example, allocation of resources to professional supervision or the employment of additional staff, which in turn affects caseloads)
- program or team decisions about the adoption of particular programs, intervention models, practice principles, or service types (for example, adoption of an assessment tool or a model of practice)

- practitioner decisions about how to intervene or respond in individual practice circumstances (for example, weighing risk and protective factors, potential for change, intervention options, and potential negative consequences in families)

There are particular dynamics associated with each of these forms of practice decision making. However, within an EIP strategy, reference to evidence can be enhanced in each. The first three forms of decision making may allow more time for a planned and considered approach than may be possible in frontline practitioner decision making. Examples of organizational impacts of decisions made by management include the adoption of particular programs (for example, transition from care program), practice tools (for example, assessments), and practice guidelines and the direction of resources to professional supervision. Because these decisions define the context and boundaries within which practitioners make decisions, they are as important to consider in an EIP approach as decision making at the front line of practice. Although the SPJ approach described earlier is intended for use by practitioners, it can also usefully be applied to organizational and program-level decision making.

EIP decision making is supported by ongoing opportunities for reflection on practice in which evidence is considered in the context of practice scenarios. These opportunities can occur through supervisory relationships or reflective practice groups. Practitioners are given a chance to build, develop, and share their knowledge of evidence in an integrated way with practice theories and professional experiences. Enhancing the role of evidence in practice decision making does not replace reference to past practice experiences, value stances, or theoretical positions. Evans (2015) pointed out the reciprocal way in which evidence and theory can enhance social work decision making. First, theoretical clarity provides a framework for understanding evidence and seeing when and how it can be incorporated into practice. Second, evidence can challenge the values and assumptions underpinning theories or practice models and prompt a more critical stance that is open to alternative explanations and ways of practicing.

LINKING EVIDENCE TO PRACTICE IMPLICATIONS

The link between evidence and practice decisions is often tenuous in the real world of human services provision. Chapter 6 proposed an evidence-mapping process as a strategy for negotiating the weight of evidence for different practice alternatives. Using this process, evidence and local knowledge are considered and evidential arguments proposed for practice responses that suit the local practice setting. Drawing out practice implications is, however, as much a creative, lateral thinking task as it is a rational process. For example, a review of evidence may indicate the benefits for children gained from human services engaging and working with fathers and reveal practice principles that may offer guidance for this work (Fleming, King, & Hunt, 2015). However, translating this evidence into actual practices, strategies, programs, and interventions requires creative thought that is grounded in an understanding of the evidence, the theoretical basis of current practices, and contextual knowledge. What will the new practices to engage and work with fathers look like? How can these new practices be incorporated into, or replace, current practices? These are questions that are best collectively developed by a range of stakeholders in the organization, including managers, leaders, practitioners, and service users, with input from external service providers and others with expertise in the field. A creative process that is grounded in the realities of practice in the organization will be enhanced by the involvement of stakeholders with different perspectives and experiences of service provision.

LINKING PRACTICE DECISIONS TO PRACTICE BEHAVIORS

Like the link between evidence and practice decisions, the link between practice decisions and practice behaviors is tenuous (Figure 7.1). Decisions about exercising more or eating less refined sugar are made daily by numerous individuals in wealthy nations, but these decisions often do not translate into lasting changes in behaviors. Similarly, in human services organizations, decisions about practice implications that are drawn from a critical appraisal of evidence do not always lead to changes in practice or to changes to the extent envisaged.

Fleming et al. (2015) outlined implications for assessment and practice with fathers derived from a review of research evidence into father engagement and the role of fathers in child well-being. These practice implications include specific principles, practical strategies, and gender-specific language that help engage fathers and focus on their contributions. On the basis of this evidence and local knowledge, a family services organization

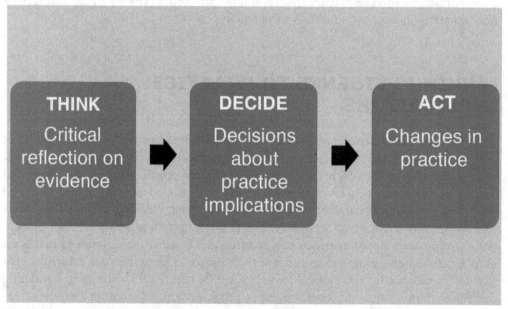

Figure 7.1 Linking Evidence, Decisions, and Behaviors

may generate a range of strategies to improve outcomes for families through stronger engagement and improved practice with fathers. There may be clear practice implications and strong practitioner commitment to this decision. However, a long history of focusing on the needs and roles of women as mothers, and the associated language and accepted ways of practice, can result in inertia that prevents incorporation of new ways of working and thinking among practitioners. In such situations, strategies that challenge entrenched attitudes and practices and provide ongoing input, support, monitoring, and review are needed if practice decisions are to lead to actions and sustained practice changes.

The implementation of new practices is supported when practitioners understand the thinking behind particular practices and have had the opportunity to reflect on how and why these practices can be incorporated with their current ways of thinking and working. This is a cautionary message in the development of practice guidelines: Enshrining decisions about procedures and practices in practice guideline documents will not be sufficient to change practice, even when guidelines are widely disseminated and staff are trained in their implementation (Fixsen, Naoom, Blase, Friedman, & Wallace, 2005). Along with practice decisions, attention must be paid to the practice culture and the development of appropriate organizational change strategies that support practice decisions.

Decisions to adopt standardized empirically supported interventions or evidence-based programs can also face challenges in their execution. Practitioners may adapt and modify standardized programs to the point where the resemblance to the original program, and links to the evidence for that program, becomes questionable. Strategies to support the adoption of standardized interventions and programs are discussed later in this chapter, along with guidance on the adaptation of standardized programs.

Based on a review of implementation science research and literature, Fixsen and colleagues (2005) identified three levels of implementation of EIP: paper implementation, process implementation, and performance implementation. These levels illuminate the extent to which this fourth phase in the EIP model may be achieved, highlighting constructive engagement with practitioners as a key element for the implementation model:

1. *Paper implementation:* EIPs, policies, and procedures are adopted at a formal level in the organization. Decisions about these practices are recorded in reports, manuals, or guidelines, largely to meet the requirements of management, funders, or external accreditation bodies. Although this level of implementation may meet certain bureaucratic requirements, it does not engage the practitioners who provide services and, consequently, does not translate into changes in practices that lead to benefits for service users.

2. *Process implementation:* Organizational strategies and procedures are implemented to raise awareness of and monitor new EIPs. Such strategies and procedures may include training, reporting forms, and supervision. Practitioners attend training, aspects of practice are monitored, and new language is adopted to describe practice. The emphasis, however, is on organizational compliance. Practitioners may feel alienated if their professional knowledge and experience are undervalued. Although some behaviors may change, there is minimal impact on practice decisions at the front line or changes for service users.

3. *Performance implementation:* Careful and thoughtful analysis of the practice culture of the organization is undertaken. Systems and processes are set in place to engage practitioners and support organizational change. Some of the strategies may resemble those adopted for process implementation (that is, level 2), but attention is paid to building relationships among managers, supervisors, practitioners, service users, and researchers. The organizational culture values practice knowledge, supports critical thinking, and strengthens links between practice understanding, behaviors, and outcomes.

In moving organizations and programs from paper implementation to performance implementation of EIP, attention must be paid both to decision-making processes that translate evidence into practice implications and to follow-through actions that support actual changes in practice in the organization. Strategies that support and strengthen these two critical links are discussed in the following sections. The introduction to organizational theories presented in chapter 3 is useful in providing a framework for understanding how organizational culture can mediate both practice decision making and behaviors.

STRATEGIES TO STRENGTHEN EIP DECISION MAKING

The earlier phases in the EIP implementation model create the groundwork for this fourth phase. That is, well-designed practice questions reflect clarity about the aspect of practice for which decisions need to be made; evidence-gathering strategies generate the knowledge base to inform decisions; and critical appraisal enables judgments about the quality, relevance, and applicability of evidence to the decisions being made. The engagement of stakeholders across the organization, attention to relationship building, and a focus on critical reflection in the earlier stages contribute to an environment for EIP decision making in this phase.

Decision making in human services organizations has ethical, political, legal, pragmatic, and relational dimensions, as well as an evidence-informed dimension. Strategies to strengthen EIP decision making need to take into account the complex nature of human services decisions and the political context, competing interests, organizational constraints, personal interests, and uncertainty that characterize the human services environment. A number of interrelated elements are required to raise the profile of evidence in this complex arena of practice decision making. First, evidence needs to be disseminated to those who make and implement decisions. Second, stakeholders need to engage actively with the evidence. Third, a critically reflective approach to decisions that influence practice is required, including formal organizational statements, management decisions, team or program decisions, and frontline practitioner decisions.

Evidence Dissemination Strategies

In order for evidence to be considered in decision making, it needs to be available and accessible. Although the involvement of relevant players from within and outside the organization has been advocated in the design of practice questions, gathering of evidence, and critical appraisal of that evidence, circumstances may make it inappropriate or impossible for some key people to be involved. The demands of other work commitments, the arrival of new staff, a lack of interest, or the logistics of involvement across a large organization are reasons why some or many stakeholders may not be informed about EIP strategies in the organization. A range of relevant staff in the organization may not be aware of the evidence that has been gathered and the purpose for its collection. Finding new ways to engage people across the organization in sharing knowledge and evidence is therefore still a high priority in this decision-making phase. Disseminating evidence in creative and appealing ways is one part of engaging staff with EIP.

Because of the cyclical nature of the EIP model, engagement with the process can occur at any point in the cycle. Different events in the life of an organization could trigger a new cycle of EIP activity. Evidence related to human services practice is constantly being disseminated through training workshops, conferences, and evidence dissemination organizations. This evidence can be critically appraised and used to inform practice decision making or the adoption of new tools or interventions.

Evidence dissemination is an important part of the wider EIP process, but it has been found to be ineffective on its own in driving EIP (Fixsen et al., 2005). Evidence dissemination has a greater impact on the decision making of practitioners and managers if it is linked to identified practice questions and knowledge needs. In this way, the consideration of evidence is construed as helpful rather than as additional information to digest. To gain traction and make an impact in the busy world of human services organizations, evidence should be presented in easily accessible and engaging ways. Evidence dissemination can be incorporated into other daily activities, such as team meetings and supervision sessions. Audio recordings could make evidence accessible to be listened to while driving to client home visits or to meetings (Hagell & Spencer, 2004).

As well as being relevant and accessible, the dissemination of evidence should be timely if it is to be taken up by decision makers. Practice questions and knowledge needs are continually changing in human services organizations. It is challenging to locate evidence at the same time as practice questions are being asked or program-planning decisions need to be made. Although it is idealistic to think that it will always be possible to disseminate evidence just when it is needed, timing remains a factor that should be considered in planning evidence dissemination strategies.

Evidence may be disseminated to practitioners, managers, and other relevant decision makers in the organization in a variety of ways. Creative thought and consideration of the requirements and dynamics of the organization are needed when planning evidence dissemination strategies to suit the setting. There are four questions to consider in this planning process:

1. What are the key practice questions, and is the evidence directly relevant to these questions?
2. How can the evidence be presented in engaging and accessible ways?
3. When is the best time to disseminate this evidence?
4. Who are the recipients who can make use of the evidence?

The following are examples of possible forums and methods for sharing evidence:

- evidence fact sheets and summary sheets (via e-mail, social media, or hard copies)
- posters and postcards with key messages from the evidence
- podcasts and other audio recordings
- training workshops
- seminars and webinars
- professional supervision sessions
- group discussion forums, such as team or program meetings, peer supervision, journal groups, or communities of practice

Engagement of Practice Decision Makers with the Evidence

Evidence dissemination will have minimal or no impact on the decisions practitioners and managers make if they are not engaged with the evidence in meaningful ways. Although the evidence may be relevant, accessible, and timely, decision makers need to recognize it as such if it is to have an impact on decision making and practice. Strategies are therefore needed to engage decision makers with the evidence so that they can derive its implications for their own practice and decision making and develop a sense of ownership and responsibility for the evidence-informed nature of their practice decisions. Professional supervision, workshops, and evidence support professionals are mechanisms through which evidence-informed decision making can be facilitated and supported.

Professional Supervision. Professional or clinical supervision has been identified as an important mechanism for engaging practitioners with evidence (Collins-Camargo, 2007; J. L. Jones, Washington, & Steppe, 2007; Straussner et al., 2006). In a supervisory relationship, practitioners can be guided to refer to evidence in timely and relevant ways as issues from current practice emerge for discussion and reflection. Supervisors can help practitioners identify where and how the incorporation of evidence may be helpful and examine the implications of evidence for particular aspects of practice. Organizational systems and resources are required to support the supervisory relationship if it is to be successful, including allocating sufficient staff time to engage in supervision and ensuring that supervisors are trained, skilled, and provided with resources to carry out the role. Supervisors should be skilled in facilitating reflective discussions that assist practitioners in analyzing practice and making informed clinical decisions. To support evidence-informed decision making, supervisors need to understand the EIP process and have access to relevant evidence that can be brought into supervision discussions as required.

Workshops. Workshops to examine evidence and draw out implications for practice are another way to engage decision makers with the evidence. Whereas professional supervision has the flexibility to respond to emerging issues in practice at the front line, workshops provide a space in which evidence and practice implications can be examined proactively. Skilled facilitation is important in such workshops so that participants' experiences and insights can be mined and put to creative use in generating the range of practice, policy, and resource implications for the organization that could be informed by the evidence. Such workshops are also opportunities for service users to be involved in decision making in the organization.

A range of participants with different experiences of and roles in the provision of services can offer diverse perspectives that can fuel creative and lateral thinking about practice implications. Workshop facilitators should be skilled in planning workshop processes and managing different views and perspectives in the group, including tensions that can emerge between service users' views and what is regarded as clinical expertise.

Contextualizing the implications of evidence for the particular needs and circumstances of the organization can support the development of relevant practice strategies, such as the adoption of a standardized tool or intervention or the design of EIPs that are tailored to the practice setting. An organization or team may, for example, decide to revise the language in standard letters and publicity material and adopt new evidence-informed family assessment protocols that support engagement and work with fathers. In response to practice questions in other settings, workshops could be designed to make decisions about the key pieces of evidence that must be included in decision making in certain areas of practice, such as safety assessments for suicide or family violence. Workshops could also be run after staff attendance at conferences or seminars. Rather than staff simply reporting back on their learning, a more active approach can be taken in which workshop participants examine how their new knowledge contributes to the body of evidence that has been gathered over time and identify practice implications for the organization.

Drawing practice implications from evidence, like all practice decision making, involves both rational and intuitive elements. When decisions are examined in a group forum, there will inevitably be various interpretations of the evidence and different views on the implications for practice in the organizations. Use of evidence in decision making in human services organizations is a negotiated realm, and the process can be frustrating if participants expect a purely rational process with definitive consensus outcomes. Successful workshop processes prepare participants for both the interpretive and rational aspects of drawing practice implications from the evidence and making practice decisions. Workshops can also be an empowering process if facilitators provide space for the voice of service users to be heard.

Evidence Support Professionals. Evidence support professionals can work with practitioners to identify evidence needs and to locate, appraise, and summarize evidence in response to practice questions. Evidence can then be provided to decision makers in timely and relevant ways through workshops, supervision, and other evidence dissemination methods. Evidence support professionals need to work closely with practitioners to ensure that there is a good fit between evidence summaries and the requirements of practice, program, and policy decision making (Stevens, Liabo, Frost, & Roberts, 2005).

For evidence-informed decision making to become integrated into an organization, resources need to be directed toward staffing to support the implementation. Champions of EIP can be effective in keeping evidence on the agenda and inspiring engagement with the process, but allocation of staff and staff time is also needed. Evidence support professionals could be appointed, or existing staff could have their work role altered to include evidence implementation duties. It is unreasonable to expect changes in organizational systems, culture, and decision-making practices to be achieved if staff are expected to work toward such goals alongside their usual workload. Without additional resources, work is likely to continue as usual. Like supervision and workshop facilitation, evidence support professionals require resources.

Critically Reflective Approach to Practice Decisions

Practitioners who feel undervalued or burdened by work demands will adopt shortcuts in decision making. Time for critical reflection on practice decisions is needed to make considered judgments that incorporate evidence. The critically reflective approach discussed in chapter 6 is also important in practice decision making because it promotes openness to alternative ways to view service user circumstances and potential service responses. This approach entails questioning assumptions and accepted practices and seeking evidence that may suggest better alternatives. Without a critically reflective approach to evidence-informed decision making, practitioners may take shortcuts and seek out evidence simply to justify existing practices.

The organizational systems and resources that support evidence-informed decision making discussed in this chapter, such as supervision, decision aids, and workshops, should incorporate opportunities for critical reflection to examine personal and experience-based dimensions together with the rational dimensions of decision making. Time for critical reflection can help practitioners make sense of the multiplicity of evidence, information, feelings, and competing work demands so they can make balanced and informed professional judgments. De Bortoli and Dolan's (2015) SPJ decision-making aid presented earlier in this chapter offers a useful starting point for critical reflection on aspects of decision making. The following list of questions can be used in supervision or other forums to support reflective decision making in response to practice situations that incorporates knowledge from evidence and past experiences:

- What emotional responses arise in this situation, and what effect could they have on decision making?
- What past experiences relate to this situation, and how could these past experiences aid, hinder, or otherwise affect decision making in this situation?
- What theoretical, value, and ethical frameworks help make sense of this situation?
- What information and evidence would need to be considered in making a professional assessment of this situation (for example, risk and protective factors)?
- What alternative responses or options are available? What evidence is available about these alternatives?
- What are the characteristics of the worker–service user relationship, and how could this relationship influence alternative responses?
- What worker or organizational skills, capacities, and resources affect the alternative responses that are available?
- What are the information and evidence gaps? Is it possible to fill these gaps in the time frame?

These questions could equally be used by practitioners reflecting on decisions about interventions in a clinical, client situation and by managers deciding on the establishment or modification of a program. Discretion, judgment, and a degree of uncertainty are features of human services decision making, but by using a framework that prompts critical reflection on the factors affecting decisions, alternative responses, and relevant evidence, more considered, evidence-informed judgments can be made. When this reflection occurs in a timely fashion, it can contribute to ongoing knowledge development and increase the capacity for professional judgment in the future.

Organizational strategies that can support decision making include the provision of evidence-informed assessment tools, decision aids, and practice protocols. Adherence to such protocols will be enhanced if practitioners have the opportunity to reflect on and understand their origins, evidence, and purpose. The critical reflective process facilitates consideration of the logistical, resource, relationship, skill, and other contextual constraints on intervention alternatives alongside consideration of evidence. Critical reflection supports the contextualization of evidence in the real world of human services practice.

STRATEGIES TO STRENGTHEN LINKS BETWEEN DECISIONS AND PRACTICE

Strategies to support translation of decisions into sustained actions include training, monitoring, follow-up, and support. However, if behavioral changes are to be achieved, attention also needs to be paid to the organizational culture and strategies for organizational change. In particular, an organizational culture of inquiry and learning must be developed that supports the implementation of EIP.

The approach to organizational implementation of EIP taken in this book respects experiential knowledge and promotes collaborative responsibility and accountability for the use of evidence. Rather than a culture of blame in circumstances when practitioners do not follow evidence-informed procedures or practices, a collaborative, engaged approach is advocated to promote ownership of the EIP process across the organization. This approach entails finding strategies that support the translation of decisions into actions. Workers who are not valued and supported tend to become frustrated and leave organizations. When staff retention rates are low, organizational knowledge and learning built up over time through EIP processes are lost, causing the implementation cycle to stall. Workers leave organizations for a variety of reasons. It is therefore important to have wide engagement in EIP activities, with systems in place to monitor, record, and support evidence-gathering and implementation activities. An organizational culture that values inquiry and critical reflection on practice helps to sustain the implementation process.

Strategies to Facilitate an Organizational Learning Culture

Organizational culture encompasses the complex interplay among systems, objects, meanings, values, language, and behaviors that produce the particular work environment, experience, or feel of the organization. Culture comprises the often intangible and covert aspects of an organization that are produced through interpretations and experiences. Organizational culture tends to endure above and beyond the efforts of individuals in the organization, who come and go.

It is important to give consideration to organizational culture at this point in the EIP cycle because the culture of the organization mediates whether and how formal and informal decisions are translated into behaviors. An analysis of organizational culture can help identify the areas in which change needs to occur to develop a culture of inquiry and learning, which is a foundation for the implementation of EIP (Austin & Claassen, 2008; Dill & Shera, 2015). A culture of learning and the development of learning organizations have been associated with a range of valuable outcomes for human services organizations (Gardner, 2006; Lee & Austin, 2012; Lindberg & Meredith, 2012). A learning organization uses "evidence, successes, and even failures to transform the culture from being reactive to focusing on promoting change through knowledge and innovation" (Dill & Shera, 2015, p. 13).

A. Jones and May (1992) defined *organizational culture* as the shared meanings within an organization. These shared meanings incorporate values, beliefs, ideologies, and norms, which are expressed through shared symbols such as myths and stories about organizational life; rites, activities, and events; language that expresses shared understanding; and physical objects or artifacts that convey the values, history, and norms of the organization.

A culture of inquiry and learning may be demonstrated in an organization by team discussions on *why* certain practices are undertaken, rather than merely what is or what should be done. It is further illustrated through regular events such as annual service planning and review days, in which participants have the opportunity to take a step back from their work and consider alternatives. There may be awards for innovation and creative thinking. A learning organization is a safe place to express uncertainty, which is valued as part of the process of seeking out and discovering new knowledge. There is an overarching philosophy in the organization, which is more than a written mission statement, reflecting the commitment of staff to ongoing learning and critical analysis of practice to achieve better outcomes for service users. Money is directed toward professional development, and there is an expectation that staff will participate in learning opportunities and share new knowledge with others in the organization. Mottos, logos, letterheads, and other organizational materials make reference to learning, discovery, and innovation. There are physical spaces and resources available for collaborative learning and discussions.

All of these examples are representations of meanings. There is a link between the outward expression (for example, logo, collaborative learning area, awards event) and what is valued by members of the organization (inquiry, critique, discovery of new knowledge, outcomes for service users). A symbolic representation may, however, exist without an associated shared meaning in the organization. A new logo, learning space, or award, does not necessarily reflect changing values and ideologies of members within the organization. Staff members may be cynical, question intentions, and refuse to participate in events and programs. Rather, the symbols should be outward expressions of commonly held values if they are to be representations of the organizational culture. The outward symbols and internal meanings can feed off each other over time as values begin to shift with experiences and new employees are attracted to the organization by the values it is seen to promote.

Even with a strong organizational culture, there will always be some variation in values and beliefs within an organization. A common culture reflects dominant trends and positions, but variety will result from individual differences and changes over time. In medium-sized and large organizations, there may also be subcultures in different units, levels, or networks within the organization. The values and meanings of service users may be quite different from those of workers, which may in turn be different from those of boards and management. Within each unit and level, there may also be subgroups and individual differences. These differences between groups and individuals in organizations offer avenues to support organizational change. Differences and subcultures can, however, also work to thwart change efforts.

Organizational culture is shaped by the past and present members of the organization, but it is also shaped by the external environment in which historical, political, economic, and social factors place overt and covert pressures on the organization. Gardner (2006) highlighted shifts in the culture of human services organizations over recent decades; economic rationalism, managerialism, and business systems have come to dominate government policies, legislation, and public expectations about how organizations should be run. External pressures regarding the implementation of EIP also influence organizations. The way in which organizations respond to these pressures can, however, vary. Some organizations respond with a reluctant submissiveness to what is regarded as a bureaucratic requirement to demonstrate evidence for practice; these organizations tend to take a similarly bureaucratic tick-the-box approach to EIP. Other organizations approach such pressures as an opportunity to develop a more critical, reflective approach to practice in which inquiry and new knowledge are valued and efforts are made to use new knowledge to create better outcomes for service users. Of course, the latter response is promoted here, but how can such a culture be promoted in organizations?

Time and effort are required to shift organizational culture through the development of shared meanings and values. This effort involves persevering in an incremental way, being prepared for trials and errors, and learning from experiences. The change process entails building relationships and developing a sense of ownership over the new directions in which the organization is heading. An organizational culture shift can take years to achieve, with challenges and obstacles likely to surface along the way.

Strategies to Facilitate Organizational Change

An organizational culture that values inquiry, new knowledge, and innovation can take many different forms. Human services organizations already have existing strengths that could contribute to EIP. Effecting cultural change in the organization involves identifying and building on these strengths so that preparedness and capacity to develop new knowledge and critically review practice are enhanced over time.

An active strategy for change recognizes both the formal and informal processes required for organizational change. The formal organizational processes required to implement EIP include proposing, endorsing, and approving decisions that lead to formal statements of strategic intent and policy, allocation of resources, formation of working groups, and establishment of structures and systems. Possible strategies to support the adoption of EIP at the formal organizational level include

- education of executive management or the board on the value of adopting an EIP strategy;
- decision by the board to implement the strategy;
- budget allocation to support implementation;
- formation of an implementation leadership team;
- nomination of staff or units in the organization to work on different aspects of implementation; and
- systems and resources set in place to support the process through the five phases, including systems to monitor decision making and practices.

In conjunction with formal processes, informal changes can be understood in terms of the human relations and conflict-based theories of organizations (for example, neo-Marxist, political economy, feminist, Indigenous) presented in chapter 3 (A. Jones & May, 1992). Informal, or covert, processes involve identifying and working with the social relationships and power dynamics in the organization to achieve change through networking, influence, support building, and advocacy. Discussions on what EIP implementation is about, how it will involve and affect individuals, what the challenges will be, and how the use of evidence could be helpful for employees, service users, and the organization can take place in a variety of meetings, forums, and training sessions across the organization. Providing information and encouragement across the organization and gently beginning to challenge resistant positions are part of the change process and may take several years. The support of individuals and groups from outside the organization, such as other human services organizations or university faculty, may be helpful in promoting the message and gaining support. Finding avenues for service users to have their say about proposed changes to practice is also important. Focusing on the benefits to clients as the key purpose for the implementation process can be used as a way to challenge accepted power and authority relationships that support entrenched practices.

The goal of building shared meanings about the value of inquiry and learning, and, in particular, evidence-informed approaches to practice, relies on engagement and relationship building. Without this grounding, efforts to make changes to practice at the front line are likely to be met with opposition and resistance.

The major components of organizational culture that are supportive of EIP, as proposed by Austin and Claassen (2008), include

- leadership provided by a change management team and champions of EIP,
- involvement of stakeholders at all levels and phases of implementation,
- cohesive teams,
- resources allocated by the organization to support the implementation, and
- readiness to become a learning organization.

These contributors to organizational culture can be attended to before embarking on the implementation strategy, but they also need to be addressed throughout the process.

A number of strategies can be implemented to strengthen the links between decision making and changes to practice. Discussion, planning, trialing, and monitoring will be needed to determine how these activities can be translated into appropriate strategies for particular organizations. Leadership strategies that support cultural change for EIP include the following:

- Analyze the organization and identify strengths, challenges, and opportunities for change, input, guidance, and influence to support EIP.
- Build relationships, share information, and involve stakeholders across the organization in all phases of the EIP implementation process.
- Communicate strengths, provide encouragement, and acknowledge emotions and challenges to staff and teams in implementing EIP.
- Rrecognize and encourage champions of EIP in the organization who can support and mobilize others.
- Take on a role as coach to other key people in the organization.
- Negotiate conflicts about EIP.
- Engage staff and service users in the development, application, and review of practice guidelines and protocols.
- Identify support and training needs to facilitate practice changes.
- Allocate time for staff to monitor and review their practice.
- Allocate resources for staff training and supervision.
- Implement a system to monitor and review practice changes over time: What practices are implemented? How do practices relate to evidence-informed decisions and program logic? What can be learned from discrepancies between decisions and actions?

Strategies for promoting research-minded practitioners and teams include the following:

- Use supervision to support practice changes through use of critical questioning, critical reflection, research-informed practice judgments, and feedback on service user outcomes.
- Use a team approach to reviewing and supporting evidence–decision–practice links in which there is collective support and responsibility rather than individual responsibility.
- Engage in case conferences, review meetings, and critical incident analyses that draw on evidence and analyze practice–consequence associations.
- Form communities of practice that provide opportunities to reflect on evidence, practice implications, and outcomes in collaboration between practitioners and researchers across human services organizations and universities or research units, encouraging openness to new ideas and practices.

- Recruit practitioners who demonstrate the capacity for innovation and the application of new knowledge to practice.
- Offer training and professional development opportunities.
- Collaborate and share knowledge and experiences through learning groups of participants drawn from different units across the organization.

Strategies to increase service user participation include the following:

- Seek out service user views both to empower service users and to generate alternative perspectives to those held by practitioners, encouraging openness to new ideas within the organization.
- Incorporate service user input into planning practices that are informed by evidence.
- Form service user reference groups to check practice decisions and practices against the lived experiences and views of service users.
- Present feedback on the impact and outcomes of practice interventions from service users in supervision and practice review meetings as part of critical reflection and practice decision making.

IMPLEMENTING AND ADAPTING EMPIRICALLY SUPPORTED STANDARDIZED INTERVENTIONS

The implementation of empirically supported standardized interventions has particular requirements related to maintaining the fidelity of the program or intervention. Fidelity is maintained through standardized delivery in accordance with how the program was designed by the developers and evaluated by research. Although inquiry into evidence and critical reflection on service user requirements may precede the decision to adopt a standardized intervention or evidence-based program, once selected, the goal is to implement the intervention in its standardized form. For the organization, standardized implementation requires strategies to support compliance and sustainability over time, including identifying and addressing potential barriers and facilitators to sustaining implementation.

A review of research on the implementation of empirically supported standardized interventions by Fixsen and colleagues (2005) found that systematic strategies are required at multiple levels in an organization to support fidelity and that implementation appears to be most successful when

- carefully selected practitioners receive coordinated training, coaching, and frequent performance assessments;
- organizations provide the infrastructure necessary for timely training, skillful supervision and coaching, and regular process and outcome evaluations;
- communities and consumers are fully involved in the selection and evaluation of programs and practices; and

- state and federal funding avenues, policies, and regulations create a hospitable environment for implementation and program operations. (p. vi)

Aarons, Wells, Zagursky, Fettes, and Palinkas (2009) found that resource factors (staffing, cost of the intervention, and funding), suitable staff development and support, research and outcomes supporting the intervention, and the political dynamics surrounding the intervention were the most important factors influencing the successful implementation of an evidence-based standardized program. Other influential factors were consumer concerns and values, the impact of the program on other clinical practice, and system readiness and compatibility (Aarons et al., 2009). These are useful indicators of the factors that should be analyzed in organizations and incorporated into the decision about whether or not to adopt a standardized program or intervention.

Detailed understanding of standardized interventions is required for implementation. In particular, the core components must be preserved for fidelity. There will, however, be occasions when the program is not well matched to an individual, family, or the target population because of cultural, language, social, gender, or other characteristics. Tensions can consequently emerge between the professional judgment of the practitioner and what the program prescribes. On examining the implementation of the Maudsley model of family treatment for adolescent anorexia nervosa (Lock & Le Grange, 2013) in an Australian health service, our team found that all clinicians in the study adapted the program for some clients in response to perceived cultural barriers or an assessment of risk of withdrawal from the program (Plath, Williams, & Wood, 2016). Professional judgment by the practitioner in these cases overrode the fidelity requirements.

Human services organizations often are committed to providing services to all clients in a target group, not just those who are able or prepared to conform to a particular program requirement. Flexibility and adaptability in program delivery are therefore, at times, required. If adaptation of a standardized program is necessary to engage or retain service users in the program, the core components of the program should be reviewed to ensure that the adaptation remains true to the theory, knowledge, and principles that underlie the program. Rather than taking out content, the goal should be to make the content accessible. Questions of interpretation and degree in this process can, however, produce uncertainty. Because many standardized interventions are licensed and controlled, developers of programs should be consulted before adaptations are made. Approval for adaptation may not be given. Adaptations to empirically supported standardized interventions should also be carefully documented, monitored, and evaluated over time; modifications to standardized programs are discussed further in chapter 8.

CHALLENGES AND PITFALLS IN EIP DECISION MAKING

By the time evidence has been gathered and critically appraised, the practice questions for which the evidence was gathered may not be the current key practice questions. The reality of human services practice is that there will always be new practice questions and that evidence will often lag behind questions and be lacking in some way. The larger cycles of EIP inquiry around key practice questions need to be juggled with the ongoing cycles of critical reflection, rapid evidence needs, and application of available evidence to practice issues as they emerge. Short-term clinical decision-making processes contribute to ongoing knowledge development for individual practitioners and the organization. This ongoing knowledge development supports the longer term, planned EIP cycle around key practice questions, service planning, and program or intervention choices. Working with this complexity and lack of definitive answers can be unsettling. Encouragement, guidance, and assurance by leaders are important.

This chapter has discussed the association between EIP and a rational decision-making model. Furthermore, it has analyzed how this model can challenge the professional judgment and autonomous decision making of human services practitioners. Experience-based and intuitive knowledge, however, can be regarded as too interpretive and contextually bound. The challenge for human services managers and practitioners is to negotiate a balanced decision-making approach that draws on different types of knowledge and integrates different decision perspectives. The provisional nature of evidence must be acknowledged. Although this uncertainty can be unsettling, it plays an important role in inquiry and learning. Likewise, failure can be informative in the learning process. Finding ways to work constructively with questions, uncertainty, and failure will contribute to the development of an organizational learning culture.

A challenge for this phase of implementation is to balance the culture of inquiry and learning with the requirements of compliance and fidelity demanded of standardized empirically supported interventions. The rigid adoption of principles, procedures, or standardized programs without ongoing reflection and evaluation is in opposition to an EIP model that values critical questioning. An important reminder at this point is that although evidence may inform the selection of practice interventions, professional judgment and the worker–client relationship remain fundamental to the effectiveness of human services interventions. An overreliance on standardized practice at the expense of building trusting and empathic relationships with service users can impede effective practice outcomes.

Relationship-building skills and the knowledge base required to deliver the standardized intervention are as important as the components of the intervention themselves. In the field of mental health, for example, the pressure to adopt evidence-based interventions has been challenged by a strong case for the individualized recovery approach that focuses on relationship building and consumer-driven agendas (Rosenberg & McDermott, 2015; Stanhope & Solomon, 2008; Tosone, 2013). A balance must be maintained among the three components of evidence, critical reflection, and relationship building, as was noted at the outset of the book as a key principle for the implementation of EIP.

Another pitfall for organizations is that the resources and costs associated with strategies to support evidence-informed decision making and interventions can be underestimated. Considerable resources are required to support long-term processes of cultural change through leadership strategies, evidence dissemination, supervision, engagement of experts, professional development, allocation of staff time, and identification of practice implications. Managers need to plan strategies and assess the associated costs because cultural change in decision making and practice is not cost neutral. The costs should, however, be weighed against the expected benefits to service users, practitioners, leaders, and the organization in the longer term. The range of benefits to human services organizations of implementing an EIP strategy were discussed in chapter 3. Inadequate resource allocation for this phase in the implementation cycle could risk wasting the effort and resources directed to the earlier phases; evidence gathering and appraisal without application and improvements to practice are of no value to service users. The political reality may be that funding is available for service development only for a particular target group. As a result, the organization may decide to direct EIP implementation activities toward a particular field of practice for which funding resources are more likely to be available.

Finally, dealing with resistance to change is a challenge for organizations implementing this phase of the EIP process. Changes to beliefs and values, accepted practices, and organizational culture are often met with resistance. Careful analysis of the organization is required, along with sensitivity to the emotional responses of people in the organization whose identity and sense of security are enmeshed with how they carry out their jobs. A planned approach is needed that gives people time to understand and engage with new information and voice their views. Both encouragement and understanding are needed if resistance is to be overcome. Rather than top-down compliance enforcement, a collaborative, participatory approach that genuinely values the experiences and input of everyone in the organization, together with a preparedness to negotiate conflicting viewpoints, fits best with the EIP implementation model.

SUSTAINING CHANGE

Sustaining a learning culture and the practices that flow from evidence-informed decisions requires ongoing commitment, resources, and organizational systems that support the change. A critically reflective approach is needed as new knowledge is incorporated into existing practices and progress is made through the stages of the EIP cycle. Seeking out and incorporating feedback contribute to learning in the human services. Information gained from evaluations of interventions in the local context is an important source of new knowledge for evidence-informed decision making. Practice monitoring and evaluation are the essential next phase in the EIP implementation cycle.

REFLECTIVE QUESTIONS

Types of Practice Decision Making

- Identify some examples of each of the four types of practice decisions that influence your own practice or practice setting:

    1. organizational requirements

    2. management decisions

    3. program or team decisions

    4. practitioner decisions

- To your knowledge, how was evidence incorporated into these decisions?

Linking Practice Decisions to Practice Behaviors

- From your own practice experience, identify an example in each of the following three categories:

  1. Evidence was obtained and considered but did not lead to any decisions about changes to practice.

  2. Evidence was considered and a decision about practice implications was made, but no actions resulted.

  3. The consideration of evidence led to decision making that resulted in changes to practice.

- In relation to your example in the third category, what supported the progression from thinking about evidence to making decisions and acting?

- In relation to your examples in the first and second categories, what were the barriers to moving toward changes in practice?

Evidence Dissemination

- What evidence dissemination strategies suit your practice setting?
- How could evidence dissemination using these strategies be made more engaging and accessible for practitioners and other decision makers?
- What circumstances would make it timely to disseminate evidence in your setting?
- What types of evidence should be disseminated to whom?

Engaging Practice Decision Makers with Evidence

- What would be required in your practice setting to make supervision a more effective way to engage practitioners with evidence? For example, consider what training, time allocation, frameworks, and other organizational systems would be required.

- Select an aspect of practice in your team or organization, and plan a workshop outline that would engage participants in developing practice implications for your setting on the basis of evidence. Who would take part in the workshop?

- What potential is there in your program or organization for one or more staff members to take on an evidence support role with practitioners? What would the role entail? How would strong relationships between the evidence support professional and other practitioners be facilitated? What links with external organizations would strengthen the role?

- What other strategies could support practitioners and decision makers in your organization in referring to evidence in their decision making?

Critical Reflection on Practice Decision Making

- Select a practice decision that you are currently faced with (or, alternatively, were faced with in the past) in your own practice, as a supervisor, as a manager, or as part of a team or group.

  - What are the emotional responses to this situation, and what effects could these responses have on decision making?

  - What past experiences relate to this situation, and how could these past experiences aid, hinder, or otherwise affect decision making in this situation?

  - What theoretical, value, and ethical frameworks help make sense of the situation?

  - What information (for example, risk and protective factors) and evidence would need to be considered in making a professional assessment of this situation?

  - What alternative responses or options are available? What evidence is available about these alternatives?

  - What are the characteristics of the worker–service user relationship, and how could these relationships influence alternative responses?

  - What worker and organizational skills, capacities, and resources affect the alternative responses that are available?

  - What information and evidence gaps are there? Is it possible to fill these gaps in the time frame?

Organizational Culture

- How would you describe the culture of your organization in relation to the use of evidence for practice?
- What are some of the shared meanings in the organization, including common values, beliefs, and norms?
- What are some of the outward symbols of those shared meanings in the organization (for example, stories, events, language, physical objects, logos)?
- What aspects of the organizational culture could be enhanced to develop a culture of inquiry, learning, and evidence use?
- Where would the challenges lie?

Cultural Change Strategies

- What strategies would facilitate an organizational culture in which practice is guided by evidence-informed decisions? Describe how these strategies could be applied in your organization.

- What additional strategies are required to support the implementation of empirically supported standardized interventions or evidence-based programs?

Challenges and Pitfalls in Creating an Evidence-Informed Organizational Culture

- What are likely to be the main challenges and pitfalls in implementing a culture of evidence-informed decision making in your organization or program?
- What might resistance to EIP look like in your organization?
- What strategies or approaches could minimize or address these challenges and potential pitfalls?

8

Phase 5: Monitoring and Evaluating Client Outcomes

The prime purpose of human services delivery is to effect positive social change for communities, groups, and direct service users. Once evidence-informed practices and programs are selected and delivered, there continue to be many questions about the effectiveness of these interventions for service users in the unique organizational context in which the interventions are delivered. These questions include the following:

- What is the range and variety of positive outcomes and experiences for service users?
- What are the characteristics of individuals, groups, and communities experiencing positive changes as a result of the services provided?
- What are the characteristics of service users who miss out on positive changes?
- What are the reasons those service users miss out on positive changes?
- How can the effects of services be assessed and recorded?
- What is it about the provision of this program or intervention that is working well?
- What influences the capacity to achieve positive outcomes?
- How can programs and interventions be improved in the future?

The monitoring and evaluation phase of evidence-informed practice (EIP) focuses on the real conditions, processes, outcomes, and experiences of services at the local level, with the recognition that the specifics of the local context shape the interventions and their impact. Findings from evaluation and monitoring activities contribute local evidence and help answer questions such as these.

Monitoring and evaluation is not the final phase in the EIP process, but rather part of the ongoing process of building, reviewing, and incorporating evidence into practice decisions. Evaluation activities can create as many questions as answers. These questions can be fed back into the design of practice questions, which is Phase 1 of the EIP process (chapter 4). The new information generated by the monitoring and evaluation activities also becomes part of the local evidence that is included in Phase 2, evidence-gathering activities (chapter 5). This local information offers a valuable reference point for the critical appraisal of the relevance and applicability of evidence obtained from external sources, undertaken in Phase 3 (chapter 6). It also provides contextual information required for practice decision making in Phase 4 (chapter 7). Service user feedback and other information on outcomes offer alternative perspectives that can be incorporated into a critically reflective approach to practice that informs practice refinement and changes.

Monitoring and evaluation are an integral part of the ongoing cycle of EIP. Monitoring and evaluation activities in Phase 5 are enhanced by a critically reflective and research-minded organizational culture in which questions such as "Why do we do things the way we do?" and "How can we improve the way we do things?" remain at the forefront of thinking.

This chapter examines organizational approaches and strategies for planning evaluation activities that support an evidence-informed approach to practice. It does not, however, provide a guide to evaluation research methods. There are many texts available that provide guidance on program evaluation and social research methods. Reference to such texts is recommended when planning the specifics of evaluation projects. The focus of this chapter is on a broad approach to evaluation and monitoring activities. In addition, it addresses the organizational processes that can help prepare for and support these activities as an integral part of an EIP strategy.

AN ORGANIZATIONAL APPROACH TO MONITORING AND EVALUATION

Individual practitioners who seek feedback from service users and maintain records of goal achievements and outcomes fulfill a fundamental aspect of professional practice. Reflection on this evaluative information can shape practice so that it is more responsive to service users. An organizational approach to monitoring and evaluation supports and complements these individual activities with a planned, systematic, and collaborative approach to the collection of information that feeds into the EIP cycle.

Unfortunately, data gathering and outcome measurement that are undertaken in human services organizations do not always lead to the effective use of information to plan improved services. Practitioners can feel alienated from data collection processes and can become resistant as they enter seemingly pointless data that are used to scrutinize, rate, and classify programs or are not used at all. As in each of the EIP phases, engagement and relationship building are vital for the establishment of useful monitoring and evaluation activities; these efforts include engaging with service users so that they can contribute constructive feedback in a safe and trusting environment and engaging with practitioners who can offer insights into relevant information for practice development. If practitioners have a sense of ownership over the data collection process, improved data entry compliance and information uptake are likely to follow.

Organizational strategies can be implemented to

- facilitate the engagement of stakeholders in designing and completing evaluation activities
- allocate resources for the collection of local evaluation knowledge in a systematic way
- maintain records of findings from evaluation and monitoring activities so that they are available for future service development and strategic planning activities
- incorporate local evaluation and monitoring knowledge into each of the EIP phases.

The types of evaluation data organizations can collect include outcome data and trends, qualitative experiential data, and information on the characteristics of the local context that influence how practice, interventions, and programs are provided. Examination of the contextual features enables additional questions beyond "Does it work?" to be examined. More detailed consideration can be given to questions about how interventions work, the circumstances under which different aspects of interventions work well, and the service users for whom interventions are effective.

When modifications are made to standardized practices supported by research evidence (for example, therapeutic interventions, group programs) in response to service user circumstances (for example, offering fewer or abridged sessions) or features of the practice context (for example, using a sole facilitator rather than cofacilitators because of an insufficient number of trained staff), the fidelity of the interventions is weakened. When programs and interventions are shortened, adapted, or modified in other ways, organizations cannot rely on the original evidence to support use of the intervention and are responsible for evaluating the interventions in the local setting. Even when standardized interventions and programs are implemented in accordance with the program manual, the way in which the program is delivered and received in the local setting can influence outcomes. Monitoring and evaluation are required to assess the impact of an intervention in each unique practice setting.

At an organizational level, decisions need to be made about the best ways to measure or understand the impact of interventions. Whether such measurement involves the use of standardized outcome measures, survey questionnaires, qualitative data from reflective discussions, observations, or a combination of measures, consideration needs to be given to how the data should be collected, analyzed, and used to inform future practice decisions. Resources are required if a planned and coordinated approach is to be implemented to gather sufficient data over a period of time and enable trends to be identified.

The evaluation data collected for a particular program or type of practice intervention may reveal significantly better outcomes for this intervention in comparison to other interventions or no intervention. Alternatively, qualitative data may provide insights into how different aspects of the program were received and the effects perceived by service users and practitioners. Some service users may decide to discontinue with the service, and for those who continue, the intervention may not result in desirable change. The benefit of evaluation in the local context is that the varied complexity of daily practice presents opportunities to examine different aspects of practice and contextual factors through examining case studies, following up with people who withdraw from services, and offering and comparing alternative interventions. Recording and evaluating responses to emerging practice issues can offer detailed and relevant insights into the nature of practice on the ground in a way that a controlled study in a remote setting cannot.

Local monitoring and evaluation activities can foster a clearer understanding of the practice circumstances and service user characteristics that contribute to positive outcomes. The provisional and cumulative nature of evidence has been discussed throughout this book, and, in the same vein, evaluation data need to be regarded as provisional rather than definitive. By implementing planned, coordinated, and goal-directed evaluation and monitoring strategies, local evaluations can move beyond impressions and reassuring client satisfaction surveys to make valuable contributions to an ongoing EIP process. How practice interventions can be improved in the unique practice context of the organization, with the range of service users who participate in the organization, is the driving concern of local evaluation and monitoring. The Family Focus example is revisited in this chapter to illustrate aspects of implementing evaluation strategies.

Case Study: Family Focus (Organizational Scenario 3)

The Family Focus organization has implemented an EIP strategy over the past 18 months that has involved working through the five implementation phases in each of its program areas. Parenting education is one program that has been modified as a result of the EIP strategy. Drawing on information obtained from online evidence repositories, a standardized parenting education program was selected as the most appropriate for the program goals, professional skill set, agency context, and characteristics of the local community. Evidence for this program showed significant improvements in parenting behaviors, parent–child relationship factors, and child behaviors that matched with Family Focus parenting education program goals.

As the center-based program got under way, data were collected to monitor the program. Data on participant characteristics, including family structure, enabled participation rates to be monitored and compared in relation to different family characteristics. Findings led to the identification of higher dropout rates among single-parent families. The question of how to better engage parents in a range of family structures became a practice question for further evidence gathering. Following the appraisal of research on family engagement, in light of the locally collected participation data, practice decisions were made about ways to make the program more accessible and engaging to a range of groups, including single parents, fathers, same-sex parents, and grandparents. A number of practices were incorporated, and some of the language and group activities in the education program were modified to be more inclusive of different family structures.

As a result of networking activities, an opportunity has subsequently arisen to deliver the program in the local primary school with a school counselor working as a cofacilitator for the groups. Family Focus parenting educators regard this as an opportunity to engage earlier with parents who may be facing parenting challenges but would not otherwise seek out assistance. Because the teachers know the families, they have opportunities to refer families whom they think would benefit from the program. With the school counselor working as a group cofacilitator, a Family Focus staff member is made available to offer a reciprocal service to the school, providing professional development and consultation for teachers on child conduct concerns and ways to support families in accessing community services.

After several months of collaborative planning with the school, the parenting program about to be offered is looking quite different from the center-based program initially delivered at Family Focus. Not only have parts of the group-based parenting intervention been changed, but the structures, processes, physical facilities, and relationships supporting the delivery of the program have also changed. The outcome goals of shifting parenting behaviors, parent–child relationships, and child behaviors are now accompanied by process goals associated with early intervention, referral behaviors of teachers, capacity building among teachers, and inclusive engagement of parents from a variety of family structures.

Family Focus wants to ensure that relevant local evaluation data are collected and appraised in conjunction with external evidence. The growing body of evidence is to be used to inform future practice decisions guiding development and improvement of the school-based parenting program into the future.

APPROACHES TO EVALUATION IN THE HUMAN SERVICES

This section discusses some different forms of evaluation used in the human services. Later in the chapter, strategies for incorporating aspects of these approaches into organizational life and the EIP process are offered.

Evaluation Focus

Evaluation activities in the human services take many different forms. Owen (2006) classified program evaluation into five forms: proactive, clarificative, interactive, monitoring, and impact. Each form of evaluation is a response to particular evaluation questions that emerge at different points in the design and delivery of interventions. Different forms of evaluation are also required to respond to varying organizational information needs. The five forms of evaluation are explained briefly, using the Family Focus scenario to illustrate how they can apply in practice:

1. *Proactive:* Proactive evaluation assesses the needs for certain types of interventions and includes synthesizing knowledge, research, and evidence to identify needs and programs or interventions that can address the needs.

Family Focus conducts a survey of teachers and parents to assess the local need for and interest in interventions to address parenting practices and child behavior. Results of the survey are examined in light of the evidence on parenting programs and parent engagement that was gathered and appraised in earlier phases in the EIP process.

2. *Clarificative:* Clarificative evaluation clarifies the intended outcomes, values, elements, and reasoning of the program.

   Family Focus runs a workshop to discuss and define the types of changes and outcomes related to parenting, child behavior, parent–child relationships, and teacher referral patterns that are desired from a school-based parenting program. The workshop also sets goals for the number and diversity of participant families. Based on knowledge, values, and practice principles around family engagement, early intervention, partnerships, group program delivery, and other factors, an explanatory model is negotiated and developed for how the program elements are expected to work together to achieve program goals and outcomes.

3. *Interactive:* Interactive evaluation examines how well the program or intervention is going and how the responsiveness of the program could be improved.

   Once the parenting program is under way, Family Focus uses forums and interviews to engage with schools and families. Information is gathered on experiences and effects of the program and ideas for how it could be improved.

4. *Monitoring:* Monitoring evaluation records details of the program or intervention to monitor fidelity to the standardized intervention model and adherence to targets and benchmarks. This type of evaluation provides information to help refine and fine-tune the intervention for greater efficiency and effectiveness.

   Family Focus implements a data collection system to record attendance information and collect data on characteristics of program participants. Program sessions are reviewed and reported on each week to record features of the program, monitor compliance, and identify areas of deviation from the standardized parenting program.

5. *Impact:* Impact evaluation assesses intended and unintended outcomes, the ways different aspects of the program influence outcomes, variation in outcomes between participant groups, and cost-effectiveness.

   Family Focus collects pre- and postintervention scores on standardized scales of parenting practices and child behavior. Qualitative data on the impact of the program are collected from parent interviews at the completion of the program and six months later. Staff time and other program resources are priced to calculate cost-effectiveness. Review meetings are held with school, parent, and Family Focus representatives to examine and record views on how aspects of the program delivery context influence program delivery and where changes could be made.

It can be seen from the Family Focus example that the five forms of evaluation are complementary approaches that respond to differing information requirements in the process of developing, reviewing, and refining the delivery of a program. Each of the five forms of evaluation is likely to generate further evaluative questions that could be taken up as the foci of later evaluation activities.

Related to these five forms of evaluation, there are four common approaches to evaluation in the human services: assessment of needs and strengths, program theory or logic evaluation, process evaluation, and outcome evaluation. The following sections explain these approaches and identify parallels with the preceding five forms of evaluation.

Assessment of Needs and Strengths. Assessment of needs and strengths logically occurs prior to the planning and implementation of interventions and, as such, is a proactive form of evaluation based on Owen's (2006) schema. The circumstances and contexts for service delivery are dynamic, however, and reevaluation of need is also required after a program or intervention has been offered for some time. Need may be assessed against norms or standards for society, as a comparison between social groups, or in terms of what people are demanding or feel they want. Data used for the assessment of need can be obtained by measuring indicators, conducting surveys, and gathering information from published research and reports on demographic data. In this way, needs assessment can draw on evidence that was gathered and appraised in earlier phases of the EIP process. To build a balanced view of service target groups, strengths and assets should be assessed as well as needs and deficits.

Program Theory or Logic Evaluation. Program theory or program logic is an explanatory depiction of why and how the elements of a program or intervention lead to what outcomes. Program theory or logic evaluation aligns with the clarificative form of evaluation in Owen's (2006) schema. Development of program theory or logic is best undertaken as a collaborative process that involves critically thinking through and articulating the theories, principles, values, and assumptions that underlie and guide an intervention. Potential outcomes are examined, and desirable outcomes are negotiated recognizing that the effectiveness of a program or intervention can be interpreted in a variety of ways and from different perspectives. A reasoned process is then articulated to operationalize the steps, strategies, processes, and program components, derived from the theoretical stance and informed by evidence, that work to achieve the desired changes and specified outcomes.

Program logic is generally depicted diagrammatically using a framework such as that in Figure 8.1. Such diagrams simplify complex and multifaceted intervention processes. Developing program logic diagrams prompts critical reflection on the theoretical and evidential grounding for interventions and the types of inputs, outputs, and outcomes associated with a theoretical framework. Such diagrams also highlight gaps where additional information or revisions to interventions are required. The development and review of program logic models play an integral role in focusing and designing process and outcome evaluations.

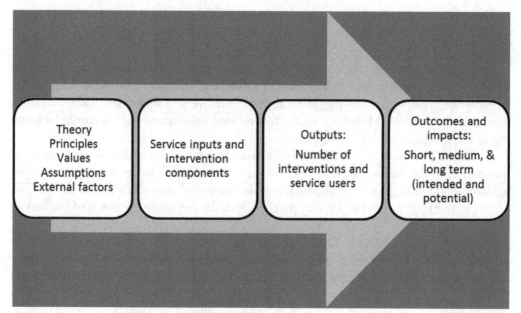

Figure 8.1   Program Logic Framework Diagram

Process Evaluation. Process evaluation examines all of the aspects involved in the day-to-day organization, management, and delivery of a program or intervention, including structures, resources, communication, professional supports, client services delivery, client pathways, decision making, documentation, alignment with or deviation from intervention plans, and compliance with policies and standards. Process evaluation incorporates both the interactive and monitoring forms of evaluation in Owen's (2006) schema. A vast array of data sources can be drawn on in conducting process evaluations. The information that is gathered can be checked against the program logic model for the intervention and also used to fill gaps in understanding identified by the program logic model.

Outcome Evaluation. Outcome evaluation examines the effects and changes that occur for service users and target groups or communities as a result of human services interventions. Outcome evaluation is aligned with the impact form of evaluation in Owen's (2006) schema. Clearly articulated program logic is required for the outcomes of programs and interventions to be evaluated because the conceptualization of effectiveness and desirable outcomes from interventions is open to interpretation and shaped by theories, values, and assumptions. The program logic model describes and explains the nature of outcomes, which are then assessed in outcome evaluations. Outcome evaluations include the measurement of program effects using experimental designs and standardized outcome measures, but they also include qualitative depictions of the impact, outcomes, and experiences of interventions for service users. Differential effects for subgroups of service users may also be examined in outcome evaluations. Cost–benefit evaluation is a type of outcome evaluation that attributes monetary values to service user outcomes and assesses these benefits against the costs of service provision.

Evaluation Methodology

As discussed earlier, evaluation of human services interventions takes on different forms in response to a variety of questions and information needs. Evaluation is a type of social research, and as with all social research, the choice of an appropriate evaluation methodology is guided by research or evaluation questions. Coverage of evaluation methods, sources of data for evaluation, and techniques for the analysis of data is beyond the scope of this book, but some general comments on the choice of methodology are offered.

Evaluation research questions about experiences or meanings tend to suit qualitative, interpretive methodologies. For example, in evaluations of the Family Focus parenting program, qualitative methods would be suited to the examination of questions about parents' understandings of how the program affected the way they parented, what factors assisted their engagement with the program, and what the obstacles to engagement were.

Questions about categorically defined or measurable events or outcomes are more suited to quantitative methodologies and experimental or quasi-experimental designs. Changes in the behaviors of the parents and children who attended the Family Focus parenting program could be assessed using standardized scales completed by parents, teachers, or practitioners. Questions about process features, such as the best time and location of a program, could be answered with categorical questions in a survey questionnaire.

Along with evaluation questions, theoretical perspectives and value stances on the nature of the social world influence choice of methodology. Qualitative methodologies are aligned with the stance that meanings in the social world are created by subjective experiences and interpretations of social events, whereas quantitative methodologies involve the assumption that the social world can, to a certain degree, be controlled, quantified, and measured. Mixed-method approaches entail the position that single social research methods produce inadequate findings for understanding the social world or social phenomena such as the delivery of human services interventions. Using a mixed-method approach that involves gathering data from a number of different perspectives and sources can produce a fuller picture of this social complexity. In the Family Focus example, outcome data from standardized measures were complemented by qualitative, explanatory data from qualitative interviews.

In designing an evaluation methodology, it is important to recognize that social research can be alienating and disempowering for research participants and can serve to further entrench power relationships between privileged, so-called experts and service user participants. If a social justice perspective is upheld, attention should be paid to the nature of service user participation in the evaluation process. There are ethical issues around how participants are engaged and treated throughout the research process, but there are additional questions about who defines and leads the research agenda. Parents who have previously participated in the Family Focus parenting program, for example, may be interested in designing and implementing evaluation activities. Participation in evaluation activities can assist with service user engagement and offer insights into an appropriate evaluation design.

Realist Approach to Evaluation

There are practical, ethical, and contextual constraints on how data can be gathered and used to evaluate practice. For EIP purposes, the goal is that the data will complement other evidence that has been gathered and usefully inform practice decision making.

A thorough evaluation of practice could technically entail a multifaceted evaluation design with an array of mixed research methods that investigate needs, program logic, and process and outcome components of interventions drawing on several different data sources and perspectives. The resources required to implement such an evaluation plan would, in many cases, outweigh the resources directed toward delivery of the intervention. In the face of limited resources available to human services organizations, a balance between service provision and service evaluation is required. Limited by the constraints of time and resources, evaluation plans need to be strategic, focused, and realistic.

Realist evaluation focuses on priority questions and practical methodologies that produce findings to inform future practice decisions. Realist evaluation recognizes that human services interventions affect people in a variety of ways. Different change mechanisms operate to achieve change, which is shaped by individual, social, economic, political, organizational, staffing, geographic, cultural, and historical factors (Pawson & Tilley, 1997). Although it may offer reassurance to practitioners, managers, and funders to have findings showing that a program produces positive outcomes and satisfies service users, an evidence-informed approach to evaluation aims to identify how practice could change to increase or better focus the positive impact of interventions. A realist evaluation plan avoids generating data that are never put to practical use in the organization.

If interventions are to be adequately evaluated, time and resources need to be directed toward evaluation activities. Organizations embarking on an EIP strategy must commit resources to support local evaluation and monitoring activities. This commitment ensures that context-specific evidence is produced. Seeking out external funding opportunities; forming partnerships to support evaluation activities, such as with university researchers and student practicum placements; and redirecting internal funds are ways to finance and support evaluation activities.

Pawson and Tilley (2009) advocated a realist approach to evaluation in social work that prioritizes theoretical explanation during the evaluation process. Clarity on the theoretical principles underlying an intervention helps guide decisions about the types of evaluation data needed for future decision making and informs explanations of practice that can be transferred to other settings. The goal is to produce a tested theory about what works for whom in what circumstances and in what respects. This end product is never a pass–fail verdict on an intervention but rather an understanding of how its inner workings produce diverse effects. Strong realist evaluations are thus intended to lead to better focused and more effective programs (Pawson & Tilley, 2009).

The ongoing development and review of program theory or program logic for interventions is integral to the realist approach to evaluation. Realist evaluation entails gathering targeted pieces of information that help build a theoretical argument about, and explanations for, what is working and how. Locally gathered evaluation data can be used in combination with theoretical principles and evidence from external sources to build such explanatory arguments.

A realist approach to evaluation fits well with the EIP process advocated in this book. The provisional and limited nature of evidence is acknowledged, along with the value in continuing to build knowledge and understanding in a critically reflective way. Critically appraising evidence from a variety of sources for credibility, relevance, and applicability to the practice setting is recognized as part of the ongoing process of understanding and improving practice. Incorporating evaluation findings and external evidence into program logic models assists with practice decision making because it addresses questions of *how* and *why* as well as *what*.

Seeking out targeted pieces of information to fit a theoretical explanation for how and why an intervention works does, however, present the risk of adoption of a biased explanation that supports existing practices and associated explanatory models. Critical reflection is needed to prompt consideration of the full range of explanations that could make sense of program outcomes. Explanations should be adopted or discarded only after critical analysis that considers different theoretical perspectives and potential change mechanisims and incorporates different stakeholder viewpoints. Close attention also needs to be paid to the values and assumptions that inform explanations. As Pawson and Tilley (2009) argued, the reasoning process can focus attention on the aspects of practice that are open to change and improvement.

There are an infinite number of explanations for why, when, and how a program works, but there are only so many ways in which a program might be improved. Realist evaluators need not wait to figure out the totality of explanations but should concentrate, therefore, on program ideas and variations that are feasible to implement (Pawson & Tilley, 2009).

In the Family Focus school-based parenting program, a traditional outcome evaluation could, for example, seek to identify whether there is a significant improvement in parenting behavior and child behavior scores on standardized measures after the intervention. In addition to constraints associated with implementing an experimental design and forming a suitable control group in this real-world setting, questions of how, why, and for whom positive changes are made would largely remain after obtaining such findings. If significant improvements are found for the group of participants overall, the gains may be small and some families may not experience positive change. Even if the findings did not show a significant change for the group overall, some families may have experienced substantial positive changes. Knowledge of a significant or nonsignificant result does not actually help much in making decisions about whether and how the program should be developed in the future, particularly if the participant group is small and the research design has limitations related to real-world constraints.

To gather information to improve the program, different types of targeted information would be more helpful than a significant or nonsignificant result. Realist evaluation aims to gain understanding of how and for whom a program is working and ways to improve that program. In the Family Focus program example, groups of families who did and did not show positive changes could be selected. Qualitative information could be gathered from these families on their experiences of what was helpful and unhelpful in their particular circumstances and what could assist them to get more out of the program. Such an approach could be taken with a small group of participants and would not require a control group because it seeks to understand the experiences and trajectory of change for these families and the role that the parenting program played or could play.

The evaluation data that are gathered could then be used to enhance the explanatory model for the program.

The process goals set for the Family Focus parenting program include providing early intervention and engaging a diversity of parents. A full process evaluation may examine all of the systems and processes associated with the program, identifying areas in which efficiencies and systemic improvements could be made. A realist approach to process evaluation, alternatively, could gather information that directly relates to the process questions about targeted engagement of participants. Participant characteristics could be reviewed, with feedback and suggestions sought from parents and teachers, to better understand how to engage families in particular circumstances and how to develop the program to improve engagement in the future.

Information gathered from a realist approach to evaluation does not stand alone. It is preceded by collaborative, critical reflection on what types of knowledge will contribute to understanding and how this knowledge can best be gathered. The gathered information is critically appraised for credibility, with consideration given to the range of ways in which the new information can be interpreted and decisions made on how the program theory or logic model can reflect the new knowledge.

MANAGERIALISM AND MONITORING OUTCOMES

One of the ways that organizations contribute to the body of knowledge on the effectiveness of interventions is to monitor the changes and gains achieved by local service users over time. This effort requires data entry and management systems that can be easily integrated into daily work routines and are not onerous for staff. Ideally, a data system is used to record service user characteristics, components of interventions, and outcome measures that reliably, consistently, and validly measure the desired change in a culturally sensitive way.

If the goal of a program is to support Indigenous children to remain in high school until graduation, then high school completion rates are an appropriate measure of success. If the goal of a program is to improve parenting practices and the quality of parent–child relationships, as in the Family Focus example, then the appropriate outcome measure is not as obvious. There are many parenting scales, generally relying on parent self-report, that have been tested in different contexts for reliability and validity. Because parenting is a culturally bound practice, a process of consultation, appraisal of the research conducted on these scales, and trial periods in the organization will assist in decisions on which scale is most appropriate for the setting and is the best measure of desired changes in the service user group. If the experiences, barriers, and issues with adopting different parenting practices are to be understood, however, then qualitative feedback also needs to be gathered to consider alongside the outcome data.

Unfortunately, the managerial approaches that have been widely embraced by government departments and human services organizations tend to emphasize data collection for work inspection, output monitoring, management control, and performance review purposes rather than for the constructive evaluation of practice. Data management is often the domain of administrative and information management staff. It is often very difficult for practitioners or service users to have input into the types of data collected and how the data are put to use as a source of information that contributes to practice decision making. Data systems can be experienced as oppositional, rather than helpful, for practice.

Developing evidence-informed approaches to practice requires consideration of how service users and practitioners could be included in decision making about the types of data to be collected. Including these perspectives entails building relationships between information management and other units in the organization. Because there are likely to be various views on what information is valuable and why, a collaborative process of reflection and negotiation on what data are collected and how the data can be accessed, analyzed, and used may be helpful. Strong leadership is needed to manage such a process, with a clear notion of how data collection can be used to gather local knowledge that contributes to the body of evidence for practice decision making.

Decisions on the types of data to be collected should be informed by an understanding of how the data could be used for service improvement. In addition, the demands that the collection and entry of data place on clients, practitioners, and other staff should be considered. The goal is that data systems are designed with clear purposes in mind, do not compromise the quality of work with service users, and are user friendly to ensure compliance with data entry.

ORGANIZATIONAL STRATEGIES FOR THE IMPLEMENTATION OF EVALUATION ACTIVITIES

Organizational support is required to ensure that evaluation activities are well considered and integrated with the overall EIP process. The sections that follow discuss organizational strategies in four areas:

1. Provide leadership and direction.
2. Establish systems and processes.
3. Engage and build relationships with stakeholders (managers, practitioners, service users, researchers).
4. Promote critical reflection on evaluation design and the ways findings are to be integrated into the knowledge and understanding of practice in the organization.

Provide Leadership and Direction

Evaluation and monitoring activities take a variety of forms and approaches and use different data collection methods. Leaders can motivate and mobilize staff and service users to engage with evaluation activities, communicate the vision and purpose for evaluation, and educate on evaluation processes. Administrative resources are required to plan, implement, and monitor evaluation activities; maintain records of findings; and make findings readily accessible when required for practice decision making and service development activities.

Organizational leaders are responsible for ensuring that adequate resources are directed toward evaluation activities. To do so, they must audit the technical skills required to undertake evaluation and monitoring activities; identify and direct internal resources; and broker external resources, linkages, and partnerships. External expertise and resources may be required to support evaluation activities through professional development, engagement of research staff, and establishment of partnerships.

An important role for organizational leaders is to ensure that evaluation activities are integrated with the other components in the EIP process. Leaders take on the roles of analyst, integrator, and coordinator to identify how the local knowledge gathered through evaluation activities addresses key practice questions, to map and appraise evidence, and to make practice decisions. Through consultation and negotiation, leaders communicate understanding of the interplay between externally sourced evidence and local knowledge and of the ways this interplay affects practice decisions in the organization.

In the Family Focus practice example, the findings generated from the evaluation could have applications beyond informing development of the school-based parenting program. The findings can also be included in organization-wide discussions on practice questions relating to engagement with families in other programs and included as local knowledge when external evidence is appraised. Organizational coordination of evaluation activities can also facilitate sharing of skills, knowledge, and experiences in relation to evaluation activities among different units and programs in the organization, promoting organizational learning. Leadership is required to oversee and facilitate these organizational processes.

Establish Systems and Processes

Organizational systems and processes are required to support leaders in facilitating and coordinating evaluation activities. Systems and processes are needed for the purposes of

- consulting and engaging with stakeholders,
- managing evaluation activities,
- managing information and data, and
- integrating evaluation with the wider EIP process.

Forums can provide service users, practitioners, other staff, and external players opportunities to shape and inform evaluation activities in a collaborative and interactive way. As discussed earlier in this chapter, program theory or logic models and explanatory evaluation approaches entail exploring different perspectives to clarify desirable outcomes for interventions and explain how components of these interventions contribute to the achievement of outcomes. Critical reflection is also required to examine how findings from evaluation and monitoring can be incorporated into explanatory models. Workshops that facilitate collaboration and critical thinking can inform the design of evaluation projects so that useful and practice-relevant information is produced and integrated into practice decision making in the EIP process.

Evaluation involves the phases of project design, data collection, analysis, and application, which generally take place over a number of months or years. When several evaluations are occurring at the same time, it can be challenging to ensure that findings are generated, analyzed, and examined in a timely way. When practitioners are undertaking evaluations, the demands of practice often take precedence over evaluation activities. It is therefore helpful to have systems to keep evaluation activities on track and to manage information exchange between practitioners and others involved with the evaluation. A project management timeline that is reviewed and reported on by an evaluation project coordinator can be helpful.

In the Family Focus example, pre- and postintervention measures must be appropriately timed if they are to gather the intended information. Preparatory engagement and communication with group facilitators and parent participants are required to achieve high compliance with data collection. Valuable information and useful findings will be missed if attention is not paid to communication and coordination processes. If an evaluation project requires ethics approval before data can be collected, the time required to prepare and approve the ethics application needs to be included in the evaluation management timeline.

The role of data management systems was introduced earlier in this chapter. Data entry and information management systems are needed to maintain records of findings from evaluation and monitoring activities. These systems ensure that the information is accessible when appraising evidence for practice decision making and reporting to funding bodies. The term *data mining* refers to nonintrusive methods of extracting information from data systems that can be used to pinpoint trends in service use, identify who is missing out and who is dropping out of services, and map outcome trends. There are often barriers between the administration of data systems and the use of data by practitioners to inform practice. Encouraging data mining and finding ways to make data accessible to those who could incorporate it as local evidence in practice decision making are worthwhile strategies for organizations.

A data system includes service user characteristics and outcome measures that assess the desired change in a culturally sensitive way. Selecting measures requires appraisal for suitability to the local context. Clarity on the desirable outcomes from interventions, derived from the program theory or logic, is needed before measures can be selected. The next step is for potential measures to be gathered and examined for suitability to the context and purpose. The two-volume set *Measures for Clinical Practice and Research* (Corcoran & Fischer, 2013) is a valuable resource for locating suitable standardized measures for children and adults in the field of mental health that also provides guidance on the applications and limitations of the measures. Finding a suitable measure may also be included as a practice question in the EIP process. The practice question "What is an appropriate measure of parenting behavior for Family Focus?" could be posed to gather research evidence on measures of parenting behavior and appraise this research to assess the validity, relevance, and applicability of a measure for the service user group and practice context.

Finally, systems are required to ensure that evaluation activities feed into the wider EIP cycle. Evaluation activities are not isolated projects, but rather have the potential to inform other areas of practice in the organization and be part of larger, longer term monitoring and evaluation projects. Building in reporting and information sharing across units in the organization helps develop the learning organization culture. Questions raised by evaluation activities can be recorded to feed into the design of practice questions in the EIP cycle. Professional supervision also supports the EIP process by fostering critical reflection on evaluation design, implementation, and findings. Findings from evaluation activities are an important source of feedback for reviewing practice in the organization and, as such, can be useful to incorporate as a regular component of supervision sessions.

Engage and Build Relationships with Stakeholders

As with each of the phases in the EIP cycle, building relationships with parties who can offer alternative viewpoints and who have a role to play in supporting the success of EIP processes can assist evaluation activities. Implementing strategies to engage collaboratively with service users, practitioners, managers, and researchers to develop explanatory models, design and carry out evaluations, and incorporate evaluation findings with other evidence in making practice decisions will add value to the process. For example, a variety of viewpoints and experiences can aid in the selection or design of suitable outcome measures that adequately capture desirable outcomes, are well received by the service users who provide information, and are manageable for the practitioners who enter data.

It is generally necessary to engage the support of practitioners if evaluation data are to be collected on interventions. Practitioner involvement can enhance the quality and extent of data collection and, in turn, the value of the findings as evidence for practice. If practitioners do not see the value in evaluation activities, it will be difficult to gain access to worthwhile information that can contribute to the local evidence base. Insights into the components of interventions and the factors influencing the success of programs can be gleaned with the guidance and input of practitioners. Although the design of interventions or programs and the design of evaluations have separate goals and processes, they need to be planned together so that evaluation data collection is integrated with and relevant to the delivery of the intervention.

In the Family Focus school-based parenting program example, parents, teachers, and parenting group facilitators at the school could help with the design of an evaluation that is likely to be positively received in the school and to have a good response rate. Relationships with these key players are also a source of information on contextual issues with the delivery of the program, including how to coordinate with school processes and timetables so that the parenting program runs in harmony with other school activities.

It is important to consider the question of who should carry out evaluations of practice. Legitimate concerns may be raised about conflicts of interest when the practitioners who deliver interventions are also involved in the evaluation of those interventions. There are benefits in engaging evaluators who are within the organization but external to the program or organization. Potential conflicts do not, however, preclude a partnership approach to evaluation design that draws on practitioners' understanding of the types of information that are likely to yield useful findings and the best ways to access this information. It also does not preclude practitioner involvement in identifying the implications of findings for the explanatory model and practice improvements.

J. M. Jones and Sherr (2014) argued that attention to building trusting relationships and good communication between researchers and practitioners is the key to successful practice-based research. They described a continuum of approaches, including regarding practitioners as subjects in research, engaging with practitioners in the research, involving practitioners more actively as partners, and, at the end of the continuum, deriving research from community or practitioner concerns and implementing research projects in partnership using naturalistic processes. Such a collaborative approach to evaluation research fits well with the EIP model in this book. Action research models offer useful frameworks and principles for undertaking this type of collaborative research (Reason & Bradbury, 2006). Available time is, however, a factor that limits practitioners' capacity to engage in evaluation research because the priority and demands of direct practice are high. Managers need to recognize that worthwhile evaluation activities require the allocation of staff time for both evaluators and practitioners.

Strategies to engage service users in the design and implementation of evaluation activities also need to be considered. Service user–controlled research, sometimes referred to as *emancipatory research,* can be a source of empowerment that strengthens the equal standing and rights of service users in organizations. As with practitioners, there is an argument for moving from viewing service users as subjects of evaluation research to viewing them as partners in designing and implementing evaluations and allowing them to drive the research. Service user input is likely to be minimal if a one-size-fits-all model of service user engagement in evaluation is adopted, such as having service user representatives on committees. Seeking out and responding to service users who express ideas about practice interventions may require flexibility to work in unstructured ways to plan and gather evaluation information. Attention to relationship building is important. Service users can be involved in setting local practice research agendas; carrying out research, reviewing and synthesizing findings; and disseminating findings. However, barriers to engagement are often encountered. Creative ways to elicit service user input, such as through social media, may be required (Dill & Shera, 2015).

Partnership with researchers and universities is a strategy identified as a key determining factor facilitating the implementation of EIP in the human services (J. M. Jones & Sherr, 2014). Partnerships between research institutes or universities and human services organizations are particularly relevant to designing and conducting practice evaluations. Such partnerships can bring together the skills and resources of researchers with the grounded practice knowledge of practitioners and the lived experiences of service users. Because ongoing partnerships can strengthen the evidence-informed culture of an organization, they are more valuable to the EIP process than engagement around one-off projects. Joubert and Hocking (2015) described a model adopted in an academic–practitioner partnership in social work, the aim of which was "to embed research within a clinical context" (p. 353). Features of their model include the following:

- Evolving processes are not driven by academic agendas but focus on mutually agreed aims and objectives.
- A longer term commitment is made to collaboratively addressing emerging research and evaluation questions and strengthened by formal agreement between the practice and academic institutions.
- Practice questions and issues faced by practitioners are reframed as research questions.
- Findings are used to inform practice.
- A wide range of research methodologies are drawn on to suit the research questions.

- Mentoring of individual practitioners by academics promotes research-focused practitioners who integrate research skills with existing practice skills.
- A group-based approach to research projects and professional development supports a sustainable culture of integrating research and practice.

These principles are valuable pointers for undertaking evaluation research in an organization, but they also indicate how university–practice partnerships can strengthen each of the five phases in the EIP implementation model. Partnerships with research academics can contribute to the effective design of practice questions, the gathering of research evidence, the critical appraisal of evidence, and practice decision making by promoting an organizational culture in which connections between research and practice are consistently attended to. Researchers and academics can benefit from engaging in research that has direct applicability to the human services industry context.

One strategy for establishing a relationship with a university is to offer student practicum placements in the organization and to explore opportunities for evaluation research as part of the practicum or as a follow-on project. Alternatively, university Web sites provide researchers' areas of research interest and contact details, which can be reviewed to find matches with practice areas in the organization.

Partnerships with universities may influence the nature of evaluation research that is undertaken. Universities are likely to be able to provide access to research grant opportunities that would not otherwise be available to human services organizations. University researchers are also expected to engage in research that will lead to publications in academic journals, which may affect the evaluation design in some ways because the research needs to be relevant to a wide audience. The added value of these partnerships is in the potential to contribute to the body of research evidence on human practice interventions and to share knowledge and experience beyond the organization. With adequate time, resources, and planning, well-designed projects with ethics approval can be undertaken. If published, subsequent findings can contribute to a wider body of research evidence.

Promote Critical Reflection on Evaluation Design

Strategies that provide opportunities for managers, leaders, practitioners, service users, and external partners to reflect critically on different aspects of the evaluation and monitoring phase are part of the implementation process. Facilitated, collaborative workshops and forums can be used to aid critical reflection. In particular, critical examination and reflection are required in the development of explanatory theories and program logic models for interventions or programs. This effort includes examining values and assumptions, alternative explanatory theories, and ways to incorporate new findings into explanatory models. Reflective discussions are also valuable in making decisions on the most appropriate approach to an evaluation and the evaluation design, methods, and measures to be used. Forums and workshops such as these require skilled facilitation that promotes collaboration, lateral thinking, and the examination of different perspectives so that evaluation activities produce useful evidence to meet organizational and practice goals. Critical reflection on the social, economic, political, and historical context of practice can inform an understanding of constraints, opportunities, and realistic activities and goals for the organization.

Professional supervision is another forum in which critical reflection on evaluation findings can be integrated. Service user feedback and evaluation of practice are an important source of information in practice decision making. Supervision sessions should provide practitioners with opportunities to reflect on their own practice in light of service user feedback and evaluation findings and to make decisions on how individual practice can be modified in response.

Building the organizational knowledge base requires ongoing reflection on local knowledge needs, explanatory models for practice, the nature and implications of evaluation findings, and the ways these findings can be integrated with other evidence. Each evaluation builds knowledge and adds to the growing body of practice knowledge in the organization. At an organizational level, time and space for staff to engage in these reflective activities need to be allocated, together with skilled supervisors and workshop facilitators to guide the processes.

CHALLENGES AND PITFALLS IN EVALUATING PRACTICE

It can be challenging for human services organizations developing practice evaluation plans to decide what is manageable. Gathering practice evaluation knowledge for EIP requires resources and planning so that evaluation activities usefully contribute to practice understanding and development. Half-hearted, poorly planned, underresourced, badly timed, or incomplete evaluation projects are likely to be of minimal use to an organization. A realist approach is advocated that entails undertaking thoughtfully considered and purpose-driven evaluations. A long-term commitment to gathering worthwhile data and critical reflection on such data in the context of other external evidence form the foundation for building practice knowledge in the organization.

Small-scale evaluations that are well planned and integrated are more useful than large, expensive evaluations that offer little guidance for practice. A barrier to embarking on small-scale evaluation projects is the view that worthwhile evaluation and evidence should be obtained from experimental study designs that entail randomization and control groups. Experimental studies play a vital role in generating an evidence base for human services interventions, but there is value in other research methods that generate qualitative, experiential, case study, client profile, and explanatory information that throws new light on service provision in the local context. Such local evidence does not replace evidence from controlled experimental studies conducted by external sources. Rather, it informs decisions on which interventions to provide and how best to provide them in a particular organization.

Staff turnover can be a challenge to evaluation projects, especially if an exiting staff member has been a key driver of the project. Although a loss of momentum in certain activities may be unavoidable when a staff member leaves, established leadership roles, systems and processes, and collaborative engagement with stakeholders, as discussed earlier in the strategies section, can sustain evaluation activities and support the evidence-informed culture of the organization. Efforts directed toward building organizational systems to support evaluation activities mean that less reliance is placed on the energies of individuals in the organization.

Making use of information and data management systems for evaluation purposes can also present challenges for organizations. Information systems can develop a life of their own and may not be used effectively to monitor, evaluate, or improve practice. Information may be gathered but not used; alternatively, a managerial approach may be taken to data management in which outcome data are used to control and rationalize practice rather than to provide a genuine source of evidence for practice. Critical review of the purpose and potential for ongoing data collection and ways to make data systems accessible for evaluation activities is important for organizations embarking on an EIP strategy.

INCORPORATING EVALUATION FINDINGS INTO THE EIP CYCLE

Monitoring and evaluation has been presented here as the fifth phase in the EIP cycle. However, practice evaluation activities produce valuable local evidence that feeds into each of the phases in the evidence-informed process as follows:

- Evaluation of local practice generates new questions that are an important part of the process of deeper enquiry and cumulative practice knowledge development in an organization. New practice questions are generated for consideration in Phase 1 of the EIP cycle.
- Findings from the evaluation of practice offer local contextual knowledge and a more detailed understanding of intervention processes and outcomes. This local evidence is gathered, together with external research evidence, in Phase 2 of the cycle.
- Findings from practice evaluations will have limitations and should be appraised for quality, relevance, and applicability to the local practice setting. The critical appraisal of findings is undertaken along with the critical appraisal of external evidence in Phase 3 of the cycle in a process of developing an integrated map of evidence.
- The feedback and knowledge gained from the evaluation of practice are important in critically reflecting on practice, informing practice decisions, and implementing interventions, which is Phase 4 in the EIP cycle. Monitoring and evaluation are incorporated as an integral part of practice implementation.

Although the strength of findings from local evaluations of practice is sometimes questioned, monitoring and evaluation activities at the organizational level play a fundamental role in the implementation of an evidence-informed approach to practice. By coordinating, providing resources for, and supporting practice evaluation and integrating findings with external research evidence, organizations are better placed to ensure the relevance, positive impact, and ongoing improvement of practice for their service users.

REFLECTIVE QUESTIONS

Forms of Evaluation

- Choose an intervention from your own practice setting, and identify the type of information gathering that could be carried out for each of the five forms of evaluation:

  1. proactive

  2. clarificative

  3. interactive

  4. monitoring

  5. impact

Approaches to Evaluation

- Select a program or intervention from your own practice setting. How might each of the following types of evaluation contribute to the future development of the intervention?

  - needs and strengths assessment

  - program theory or logic evaluation

  - process evaluation

  - outcome evaluation

  - realist evaluation

- What practice questions could each of these types of evaluation help answer for your organization or program?

- Consider an evaluation of an intervention or program that you are aware of in your own field of practice or organization:

  - In what ways did the findings contribute to explanations of how the program works to achieve positive outcomes? What were the limitations in these explanations?

  - In what ways were findings used to inform improvements to the experiences of and outcomes for service users?

  - Are there other types of findings that could have given other insights into how practice could be improved?

Information and Data Systems

- Consider the information and data systems in your organization.

  - What data are analyzed and reported internally to stakeholders, including managers and frontline staff?

- How useful are the data for evaluation purposes?
- What changes could enhance the usefulness of the data for evaluation purposes?
- How could organizational data be made more accessible for evaluation purposes?

Leadership in Evaluation Activities

- What leadership roles will be required to support monitoring and evaluation activities in your organization?
- Who could take on those leadership roles?
- What internal and external resources would be required to support those leadership roles?

Evaluation Systems and Processes

- What systems and processes are needed in your organization to support the following evaluation and monitoring activities?
  - consulting and engaging with stakeholders
  - managing evaluation activities
  - managing information and data
  - integrating evaluation with the wider EIP process
  - other evaluation activities
  - engaging stakeholders with evaluation activities
- What contribution could the following groups make to evaluation activities in your organization?
  - practitioners
  - service users
  - external research partners
- How could you engage these groups in evaluation activities?
- Which aspects of evaluation would be appropriate to engage each group with?

Critical Reflection on Evaluation

- What are the existing forums and groups in your organization within which critical reflection on evaluation activities could be incorporated?
- How might critical reflection on evaluation be promoted in your organization?

- How could practitioners be supported and guided to incorporate service user feedback and evaluation findings into practice decisions?

Challenges and Pitfalls

- What challenges and pitfalls are likely to be encountered in undertaking monitoring and evaluation activities in your organization or program?
- What strategies or approaches could minimize or address these potential challenges and pitfalls?

9

Are We Ready?

Embarking on a new organizational initiative or strategic direction is both exciting and challenging. Assessment of the current conditions in the organization and a planned framework for change will help avoid a fragmented, directionless approach. Human services organizations may experience coercion from external political, economic, and social forces to adopt an evidence-informed approach to practice, but there are internal choices to be made on the nature of the evidence-informed approach to be adopted and the ways it will be implemented within the organization. The framework in this book is designed to assist human services organizations in planning for the implementation of evidence-informed practice (EIP).

In the preceding chapters, attention was drawn to a range of issues for consideration within organizations embarking on an EIP initiative. Principles, processes, strategies, and challenges have been discussed. The purpose has been to guide, inform, and prompt critical reflection rather than direct readers in a particular approach. Many different implementation strategies have been suggested and discussed, but decisions need to be made within organizations on the approaches and strategies that suit the features of the particular organization.

Some of the organizational features to consider in developing an EIP implementation plan include the following:

- size and diversity of the organization
- existing engagement with research and evidence
- attitudes toward EIP
- resource opportunities to support EIP strategies

- competing priorities
- staff qualifications and skill sets
- opportunities to partner with or contract external organizations

Implementation of EIP has been presented as a process of organizational change in which shifts are made in the organizational culture to support a more critical, research-minded approach to decisions about programs, interventions, and practices at all levels in the organization. Organizational change is generally slow and incremental. Strategic plans for the adoption of EIP should therefore include both short- and longer term goals and strategies. If, for example, the organization is large and diverse, decisions need to be made on where change should start in the organization and how to propagate changes across the organization over time. Focusing on ways to build on existing strengths and capacities is a useful principle when planning for change.

Attitudes and values of workers play an important part in the culture of an organization. Assessing attitudes toward EIP is therefore helpful in determining readiness to embark on an EIP strategy and ways to prepare for change. Views can be assessed through discussions and consultations with staff or more formally through a survey questionnaire. There are scales available to assess attitudes toward the adoption of empirically supported interventions; they include the Evidence-Based Practice Attitude Scale (EBPAS) (Aarons, 2004) and the Brief Individual Readiness for Change Scale (BIRCS) (Goldman, 2009). The EBPAS comprises 15 items and measures four domains or constructs: intuitive appeal of evidence-based practice (EBP), attitudes toward organizational requirements to adopt practices based on evidence, openness to innovation, and perceived divergence of research-based practice from normal practice. The BIRCS is a four-item scale that measures practitioners' beliefs about their skills, flexibility, training, and resources to implement interventions based on research as part of an assessment of overall readiness for EBP. Before adopting an attitude questionnaire, the degree of match should be determined between the constructs the questionnaire measures and the approach to EIP that the organization is working toward.

A vision of EIP in the organization is needed to guide an implementation plan. Organizational leaders, practitioners, service users, researchers, and service development staff have roles to play in the implementation of EIP and therefore should be included in the collaborative design of that vision. Understanding attitudes toward EIP and educating all those with a role to play on the possibilities and opportunities for an evidence-informed approach can also contribute to the development of the vision.

Different views on EIP have been examined throughout this book, as have different approaches to gathering and appraising evidence. Decisions need to be made on the approach to evidence-informed practice that fits best with the nature, history, priorities, capacities, and context of the organization and the changes that are realistic to work toward. Different approaches will suit different circumstances. Engagement, consultation, and collaboration across the organization will help determine what approach is appropriate, why it suits the circumstances of the organization, and how it is to be implemented.

The remainder of this chapter provides an overview of the main aspects of the implementation framework presented in this book. This overview includes a summary of the guiding principles, resource requirements, tensions and challenges, and implementation strategies.

WHAT PRINCIPLES SHOULD GUIDE OUR IMPLEMENTATION OF EIP?

The five phases for organizational implementation of EIP—practice question design, evidence gathering, evidence appraisal, practice decision making, and evaluation—are derived from the five steps for evidence-based clinical decision making. The application of these five steps to an organizational context requires that the complexities of organizational processes, systems, and culture be addressed. In the organizational context, a goal is to continuously build organizational knowledge, which is developed over time and used to inform and improve practice. This goal is advanced by developing a learning organization in which knowledge is valued, sought, shared, and used in decision making about interventions, programs, and practices. A cyclical, rather than linear, model emphasizes the cumulative, iterative process of knowledge generation and application to practice over time. The phases of the five-phase cyclical model, presented initially in chapter 3 and detailed in the subsequent five chapters, are shown in Figure 9.1.

The approach to the implementation of EIP advocated in this book is guided by three key principles related to the nature of evidence, the role of critical reflection, and

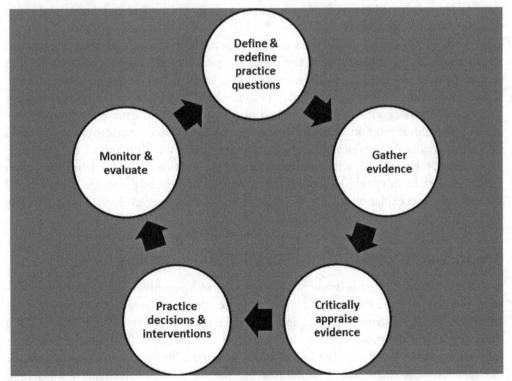

Figure 9.1 Five-Phase, Cyclical Process of Evidence-Informed Practice Implementation

the importance of building social relationships. These are recurring themes throughout the book and underlie the organizational strategies.

Nature of Evidence

Evidence in the human services comprises knowledge drawn from a range of sources, including qualitative and quantitative research, local information gathering, and professional practice wisdom. Evidence needs to be critically appraised for credibility, relevance, and applicability to the particular features of human services practice settings. Evidence is provisional, well-informed, negotiated knowledge that can be used to explain and improve practice and to inform practice decisions. Evidence is gathered with the understanding that individual, organizational, and social worlds cannot be fully understood. Evidence is continually reviewed, updated, and refined to suit the practice context. The approach to evidence is pragmatic in response to contextual forces and constraints and in efforts to make evidence applicable to real-world human services practice settings.

Role of Critical Reflection

Critical reflection is concerned with finding and challenging values and assumptions that can limit understanding. Critical questioning is used to move beyond the acceptance of information or situations at face value and to examine the range of factors that shape understanding of a situation, including personal, relational, historical, social, and political factors. The role of critical reflection has been explained in relation to each of the five phases in the implementation of EIP.

Critical reflection can be used to challenge assumptions about accepted ways of practicing, which is important in the design of practice questions. Critical reflection is used to map out the range of information that can be used as evidence for practice. Critical reflection moves the appraisal of evidence beyond a technical process to consider the social, cultural, political, economic, and historical forces influencing knowledge production and interpretation of evidence. In relation to practice decision making, critical reflection facilitates consideration of alternative ways of working and of the influence of evidence, relationships, and contextual factors on practice choices. Critical reflection is also important in the development of explanatory models as the range of theoretical frameworks and explanations are considered and monitoring and evaluation data are integrated into program logic models.

Importance of Building Social Relationships

Social relationships are fundamental to human services organizations. Both human services delivery and the interpretation and use of evidence are negotiated through relationships among management, employees, service users, and external players. EIP is a collective, relational process within and between organizations. Engagement and collaboration with stakeholders have been emphasized in the implementation framework for several reasons. First, different stakeholders contribute a variety of views, perspectives, and experiences to a fuller understanding of human services delivery and EIP. Stakeholders in this context may include board members, managers, service users, practitioners, service development staff, researchers, partner organizations, and community members. Second, the organizational implementation process relies on cooperative and collaborative relationships across and beyond the organization. Cooperation and understanding among stakeholders are required so that practice questions lead to the gathering of relevant evidence, evidence is disseminated in timely and appropriate ways for use in practice decision making, and evidence-informed decisions about interventions result in corresponding changes in practices or behaviors. These relationships may not develop without strategies to foster them.

Finally, relationships need be developed to bring together the different skill sets and expertise required for the organizational implementation of EIP. For the implementation of EIP in social work and the human services, both practice expertise and research expertise are necessary. Establishing and nurturing partnerships between research-oriented and practice-oriented experts, both within and beyond the bounds of the organization, are valuable in an implementation strategy.

DO WE HAVE THE RESOURCES?

As with any organizational change process, the implementation of EIP requires resources for planning, implementing, and maintaining the approach. One of the reasons for advocating an organizational approach is the unreasonable expectation that practitioners will adopt EIP without any change to their normal practice workload and without organizational support and resources to do so. Resource implications have been discussed in the preceding chapters in relation to each of the five phases of implementation. In summary, the organizational resources required to implement the approach to EIP advocated in this book include leadership resources, staff resources, financial resources, and external resources.

Leadership Resources

A leader or leadership group takes on a range of roles in the implementation of EIP, including the following:

- inspire a vision of EIP for the organization
- connect EIP with organizational strategic planning processes
- educate stakeholders on the nature of EIP and promote access to specific skill development
- enable and encourage engagement with the phases of implementation
- facilitate relationships that support the EIP process
- coordinate evidence-gathering, appraisal, evaluation, and knowledge-sharing activities across the organization
- negotiate conflicts and resistance to change
- mobilize and broker resources to support the implementation

Staff Resources

Staff workloads and skills need to be reviewed to ensure that the following resources are in place:

- staff time to engage in workshops and other strategies in each of the implementation phases
- appropriate supervision and guidance in the EIP process
- time for critical reflection on evidence and practice
- access to research expertise
- access to group facilitation skills

Financial Resources

Operating budgets may need to be directed toward the following:

- training for staff in critical appraisal of evidence, implementation of empirically supported standardized interventions, and provision of evidence-informed professional supervision
- purchase of empirically supported interventions
- engagement of external experts to facilitate workshops, undertake evidence searches or reviews, or advise on evaluation projects

External Resources

Links with external organizations can provide access to resources and support for the implementation of EIP. External resources could include the following:

- evidence dissemination services, including repositories of evidence-based standardized programs
- partnerships with universities or research organizations to undertake research reviews or implement practice evaluation projects
- communities of practice to share evidence and knowledge on practice

The resource implications of implementation strategies should be considered in advance. Some of these implications are associated with the enhancement of existing processes in the organization. The uptake of EIP will be aided by the integration of each of the five phases with existing organizational structures and processes.

Planning for the implementation of EIP includes reviewing where attention to the EIP approach can be heightened in the organization and where processes may be integrated. For example, the design of practice questions may occur as part of an annual service review process. The critical appraisal of evidence could be incorporated into case review or team meetings. The integration of evidence into practice decision making could be used to enhance professional supervision processes. Organizational resources will be used more efficiently if existing processes, strengths, and skills in the organization are identified and capitalized on. When the required skills and capacities are not available within the organization, external partnerships, staff recruitment, or the engagement of external consultants provide other options.

CAN WE COPE?

Potential challenges and pitfalls have been identified in relation to each of the five implementation phases in the preceding chapters. Perspectives on ways to understand and approach these challenges have also been offered. The context and characteristics of each organization are different, and the issues faced will be unique to the organizational setting. Consideration of potential challenges and pitfalls in advance, however, facilitates strategies being put in place in a proactive rather than reactive way. Three general challenges for organizations are tensions between different views on the nature of EIP, struggles to balance priorities in the context of direct service demands, and resistance to change.

Different Views on EIP

Tensions exist in social work and the human services with regard to how evidence is defined and what evidence is deemed to be acceptable for practice. EIP is also viewed in a variety of ways, which can challenge collaborative approaches to its application. Four common views of EIP were introduced in chapter 2 and discussed throughout the book: empirically supported standardized interventions, research-informed clinical decision making, best practice guidelines, and local practice-based research activities. Given the reality of these perspectives within the human services, the implementation framework includes all of these different understandings. These approaches to EIP can be complementary within an organization as long as the different approaches are clear and there are appropriate strategies for implementation.

An inclusive approach has also been taken to the definition of evidence, with the proviso that all evidence must be critically appraised for quality, relevance, and applicability to the local practice context and must help explain and improve service provision. Preparatory work is needed in organizations to clarify how EIP and the nature of evidence are to be understood and the impact that these understandings have on implementation strategies. With differing perspectives on EIP, implementation strategies need to be multifaceted but coordinated around a clear vision for the organization.

Struggles to Balance Organizational Priorities

Human services organizations tend to face challenges associated with high levels of service user demand and limited resources to meet that demand. Practitioners often have limited time and give priority to direct service provision. Both practitioners and managers can experience introduction of a critically reflective, evidence-informed approach to practice as a challenge to the direct service provision priority. Decisions about whether an

EIP approach is to be implemented and to what extent must be made within the context of other organizational priorities and service demands. A realist, pragmatic approach is advocated in which targeted information is gathered in response to key practice questions. The implementation of EIP requires a strategic approach to the promotion of an organizational culture in which accepted practices are critically questioned and the profile and value of research and evidence for practice are raised.

Tensions associated with organizational change are likely to present as challenges that must be negotiated over time. Commitment to dealing with these challenges depends on a clear rationale for the implementation of an evidence-informed approach. The range of reasons why human services organizations adopt an EIP approach was discussed in chapters 1 and 3. These reasons relate to the viability of the organization in the current human services environment and the ethical responsibility to strive for the best outcomes for service users. The role of service users in the implementation of EIP has been a theme throughout the book. Importance is placed on engaging and building relationships with service users as stakeholders and maintaining a focus on improving service user experiences and outcomes.

Resistance to Change

With competing priorities and different views on EIP, efforts to establish evidence-informed cultures and learning organizations can be met with resistance. Divisions can emerge between practitioners and staff engaged in evidence-gathering activities and service planning. Practitioners may become disengaged from the EIP process or view it as a threat to professional autonomy.

Resistance is a common response to organizational change. Leaders need to be prepared to negotiate this resistance and deal with conflicts in a sensitive and encouraging way. Engagement with practitioners has been emphasized in each phase of the implementation. Practitioners have important roles to play in establishing the key practice questions, identifying relevant evidence, gathering and producing local evidence on practice, interpreting findings, and integrating evidence with decisions about practice implications. Engagement and partnerships with practitioners in the design and implementation of EIP are one way to overcome resistance and also ensure that practice is informed not only by formal evidence, but also by the professional judgments, practice wisdom, and detailed knowledge of the dynamics of practice held by practitioners. Close integration of practice with evidence is essential if evidence is to translate into real changes at the front line of practice that will benefit service users.

WHAT IMPLEMENTATION STRATEGIES ARE AVAILABLE TO US?

Strategies that could be included in an organizational plan for the implementation of EIP have been suggested throughout the book. Selected strategies relating to each of the phases of implementation are summarized in the following sections. Additional detail and discussion on issues surrounding implementation are provided in the respective chapters. It is up to each organization to select implementation strategies that fit with their vision of EIP and with the features of their organization, service user characteristics, and service provision context.

Strategies across All Phases

Common strategies across all phases include the following:

- strong leadership to guide, support, and motivate the implementation process
- capacity building of people and systems to support EIP
- collaborative engagement with stakeholders, including boards, executives, managers, service users, practitioners, service development staff, researchers, partner organizations, community members, and other experts through the facilitation of interactive processes in which experiential knowledge is valued
- integration of EIP strategies with existing structures and forums such as supervision and team meetings
- external expertise drawn on as required and establishment of research–practice partnerships to support and sustain the implementation process

Preparatory Strategies

The goals in the preparatory phase (see chapters 2 and 3) are as follows:

- Ensure that the organization is ready to adopt EIP.
- Allocate resources to EIP implementation.
- Achieve clarity and agreement in the organization on the following:

  - understanding of what constitutes EIP

  - rationale for adopting an EIP strategy

  - what counts as evidence

  - vision for an EIP organization

  - implementation plan

- Develop an implementation plan.

Potential strategies include the following:

- Undertake organizational analysis of readiness for EIP using questionnaires, the information outlined in Table 3.2, and the questions for analyzing organizations at the end of chapter 3.
- Identify leadership potential and leadership roles for the implementation of EIP and establish a leadership team.

- Have conversations and hold forums with stakeholders to educate them on and mobilize interest in EIP.
- Run workshops with participants from across the organization to gather views and establish a position on the vision and rationale for EIP in the organization.
- Enlist a guest speaker on EIP (for example, from an organization that has implemented an EIP strategy).

Phase 1 Strategies: Define and Redefine Practice Questions

The goal of Phase 1 (chapter 4) is as follows:

- Formulate clear practice questions that reflect key practice issues and concerns for practice decision making in the organization.

Potential strategies include the following:

- Set parameters for the scope of the practice question design process (for example, program, service user group, field of practice).
- Ask staff to record key practice concerns and questions as they emerge in practice.
- Use a skilled facilitator to work with stakeholders to canvass ideas about practice issues and concerns; formulate practice questions; and reflect, review, and fine-tune the practice questions (for example, in a designated workshop or existing forums in the organization).
- Maintain a schedule of practice issues, practice questions, priority questions, next steps, responsibilities, and time frames.

Phase 2 Strategies: Gather Evidence

The goal of Phase 2 (chapter 5) is as follows:

- Gather relevant evidence from a range of sources offering organizational, practitioner, policy, service user, and research knowledge to inform practice questions.

Potential strategies include the following:

- Work collaboratively with stakeholders to map out potential sources of relevant evidence that could inform the practice questions.
- Gather local knowledge from organizational, policy, practitioner, service user, and practice research sources.
- Train staff to access online evidence for practice.
- Choose and implement methods for gathering research evidence that match organizational requirements and capacities, including primary searches, systematic reviews, external experts, online repositories, and knowledge dissemination and organization sources.

- Have leaders coordinate evidence-gathering activities, ensure they are focused on the practice questions, and keep stakeholders engaged and updated on progress.
- Maintain an evidence log to which staff contribute as evidence related to practice questions come to hand.

Phase 3 Strategies: Critically Appraise Evidence

The goals of Phase 3 (chapter 6) are as follows:

- Appraise the strengths and limitations of the gathered evidence in terms of credibility, relevance, and applicability to the practice context.
- Ensure that questioning, inquiry, and learning are valued in the organization.

Potential strategies include the following:

- Identify and bring together people with skills and strengths in the critical appraisal of evidence (for example, critical questioning skill, knowledge of relevant fields of practice, knowledge of research design, group facilitation).
- Provide education on how to appreciate and critically appraise research evidence, engaging external experts to deliver as required.
- Allocate time for staff to engage in the critical appraisal of evidence.
- Incorporate critical reflection and critical appraisal of evidence into supervision and group forums (for example, team meetings, journal clubs, executive meetings) relating evidence to practice issues as they emerge.
- foster collaboration with other organizations on the appraisal of evidence (for example, communities of practice, university partnerships) and internally within and between teams.
- Engage experts to support critical appraisal.
- Enable practitioners to have input into the review of evidence for, and selection of, empirically supported standardized interventions.
- Enable stakeholders to map critically appraised evidence from a range of sources against practice questions and negotiate the weight of evidence for practice responses in light of other explanatory and contextual factors (for example, practice expertise, theoretical knowledge, policy knowledge, service user experiences, ethics, organizational capacities and priorities).

Phase 4 Strategies: Integrate Knowledge into Practice Decisions and Interventions

The goals for Phase 4 (chapter 7) are as follows:

- Make organizational, management, program, team, and practitioner decisions with reference to critically appraised evidence.

- Use evidence-informed decisions to bring about changes to practice in the organization.

Potential strategies include the following:

- Disseminate evidence that is relevant to practice questions in a timely manner, using a range of engaging and accessible dissemination strategies.
- Engage practitioners and other decision makers with evidence using professional supervision, workshops, and evidence support staff.
- Provide training and resources to supervisors to incorporate evidence into critical reflection discussions with supervisees.
- Make use of critical questioning to foster reflection on decision making and the role of evidence in decisions.
- Promote cultural change to support EIP in the organization using both formal and informal processes, including strategies for development of leadership, promotion of research-minded practitioners, and service user engagement.
- Deal sensitively with resistance to change, hear emotional reactions, seek input, and negotiate conflicts.

Phase 5 Strategies: Monitor and Evaluate Client Outcomes

The goal for Phase 5 (chapter 8) is as follows:

- Collect purposeful local evaluation data to complement evidence from other sources to inform, improve, and explain interventions and practice decisions in the local context.

Potential strategies include the following:

- Have leaders oversee coordination, resources, and integration of evaluation activities.
- Share evaluation knowledge and skills across the organization or program and engage external expertise as required.
- Organize collaborative, interactive, critically reflective forums to develop program logic or other explanatory models for interventions.
- Implement systems and processes to consult with and engage stakeholders in evaluation activities, manage evaluation activities, manage information and data, and integrate evaluation design and findings with practice.
- Establish practitioner–researcher–service user partnerships to conduct practice evaluation (for example, university partnerships).
- Review information and data systems for accessibility and utility for practice evaluation purposes.

- Design purposeful, realistic evaluations that contribute to explanatory models and practice improvements.
- Reflect on evaluation findings in professional supervision sessions as a source of feedback on practice.
- Ensure that evaluation findings are fed back into program logic and explanatory models and integrated with other evidence in each of the EIP phases.
- Feed questions generated by evaluations back into the design of practice questions in Phase 1.

ADDITIONAL RESOURCES

References to literature and research throughout the book are provided in the reference list at the end, which can be used as a resource for organizations implementing EIP. In addition, the following key online resources relating to particular aspects of the EIP process may be useful:

- Systematic reviews of research on practice topics include the following:
  - Cochrane Library: http://www.cochranelibrary.com
  - Campbell Library: http://www.campbellcollaboration.org
  - Social Care Online: http://www.scie-socialcareonline.org.uk
- Repositories of empirically supported interventions (evidence-based programs):
  - Suicide Prevention Resource Center: http://www.sprc.org/resources-programs
  - California Evidence-Based Clearinghouse for Child Welfare: http://www.cebc4cw.org
  - National Registry of Evidence-based Programs and Practices: http://www.samhsa.gov/nrepp
- Repositories of EIP guidelines:
  - National Guideline Clearinghouse, U.S. Department of Health and Human Services: http://www.guideline.gov
  - National Institute for Health and Care Excellence: https://www.nice.org.uk/about/what-we-do/our-programmes/nice-guidance/nice-guidelines
- Critical appraisal of research:
  - Critical Appraisal Skills Programme (critical appraisal resources, tools, and checklists for varying research designs): http://www.casp-uk.net/
  - Cochrane Handbook for Systematic Reviews of Interventions (guidance to authors on the preparation of Cochrane systematic reviews and detailed guidance on the appraisal of studies): http://handbook.cochrane.org/
  - Social Care Institute for Excellence (resources for the review and use of research): http://www.scie.org.uk/

BUILDING IMPLEMENTATION KNOWLEDGE

The framework for implementing EIP presented in this book is not a standardized program and has not been empirically tested. The model and associated strategies are, however, informed by the body of research on barriers and facilitators in the implementation of EIP and research case studies of organizations adopting evidence-informed approaches. The framework also draws on theoretical perspectives including theories of organizations, critical realism, and the strengths perspective. Knowledge from my own experiences of working in and with human services organizations to integrate research with practice has influenced the framework, as has the body of literature on EIP in social work.

The implementation of EIP in the human services is a relatively new field of knowledge. Explanatory models and evidence for practice are therefore still developing. How the framework in this book is translated into practice will be unique to each organizational setting. Monitoring, evaluation, and critical reflection on the challenges and successes of the implementation process will help determine how to strengthen the integration between practice and evidence in the local context. As organizations move through cycles of the EIP phases over time and in different parts of the organization, opportunities for learning about how to improve both practice and the implementation process will be revealed.

Glossary

clinical Characterized by a therapeutic or treatment orientation.

critical postmodernism Meta-theory of social and theoretical discourses that recognizes individual histories, experiences, and value systems as the basis for meanings and interpretations of social life. Critical postmodernism promotes critical reflection and analysis rather than the rigid application of a single theory. It examines the structural systems and dominant discourses that propagate power, influence privilege, and result in marginalization.

critical realism Theory that recognizes social reality as independent of the thoughts and impressions of individuals but does not reduce behaviors and experiences to causal determinism. Both objective knowledge and social meaning are regarded as important for understanding the social world. Context-dependent structures, systems, mechanisms, and interpretations are seen as contributing to outcomes. Open systems interact to produce events and outcomes for individuals and social groups. Critical realism entails close analysis of situations to identify the social meanings, systems, mechanisms, and processes that operate and to understand the likely impact of these on experiences, behaviors, and outcomes for the individuals and groups concerned.

critical reflection Systematic examination of the influences on understanding and experiences, such as personal, relational, historical, social, and political factors. The critical reflection process involves identifying and challenging values and assumptions that influence understanding; questioning dominant interpretations of information, situations, and behaviors; and considering alternative interpretations.

critical thinking Process of applying, analyzing, synthesizing, and evaluating information or a situation to make a judgment or guide action.

effectiveness Degree to which a program or intervention achieves desired outcomes in practice.

efficacy Extent to which a program or intervention is associated with measurable outcomes in controlled research studies.

empirically supported intervention *or* **treatment** Therapeutic educational or treatment program that has a degree of standardization and an associated body of empirical research studies demonstrating effective outcomes; also referred to as *evidence-based program.*

evidence Provisional, well-informed, negotiated knowledge about what is expected to work well in a particular context. Evidence comprises knowledge from robust research (both qualitative and quantitative), practice evaluation, systematic information gathering, professional practice wisdom, and critical reflection. Evidence is continually reviewed, updated, and refined to suit the practice context.

evidence-based practice (1) Clinical decision-making process in which current best evidence is appraised in the light of client circumstances to make decisions about appropriate interventions. (2) Program or intervention that has empirical evidence to support effectiveness.

evidence-informed practice Active, critically reflective approach to gathering, appraising, and using evidence to inform practice decision making that takes into account contextual and relational factors that also affect the implementation and outcomes of interventions.

fidelity Degree to which protocols, content, principles, and formats are observed in the delivery of standardized or manualized programs or interventions.

human services Programs established to address human needs and remediate social problems, including services to families and individuals across the life span who are facing hardships and challenges that result from wider social, economic, political, and environmental factors as well as physiological, psychological, emotional, and relationship factors.

intervention Purposive action undertaken with the intention of effecting change for an individual, group, or society to reduce risks or harm, mobilize protective factors, or enhance well-being. Interventions can include single events or multiple actions carried out at the individual, group, organizational, community, regional, or national level.

intuition Experience-based knowledge drawn on subconsciously to guide practice.

learning organization Organization that undertakes a proactive approach to gaining knowledge from evidence and experiences of both success and failure. New knowledge is used to promote change and innovation. Knowledge is valued, sought, shared, and used in decision making about interventions, programs, and practices.

manualized program or intervention See *standardized program or intervention.*

meta-analysis Use of statistical techniques to pool findings from a number of studies, generally randomized controlled trials, and report combined statistical trends.

narrative review of research Summary of a body of research literature that highlights themes and issues but does not provide a complete or systematic appraisal of research on the topic.

practice-based research Research undertaken in real practice settings, driven by practitioners, and designed primarily to inform the development and improvement of practice in that context.

practice question Question derived from issues or concerns encountered in practice that focuses evidence-gathering activities, the findings from which are used to guide future practice.

practice wisdom Knowledge and expertise gained through reflection on practice experiences in relation to theoretical understanding, values, and research knowledge.

program theory or logic model   Explanatory model, generally depicted in diagrammatic or tabular form, of why and how the elements of a program or intervention lead to desired outcomes. A theoretical framework and reasoned process are used to specify and operationalize program inputs or components, outputs, and outcomes.

randomized controlled trial   Experimental research design characterized by random allocation of participants to intervention and control groups. Variables are measured before and after the intervention to determine whether the intervention group experiences outcomes that are significantly different from those of the control group. In the strongest form of this design, neither participants nor researchers know which participants are in the treatment or control group (double-blinded).

realist evaluation methodology   Mixed-method approach to practice evaluation in which targeted pieces of information are sought to contribute to theoretical arguments about and explanations for what is working for which groups and how. Practical methodologies are used that produce findings in response to priority practice questions and inform future decisions about improvements to practice.

standardized program or intervention   Intervention guided by a protocol or manual that details the principles, practices, and procedures that are to be followed, generally in a step-by-step process, in implementing the intervention.

systematic review   Summary of research literature on a defined topic that uses an explicit protocol for the location and inclusion of studies. Patterns of findings across the located research studies, including contradictory findings, are reported.

validity   Degree to which research data measure what they claim to measure.

References

Aarons, G. A. (2004). Mental health provider attitudes toward adoption of evidence-based practice: The Evidence-Based Practice Attitude Scale (EBPAS). *Mental Health Services Research, 6*(2), 61–74.

Aarons, G. A., & Palinkas, L. A. (2007). Implementation of evidence-based practice in child welfare: Service provider perspectives. *Administration and Policy in Mental Health and Mental Health Services Research, 34,* 411–419.

Aarons, G. A., Wells, R. S., Zagursky, K., Fettes, D. L., & Palinkas, L. A. (2009). Implementing evidence-based practice in community mental health agencies: A multiple stakeholder analysis. *American Journal of Public Health, 99,* 2087–2095.

American Psychological Association. (2005). *Policy statement on evidence-based practice in psychology.* Retrieved from http://www.apa.org/practice/guidelines/evidence-based-statement.aspx

Asmussen, K., Feinstein, L., Martin, J., & Chowdry, H. (2016). *Foundations for life: What works to support parent child interaction in the early years.* London: Early Intervention Foundation.

Austin, J., & Claassen, J. (2008). Implementing evidence-based practice in human service organizations: Preliminary lessons from the frontlines. *Journal of Evidence-Based Social Work, 5,* 271–293.

Barlow, J., Bergman, H., Kornør, H., Wei, Y., & Bennett, C. (2016). Group-based parent training programs for improving emotional and behavioral adjustment in young children. *Cochrane Database of Systematic Reviews, 8,* CD003680.

Bellamy, J. L., Bledsoe, S. E., & Mullen, E. J. (2009). The cycle of evidence-based practice. In H. Otto, A. Polutta, & H. Ziegler (Eds.), *Evidence-based practice: Modernising the knowledge base of social work?* (pp. 21–29). Farmington Hills, MI: Barbara Budrich Publishers.

Bellamy, J. L., Bledsoe, S. E., & Traube, D. E. (2006). The current state of evidence-based practice in social work: A review of the literature and qualitative analysis of expert interviews. *Journal of Evidence-Based Social Work, 3*, 23–48.

Broadhurst, K., & Pithouse, A. (2015). Safeguarding children. In M. Webber (Ed.), *Applying research evidence in social work practice* (pp. 111–126). London: Macmillan Palgrave.

Burke, A. C., & Early, T. J. (2003). Readiness to adopt best practices among adolescents' AOD treatment providers. *Health & Social Work, 28*, 99–105.

Campbell Collaboration. (2015). *Campbell Collaboration systematic reviews: Policies and guidelines* (Version 1.1). Oslo: Author. Retrieved from http://www.campbell collaboration.org/images/C2_Policies_and_Guidelines_Doc_Version_1_1.pdf

Cargill, J. (2015). Finding the evidence for practice in social work. In M. Pack & J. Cargill (Eds.), *Evidence discovery and assessment in social work practice* (pp. 36–64). Hershey, PA: Information Science Reference.

Carr, S., & Bostock, L. (2015). Appraising the quality of evidence. In M. Webber (Ed.), *Applying research evidence in social work practice* (pp. 44–58). London: Palgrave Macmillan.

Carrilio, T. E. (2008). Accountability, evidence, and the use of information systems in social service programs. *Journal of Social Work, 8*, 135–148.

Chandler, J., Churchill, R., Higgins, J., Lasserson, T., & Tovey, D. (2003). *Methodological standards for the conduct of new Cochrane Intervention Reviews* (Version 2.3). London: Cochrane Library. Retrieved from http://editorial-unit.cochrane.org/sites/editorial-unit.cochrane.org/files/uploads/MECIR_conduct_standards%202.3%20 02122013_0.pdf

Collins-Camargo, C. (2007). Administering research and demonstration projects aimed at promoting evidence-based practice in child welfare. *Journal of Evidence-Based Social Work, 4*, 21–38.

Comino, E. J., & Kemp, L. (2008). Research-related activities in community-based health services. *Journal of Advanced Nursing, 63*, 266–275.

Corcoran, K., & Fischer, J. (2013). *Measures for clinical practice and research* (5th ed., Vols. 1 & 2). New York: Oxford University Press.

Craig, D., & Bigby, C. (2015). Critical realism in social work research: Examining participation of people with intellectual disability. *Australian Social Work, 68*, 309–323.

Crisp, B. (2015). Systematic reviews: A social work perspective. *Australian Social Work, 68*, 284–295.

De Bortoli, L., & Dolan, M. (2015). Decision making in social work with families and children: Developing decision-aids compatible with cognition. *British Journal of Social Work, 45*, 2142–2160.

Dill, K. A., & Shera, W. (2015). Empowering human service organizations to embrace evidence-informed practice: International best practices. *Human Service Organizations: Management, Leadership & Governance, 39*, 323–338.

Dore, I. (2015). Applying evidence in practice: Isn't that straight-forward? In M. Pack & J. Cargill (Eds.), *Evidence discovery and assessment in social work practice* (pp. 65–81). Hershey, PA: Information Science Reference.

Evans, T. (2015). Using evidence to inform practice. In M. Webber (Ed.), *Applying research evidence in social work practice* (pp. 77–90). London: Palgrave Macmillan.

Fixsen, D. L., Naoom, S. F., Blase, K. A., Friedman, R. M., & Wallace, F. (2005). *Implementation research: A synthesis of the literature* (FMHI Publication No. 231). Tampa, FL: National Implementation Research Network.

Fleming, J., King, A., & Hunt, T. (2015). Recruiting and engaging men as fathers in social work practice. In M. Pack & J. Cargill (Eds.), *Evidence discovery and assessment in social work practice* (pp. 235–260). Hershey, PA: Information Science Reference.

Fook, J. (2002). *Social work critical theory and practice.* London: Sage Publications.

Fook, J., & Gardner, F. (2007). *Practising critical reflection: A resource handbook.* Maidenhead, England: Open University Press.

Gambrill, E. D. (2001). Social work: An authority-based profession. *Research on Social Work Practice, 11,* 166–175.

Gambrill, E. D. (2006). *Social work practice: A critical thinker's guide.* Oxford, England: Oxford University Press.

Gambrill, E. D. (2010). Evidence-based practice and the ethics of discretion. *Journal of Social Work, 11,* 26–48.

Gardner, F. (2006). *Working with human service organisations: Creating connections for practice.* South Melbourne, Australia: Oxford University Press.

Gibbs, L., & Gambrill, E. (2002). Evidence-based practice: Counterarguments to objections. *Research on Social Work Practice, 12,* 452–476.

Goldman, G. D. (2009). Initial validation of a Brief Individual Readiness for Change Scale (BIRCS) for use with addiction program staff practitioners. *Journal of Social Work Practice in the Addictions, 9,* 184–203.

Gough, D. (2007). Weight of evidence: A framework for the appraisal of the quality and relevance of evidence. *Research Papers in Education, 22,* 213–228.

Gray, M., Joy, E., Plath, D., & Webb, S. (2013). Implementing evidence-based practice: A review of the empirical research literature. *Research on Social Work Practice, 23,* 157–166.

Gray, M., Joy, E., Plath, D., & Webb, S. (2014). Opinions about evidence: A study of social workers' attitudes towards evidence-based practice. *Journal of Social Work, 14,* 23–40.

Gray, M., Joy, E., Plath, D., & Webb, S. (2015). What supports and impedes evidence-based practice implementation? A survey of Australian social workers. *British Journal of Social Work, 45,* 667–684.

Hagell, A., & Spencer, L. (2004). An evaluation of an innovative audio-tape method for keeping social care staff up to date with the latest research findings. *Child and Family Social Work, 9,* 187–196.

Hart, V. (2015). Using research evidence in practice: A view from the ground. In M. Webber (Ed.), *Applying research evidence in social work practice* (pp. 91–107). London: Palgrave Macmillan.

Houston, S. (2001). Beyond social constructionism: Critical realism and social work. *British Journal of Social Work, 31,* 845–861.

International Federation of Social Workers. (2014). *Global definition of social work.* Retrieved from http://ifsw.org/get-involved/global-definition-of-social-work

Jones, A., & May, J. (1992). *Working in human service organisations: A critical introduction.* Melbourne, Australia: Longman Cheshire.

Jones, J. L., Washington, G., & Steppe, S. (2007). The role of supervisors in developing clinical decision-making skills in Child Protective Services (CPS). *Journal of Evidence-Based Social Work, 4,* 103–116.

Jones, J. M., & Sherr, M. E. (2014). The role of relationships in connecting social work research and evidence-based practice. *Journal of Evidence-Based Social Work, 11,* 139–147.

Joubert, L., & Hocking, A. (2015). Academic practitioner partnerships: A model for collaborative practice research in social work. *Australian Social Work, 68,* 352–363.

Kirst-Ashman, K. K., & Hull, G. H. (2006). *Generalist practice with organizations and communities.* Belmont, CA: Thomson.

LaMendola, W., Ballantyne, N., & Daly, E. (2009). Practitioner networks: Professional learning in the twenty-first century. *British Journal of Social Work, 39,* 710–724.

Lawler, J., & Bilson, A. (2005). Towards a more reflexive research aware practice: The influence and potential of professional and team culture. In A. Bilson (Ed.), *Evidence-based practice in social work* (pp. 190–211). London: Whiting & Birch.

Lee, C., & Austin, M. J. (2012). Building organizational supports for knowledge sharing in county human service organizations: A cross-case analysis of works-in-progress. *Journal of Evidence-Based Social Work, 9,* 3–18.

Lindberg, A., & Meredith, L. (2012). Building a culture of learning through organizational development: The experiences of the Marin County Health and Human Services Department. *Journal of Evidence-Based Social Work, 9,* 27–42.

Lock, J., & Le Grange, D. (2013). *Treatment manual for anorexia nervosa* (2nd ed.). New York: Guilford Press.

Macdonald, G. (2001). *Effective interventions for child abuse and neglect: An evidence-based approach to planning and evaluating interventions.* Chichester, England: Wiley.

Mathews, I., & Crawford, K. (2011). *Evidence-based practice in social work.* Exeter, England: Learning Matters.

Mosson, R., Hasson, H., Wallin, L., & von Thiele Schwarz, U. (2017). Exploring the role of line managers in implementing evidence-based practice in social services and older people care. *British Journal of Social Work, 47,* 542–560. bcw004.

Mullen, E. J. (2015). Reconsidering the "idea" of evidence in evidence-based policy and practice. *European Journal of Social Work, 19,* 310–335.

Mullen, E. J., Bledsoe, S. E., & Bellamy, J. L. (2008). Implementing evidence-based social work practice. *Research on Social Work Practice, 18,* 325–338.

Murphy, A., & McDonald, J. (2004). Power, status and marginalisation: Rural social workers and evidence-based practice in multidisciplinary teams. *Australian Social Work, 57,* 127–136.

Nutley, S., Jung, T., & Walter, I. (2008). The many forms of research-informed practice: A framework for mapping diversity. *Cambridge Journal of Education, 38,* 53–71.

Nutley, S., Walter, I., & Davies, H.T.O. (2009). Promoting evidence-based practice: Models and mechanisms from cross-sector review. *Research on Social Work Practice, 19,* 552–559.

O'Connor, L., & Leonard, K. (2014). Decision making in children and families social work: The practitioner's voice. *British Journal of Social Work, 44,* 1805–1822.

Owen, J. M. (2006). *Program evaluation: Forms and approaches.* Sydney, Australia: Allen & Unwin.

Pack, M. (2015). Navigating practice: Informed evidence and evidence-based practice. In M. Pack & J. Cargill (Eds.), *Evidence discovery and assessment in social work practice* (pp. 82–95). Hershey, PA: Information Science Reference.

Pawson, R. (2006). *Evidence-based policy: A realist perspective.* London: Sage Publications.

Pawson, R., Boaz, A., Grayson, L., Long, A., & Barnes, C. (2003). *Types and quality of knowledge in social care* (Knowledge Review 3). London: Social Care Institute for Excellence.

Pawson, R., & Tilley, N. (1997). *Realistic evaluation.* London: Sage Publications.

Pawson, R., & Tilley, N. (2009). Realist evaluation. In H. Otto, A. Polutta, & H. Ziegler (Eds.), *Evidence-based practice: Modernising the knowledge base of social work?* (pp. 151–180). Farmington Hills, MI: Barbara Budrich Publishers.

Plath, D. (2013a). Organizational processes supporting evidence-based practice. *Administration in Social Work, 37*, 171–188.

Plath, D. (2013b). Support for evidence-based practice in a human service organization. *Administration in Social Work, 37*, 25–38.

Plath, D. (2014). Implementing evidence-based practice: An organisational perspective. *British Journal of Social Work, 44*, 905–923.

Plath, D., Williams, L., & Wood, C. (2016). Clinicians' views on parental involvement in the treatment of adolescent anorexia nervosa. *Eating Disorders, 24*, 393–411.

Reason, P., & Bradbury, H. (2006). *Handbook of action research.* London: Sage Publications.

Roberts, A. R., Yeager, K., & Regehr, C. (2006). Bridging evidence-based health care and social work. In A. R. Roberts & K. R. Yeager (Eds.), *Foundations of evidence-based social work practice* (pp. 3–20). Oxford, England: Oxford University Press.

Rosenberg, R., & McDermott, F. (2015). More than pills and beds: Contemporary challenges in social work practice and mental healthcare. In M. Pack & J. Cargill (Eds.), *Evidence discovery and assessment in social work practice* (pp. 113–129). Hershey, PA: Information Science Reference.

Ross, P.D.S. (2015). Locating evidence for practice. In M. Webber (Ed.), *Applying research evidence in social work practice* (pp. 22–43). London: Palgrave Macmillan.

Rowe, S., Baldry, E., & Earles, W. (2015). Decolonising social work research: Learning from critical Indigenous approaches. *Australian Social Work, 68*, 296–308.

Rubin, A., & Bellamy, J. (2012). *Practitioner's guide to using research for evidence-based practice* (2nd ed.). Hoboken, NJ: John Wiley & Sons.

Rutter, D., Francis, J., Coren, E., & Fisher, M. (2010). *SCIE systematic research reviews: Guidelines* (2nd ed.). London: Social Care Institute for Excellence.

Sackett, D. L., Richardson, W. S., Rosenberg, W., & Haynes, R. B. (1997). *Evidence-based medicine: How to practice and teach EBM.* New York: Churchill Livingstone.

Scourfield, P. (2010). Going for brokerage: A task of "independent support" or social work? *British Journal of Social Work, 40*, 858–877.

Shaw, I. (1999). Evidence for practice. In I. Shaw & J. Lishmann (Eds.), *Evaluation and social work practice* (pp. 14–40). London: Sage Publications.

Sheppard, M. (2004). *Appraising and using social research in the human services: An introduction for social work and health professionals.* London: Jessica Kingsley.

Small, S. A., Cooney, S. M., Eastman, G., & O'Connor, C. (2007). *Guidelines for selecting an evidence-based program: Balancing community needs, program quality and organizational resources* (What Works, Wisconsin Research to Practice Series, Issue 3). Madison: University of Wisconsin.

Small, S. A., & Kupisk, D. (2015). Family life education: Wisdom in practice. In M. J. Walcheski & J. S. Reinke (Eds.), *Family life education: The practice of family science* (pp. 17–26). Minneapolis: National Council on Family Relations.

Soydan, H. (2009). Towards the gold standard of impact research in social work: Avoiding threats to validity. In H. Otto, A. Polutta, & H. Ziegler (Eds.), *Evidence-based practice: Modernising the knowledge base of social work?* (pp. 111–137). Farmington Hills, MI: Barbara Budrich Publishers.

Soydan, H. (2015). Intervention research in social work. *Australian Social Work, 68,* 324–337.

Stanhope, V., & Solomon, P. (2008). Getting to the heart of recovery: Methods for studying recovery and their implications for evidence-based practice. *British Journal of Social Work, 38,* 885–899.

Stevens, M., Liabo, K., Frost, S., & Roberts, H. (2005). Using research in practice: A practice information service for social care practitioners. *Child and Family Social Work, 10,* 67–75.

Straus, S. E., Richardson, W. S., Glasziou, E., & Haynes, R. B. (2011). *Evidence-based medicine: How to practice and teach it.* Edinburgh, Scotland: Churchill Livingstone Elsevier.

Straussner, S.L.A., Naegle, M. A., Gillespie, C., Wolkstein, E., Donath, R., & Azmitia, E. C. (2006). The SATOL project: An interdisciplinary model of technology transfer for research-to-practice in clinical supervisions for addiction treatment. *Journal of Evidence-Based Social Work, 3,* 39–54.

Thyer, B. A., & Myers, L. L. (2010). A quest for evidence-based practice: A view from the United States. *Journal of Social Work, 11,* 8–25.

Tosone, C. (2013). On being a relational practitioner in an evidence-based practice world. *Journal of Social Work Practice, 27,* 249–257.

van de Luitgaarden, G.M.J. (2009). Evidence-based practice in social work: Lessons from judgment and decision-making theory. *British Journal of Social Work, 39,* 243–260.

Vaughn, M. G., Howard, M. O., & Thyer, B. A. (2009). *Readings in evidence-based social work.* Los Angeles: Sage Publications.

Walsh, K., Zwi, K., Woolfenden, S., & Shlonsky, A. (2015). School-based education programmes for the prevention of child sexual abuse [Review]. *Cochrane Database of Systematic Reviews, 2015,* (4), CD004380.

Wampold, B., & Imel, Z. (2015). *The great psychotherapy debate: The evidence for what makes psychotherapy work.* New York: Taylor and Francis.

Webb, S. (2001). Some considerations on the validity of evidence-based practice in social work. *British Journal of Social Work, 31,* 57–79.

Webber, M., & Carr, S. (2015). Applying research evidence in social work practice: Seeing beyond paradigms. In M. Webber (Ed.), *Applying research evidence in social work practice* (pp. 3–21). London: Palgrave Macmillan.

Wike, T. L., Bledsoe, S. E., Manuel, J. I., Despard, M., Johnson, L. V., Bellamy, J. L., & Killian-Farrell, C. (2014). Evidence-based practice in social work: Challenges and opportunities for clinicians and organizations. *Clinical Social Work Journal, 42,* 161–170.

Witkin, S. L. (1996). If empirical practice is the answer, then what is the question? [Book Forum on the Scientist–Practitioner]. *Social Work Research, 20,* 69–75.

Index